PRAISE FOR *COURAGEOUS INVITATIONS*

Using the research experience gained throughout their careers, Dr Jefferson Yu-Jen and Anne Duggan provide an exceptionally researched book on goal setting, which incorporates inspirational stories of successful people pertinent to our generation.

The greatest treasures in the book are found at the end of each chapter as empowering tools and self-enrichment exercises are given to assist readers in goal setting.

At the present time, where mental wellbeing is consistently emphasized and talked about, companionship is provided throughout the book assisting readers with dealing with the emotions they will experience whilst reading the book.

The tools and support provided in this book will immensely assist the reader in being courageous and thereby changing the destiny of ones' life. Read this book and be transformed!

Thomas Kgokolo
Former CEO
South African Airways

The opposite to faith is not disbelief, but fear. What Dr Jefferson Chen and Anne Duggan accentuate resonates strongly with me: the courage to fearlessly pursue your purpose and to appreciate what is uniquely you, the product of your own unique ampersand thinking; the unique combination of what you have been and what you are becoming in seeking and fulfilling your purpose may very well be a safer option and more likely winning bet than most other old ground ruts of old paths to power and perceived routes to so-called success. Nay-sayers are the very same people who effortlessly pivot and meet your success after the fact with a resounding "I told you so!". It is a courageous and fearless initiative that follows its own heart and healthy mind to prematurely identify new courses and new solutions to challenges, while the predominant opinion still has an outdated formula for its perception. But, exploration, innovation, and pioneering behaviours may be what many dream of achieving, and yet is not everybody's cup of tea. The greater tribe is stacked like a chessboard with different kinds of which not all can be movers and shakers. And the best consistent outcome clearly comes from developing all the supporting pieces in unison, while preparing for a final strike. Leadership and Leading is not the same thing, and all of us cannot be the head, we need teamwork and support, we need the combination of rational thinking as well as the freedom of dreaming and conjuring up visions of greater realities. The co-authors masterfully bring these elements together to challenge your mind into understanding how the process of innovation and leadership comes together to beat out new paths and better routes to new horizons, in ways that do not always correlate to existing institutional thinking, expectations and formalised thinking.

Dirk J.F. Van Der Walt
Director and Co-founder
WeBuyCars

What is the point of having an innovative idea if you never let it see the light?

What if you never give yourself permission to dream bigger, think smarter and make your mark in the world?

This is the crux of *Courageous Invitations*—having the freedom to give yourself permission to be your best self and, in the process, encouraging others to do the same. Dr Jefferson Yu-Jen Chen and Anne Duggan generously share a lifetime of knowledge and experience to inspire you to "invite yourself to the party" and I am honoured to write the Foreword for such a valuable and insightful piece of work. A veritable MBA in book form.

Courageous Invitations sets out to help you find your audacious purpose and offers practical ways to set goals that lead to action. This book challenges you to question your intrinsic motivations – What's holding you back? What are you afraid of? What's the worst that can happen?

What empowers you to embrace a new way of thinking about yourself and the world? The activities at the end of each section provide ample room for self-reflection and rigorous food for thought.

Drawing on ancient history, cognitive psychology, literature, music, marketing, philosophy and modern-day phenomena like viral videos, *Courageous Invitations* explores the very nature of what it means to be creative and to recognise opportunity where others see only problems.

Firoze Bhorat
Chief Marketing Officer
Discovery Limited

Wow, what a remarkable read! We often consider disruption to be something that happens around us and never within this. This book really stretches our though processes to disrupt ourselves from within using practical real-life examples that are easy to understand which many readers will resonate with. The simple guidelines on goal setting, measuring execution and the achievement are the pinnacle for every reader. But it doesn't stop there, the authors in their true spirit of making this a two-way process have generously made themselves available to the reader for further support. A must read if you want to be courageous and disrupt your inner being to live your best life and reach your full potential.

Vinolia Singh
Chief People Officer
Adcorp Group

Courageous Invitations invites the reader to reconsider their approach to what it means to live a life of purpose. Rather than feel directionless around one's purpose, this book explores the concept of starting to explore how one can attain the reciprocal contributions. Achieving these goals in incremental steps could be purposeful in itself. Seeing that our purpose could change as we continue to re-invent ourselves, the quest for self-mastery never stops as the learning journey is continuous. Thank you to the authors for sharing valuable examples and useful exercises to explore one's own self-disruption journey into the art of the possible. It is always possible if we apply our minds and intentional energy. It is an inspiring read that makes you rethink about where to begin.

Anoka Balram
Chief Marketing Officer and
Applied Design & Marketing Transformation Leader
Deloitte Consulting, Africa

COURAGEOUS INVITATIONS

COURAGEOUS INVITATIONS

HOW TO BE YOUR BEST AND SUCCEED THROUGH SELF-DISRUPTION

DR JEFFERSON YU-JEN CHEN
ANNE DUGGAN

Copyright © Dr Jefferson Yu-Jen Chen and Anne Duggan, 2022

All rights reserved.

No part of this book may be reproduced, stored in a retrieval system, or transmitted in any form or by any means, electronic, mechanical, photocopying, recording, or otherwise, without the prior written permission from the publisher.

 A catalogue record for this book is available from the National Library of Australia

ISBN 978-1-922357-40-3
e-ISBN (ePUB) 978-1-922357-41-0

Published by Hambone Publishing
Melbourne, Australia

Text design and typesetting by David W. Edelstein
Cover design by Larch Gallagher
Digital conversion by Hambone Publishing

To the people in our lives who stand by us, encourage us, and support us on our own journey to achieving our best self. You know who you are.

Contents

Preface — 1
    The art and science of resolve — 2
    The power of goal-setting — 4
    How does this book provide a bridge between goal and action? — 5

Chapter 1: Finding Your Audacious Purpose? An Alternative Reality — 7
    Our collective obsession with audacious purpose — 11
    Purpose. Useful, but why the buzz? — 12
    Apple's place in the golden circle — 14
    The Wright brothers vs Langley — 22
    Success springs from joy and intentionality — 26
    Subjectivity and the evolving nature of 'purpose' — 30

Chapter 2: The Moment Two Stories Collide — 35
    Exercise: Examine your All-Star life — 35
    Michael Jordan & THAT defining moment — 40
    Be in the moment — 47
    Empirical evidence — 48
    Your story. Your moment. Your legacy. Be intentional and zestful about them. — 51
    An invitation to 'be more' — 58

Chapter 3: Courageous Invitations — 67
    Courage. A small word for a big construct — 69
    Nelson Mandela: The road to forgiveness — 71
    Daryl Davis: An unusual friendship — 73
    Courage brings mental freedom, even if the path ahead is treacherous — 76
    The origin of courage: Zest and bravery — 80
    How courage and fear are wired in our brains — 82

Self-regulation meets self-certainty	87
Own your fear to help you craft courageous invitations	89
Small courageous invitations cultivate profound differences	98
Savouring the sweetness of life	100

Chapter 4: Strategic Selfishness — 107

It's all about 'me' ... and the Karens	107
A key difference: Where self-centredness and selfishness diverge	111
Are we inherently selfish?	113
The happy (selfish) Vikings	117
Ayn Rand and objectivism	120
A new, strategic approach to selfishness	125

Chapter 5: Appoint Your Inner Advisors — 149

Lessons from a scrawny boy	150
Become your own bandleader	153
Your thoughts shape your world	156
Your words shape your thoughts	159
Your multiple identities shape your words	163
Personal constructivist psychology	166
Meet Mike and his identities	168
Talk to yourself. It's healthy	177
First-, second- and third-person self-talk	178
Positive and negative self-talk	180
Instructional and motivational self-talk	184
Shine brighter: An inspiring journey	191

Chapter 6: The Magic Of Ampersand Thinking — 205

The second-largest orchestra vs super-spicy chilli	207
From Baby Shark to viral videos	210
Create your own cocktail of fusions, remixes, mashups, cross-overs and blends	212
Einstein's combinatory play	214

Ampersand thinking	217
Self-innovation for personal growth	222
Offering	224
Configuration	226
Experience	230
Your unique '&' combinations	233
A word to remember	234

Chapter 7: It's Not About Fate, It's About Navigation And The Journey — 243

Your GPS satellites	245
You are not lost	247
From Polynesia to Scandinavia	251
Unlocking the strengths and virtues of your character	254
SHIFT towards a quest for zest	260
Getting to grips with the SHIFT mindset approach	264
SHIFT spirals and micro-moments	275
If it's not just fate, how will you measure your life?	277

References — **287**

Preface

Courageous invitations was borne out of life experiences and the self-mastery journey that we have been on. Through our professional and personal engagements we came to realise that most people have similar reflections on where they are at personally and professionally and often re-count how stuck they feel (on the hamster wheel of life). So putting together our knowledge of business, leadership and self-mastery we developed this book to assist you to navigate self-disruption and to re-imagine, re-calibrate and activate your best self.

Let's be honest: This desire to improve ourselves, to learn, grow and develop is not a modern-day phenomenon. Self-mastery as a concept has been around for thousands of years, and over that time it has been received with both enthusiasm and scepticism.

The earliest ancestor of self-help books is an Ancient Egyptian genre called 'Sebayt'. The word means 'teaching' and certainly that's what these tomes offered: instructional literature on how to live your best life.[1] They also served to pass down essential wisdom from generation to generation, starting with the man who served as vizier (or prime minister) to Pharoah Djedkare Isesi, the penultimate ruler of the Fifth Dynasty of Egypt.

According to scholars, Ptahhotep – who held the post of vizier from during the late 25th and early 24th centuries BC – wrote *The Maxims of Ptahhotep* (otherwise known as Instruction of Ptahhotep) for his son

Akhethotep, in which he passed down all the wisdom he had gathered over the decades so that[2] Akhethotep could establish himself as an influential vizier and successor to his father. It all started with a self-help book born out of a father's love.

Some of the gems contained in the *Maxims of Ptahhotep* still ring true today including: "Silence is more profitable unto thee than abundance of speech" and "take advice from the ignorant as well as from the wise, since there is no single person who embodies perfection nor any craftsman who has reached the limits of excellence."[3]

Another enduring favourite is this classic: "Follow your desire as long as you live and do not perform more than is ordered; do not lessen the time of following desire, for the wasting of time is an abomination to the spirit."[4]

In today's lingo: Follow your passion.

Now we know why Ptahhotep put pen to papyrus all those decades ago. The aim was to help secure his son's future and to accelerate the younger man's personal growth and development. In that respect, self-help books of today continue that tradition seeking to assist readers in solving personal problems and making meaningful resolutions.

The art and science of resolve

A New Year's resolution is the overt act of declaring an intention to change. Change leads to growth. The question is, whether human beings are really as terrible at committing and following through on change as we assume.

In an empirical study published in the April 2002 Journal of Clinical Psychology, John Norcross and his collaborators uncovered a few interesting insights about New Year's resolutions. They gathered a total of 282 participants to take part in the study, and randomly assigned these participants into two groups – 159 of whom made New Year's resolutions and

123 who were simply planning to make changes about certain aspects of their lives. Six months into the study and the researchers found that 46% of the individuals (all having similar demographics and behavioural goals) from the 'clear New Year's resolutions' group continued to follow through with their resolve. How about the group that did not? Well, apparently only a dismal 4% of them were still actively keeping their promises.[5]

Similarly, Martin Oscarsson and his colleagues investigated what resolutions people make when they are free to formulate them, whether different resolutions achieve differing success rates, and whether it is possible to increase the likelihood of a resolution's success by administering information and exercises on effective goal setting. During the one-year follow-up as part of a solid empirical investigation that divided 1,066 research participants into three groups based on the amount of support given to attain their goals, 55% of the participants considered themselves successful in achieving their resolutions. Participants who adopted approach-oriented goals were significantly more successful than those with avoidance-oriented goals (58.9% vs 47.1%).

Approach orientation kicks in when individuals are positively motivated to look good and receive favourable feedback from others. Avoidance oriented goals occur when individuals are negatively motivated to try to avoid failures and looking incompetent in the eyes of others. The important takeaway from this study is that New Year's resolutions can have lasting effects and that self-motivation and a desire to change have a greater role to play than we realise.

Another interesting study found that individuals who set goals, irrespective of whether these were ultimately fully attained or not, demonstrated signs of increased psychological well-being when the researchers interviewed them after three years.[6] Though we do not encourage you to set goals without making the effort to attain them, it is important to acknowledge the possible unexpected benefits of goal-setting and how this allows us to challenge our intentions.

The power of goal-setting

Bearing this in mind, let's now take a look at the process of goal-setting.

Clinical psychologist and professor Dr Gail Matthews conducted a seminal study into goals and goal achievement in the workplace. Her intention was to explore how the attainment of goals at work influenced how these goals were formalised by the individuals. Were they, for instance, written down? Or was a commitment made to achieving goal-directed actions? Was a level of accountability built in to ensure commitment to these actions? The participants were broken down into five groups and each was asked to identify their goals.[7]

Each groups was then asked to rate their goals according to the following factors: importance, difficulty, having the requisite skills and resources to achieve the goal, as well as commitment and motivation. They were also asked to indicate if this was a goal they'd tried to achieve previously and how successful they'd been at that attempt.

Those in group one were asked to think about the goals they hoped to achieve in the next four weeks. Then they had to rate the goal based on the factors outlined above.

Participants in groups two to five were asked to write down their goals, using an online survey format, and then rate their goals on the same factors. Groups three, four and five were also given an additional dimension:

- Group three was also asked to formulate action commitments, or a plan of action.
- Group four was asked to formulate action commitments and then to send their goals and associated action commitments to a supportive friend.
- Group five was asked to formulate action commitments and send their goals, action commitments and weekly progress reports to a supportive friend. Participants in this group were

also sent weekly reminders to email their friend a quick progress report.

So, what happened?

Matthews and her collaborators determined the following success rate per each group:

- Group 1 = 42.8%
- Group 2 = 60.8%
- Group 3 = 50.8%
- Group 4 = 64.1%
- Group 5 = 76.0%.

These outcomes confirm that in order to achieve a desired result, the highest chance of success is accompanied by a commitment to action, by being accountable to peers and through delivering regular updates about the goals and the progress being made to achieve them.

How does this book provide a bridge between goal and action?

It is our intention to equip you with the inspirations and information necessary to shift your thinking about your own life, the vision you have for your best self, and the boldness you may need to attain your goals.

As we embark on this journey, we will ask you to commit to your action plan, to share your accountability with peers, to regularly benchmark your goals and update them. In doing so we hope that you will become courageous.

We recognise that the process of self-discovery and change is both fluid and, at times, challenging.

It is our fervent hope that each chapter of this book will trigger some new thinking, affirm some of your existing views, and evoke the emotions needed to propel you forward in your journey of self-disruption (which includes significant amounts of self-mastery and change).

By the end of this book, we hope that you will have made some productive cognitive-behavioural shifts. These shifts will help you to see the world differently and will enable you to interpret your circumstances more innovatively. With these changes, we are confident that new opportunities to accelerate your personal growth will emerge.

Once you've finished this book, and hopefully made the transformation - however big or small – we invite you to share your joy with others and share your story with us to demonstrate the power of being true to your goals.

We do not see this book as a static one-way conversation, but rather as the first step in forging a meaningful friendship with you. We, therefore, hope you will take the time to write to us and share your insights, lessons, or stories – particularly as they relate to this transformational journey. As you discuss your journey with your friends and peers, ask them to bear witness to your fantastic and significant progress that you have made.

This book cordially invites you to disrupt yourself and, above all, to help others to disrupt themselves.

Dr Jefferson Yu-Jen Chen
https://www.linkedin.com/in/jefferson-yu-jen-chen-b71b153/
www.drjeffersonchen.com

Anne Duggan
https://www.linkedin.com/in/msanneduggan/
www.anneduggan.com

www.courageousinvitations.com

Chapter 1
Finding Your Audacious Purpose? An Alternative Reality

Keeping it together is Sara Blakely's business. She is, after all, the founder of the Spanx empire - the well-known American brand of slimming undergarments, body shapers and leggings which have been endorsed, praised or publicly used by big-name celebrities such as Oprah Winfrey, Katy Perry, Gwyneth Paltrow, Mindy Kaling, Tina Fey, Kate Winslet and Brooke Shields. Men wear them too, or so we've been told.

Today, Spanx is a multibillion-dollar enterprise and part of a growing global shapeware industry. But Blakely's story wasn't always so audacious or filled with successes.

Born in Florida in the United States on February 27 1971, Blakely had an eye for a business opportunity from an early age. As a youngster she used to set up a haunted house come Halloween and charge people in her neighbourhood for admission. But a career in entrepreneurship was never really her goal. Blakely's initial dream was to become a trial lawyer, like her father. Although she did reasonably well at school, and graduated from Florida State University with a major in legal communications, Blakely scored poorly on the Law School Admission Test after several attempts.

Despite not being able to achieve her initial dream, Blakely still regarded her college days as an invaluable phase of her life. "I would say college is very important," she said during a conference in 2015. "What I got the most out of in college was the experiences, and the people I met. It's this block in your life when you can learn many subjects and expose yourself to as much as you can. Our life experiences make us more interesting than a resumé or a piece of paper."[8] It was only later in her life, when she started her own business, that the value of this time, personal growth and know-how would become clearer to her.

What she seemed to have in large doses, even during her first years in college, was *chutzpah*; that wonderfully evocative word described by Leo Rosten in *The Joys of Yiddish* as 'gall, brazen nerve, effrontery, incredible guts'.[9] Here's an example. Back in the winter of 1989, Blakely was at a shopping mall in Florida when she came across an interesting ring in a jewellery store – a ruby-like droplet hung from a delicate gold bow attached to the ring. It cost US$120. As a student, she certainly didn't have that sort of money so she asked for a discount. The salesman quickly rejected her request, declaring that they never negotiated prices. Then, presumably taking in the attractive and effervescent young woman before him, added in hushed tones something along the lines of, "Only if you came in here in nothing but a bikini would I discount the price." Blakely was not intimidated nor would she be silenced. Instead, she responded to the challenge by querying the value of the discount. Without deliberating much, the salesperson laughed and said 'half off'. I'll be back, was Blakely's retort.

Blakely tells the story herself on her Instagram feed, along with photographic evidence of her wearing a pink bikini and posing with the salesman[10]. She recounts how the next day – a balmy 27 degrees below-zero – she headed back to the store dressed in her bikini, a long black coat, a scarf, a hat and jelly shoes. In the mall, Blakely took off her winter wear and walked into the jewellery store wearing nothing but a bikini. As soon as he laid eyes on her, the colour drained out of the salesman's face. "I'm here for my discount," she announced. After some deliberation with his manager, Blakely walked out of the store with her ring – having secured a 50% discount.

Sure, it was a bit of fun and an opportunity to thumb her nose to the arrogance and sexism of the salesman, but this experience stayed with Blakely. It reinforced how overcoming challenges energized her. Far more valuable than the US$60 discount, the personal affirmation she generated from that courageous stunt followed her throughout her life. That courage and personal growth would come in handy when she started Spanx. As Blakely reminisced on her Instagram page, "I got the ring for $60. I'm betting the guy never blew off or dismissed another young female customer again. And yup, I still have the ring. Hand is just older now, but I wear it from time to time to remind myself of the courage it took me as a freshman in a new college town to stand up for myself. It was terrifying and my heart was pounding, by the time I bought the ring a crowd had gathered outside the store confused and curious. My friends were in shock that I actually did it, but in the end we laughed uncontrollably, piled back in the car, and headed back to our dorm."

After college, Blakely worked for the Walt Disney World Resort for three months, then she sold fax machines door-to-door for seven years by day, occasionally performing stand-up comedy at night, before transitioning into running Spanx on a full-time basis.[11] The idea for the innovation came to her almost accidentally, when she was dressing for a party and needed an undergarment to go under some cream-coloured pants. She chopped the feet off some control top pantyhose and, Voilà. She was 26.

Even before that lightbulb moment, Blakely had taken the time to visualise her success and the lifestyle she ultimately wanted to achieve. She wrote down her snapshot of success, which you can listen to in a YouTube videoclip posted by Primeau TV in 2013.[12] Instead of focusing on her purpose, Blakely visualised herself becoming self-employed and she imagined herself inventing a product that could be sold to the masses. She also envisaged profiting from being the owner of a business that would continue to thrive, even when she was no longer involved.

It's only in recent years that Blakely has begun to discuss her purpose more publicly.[13] In the early years of her entrepreneurial pursuit, as she was creating a business and building a brand, she would most often talk about her goals, share stories about how she created values for her business through non-traditional approaches, discuss how she got her products into luxury department chain Neiman Marcus, and how she was energised by inventing and testing her products. When you listen to her speak or read her articles, you get a profound sense of her energy, her boldness and the joy she experiences by approaching life in her distinctive and enthusiastic way.

It would be fair to say that the purpose that drove Blakey during certain stages of her life is quite different to the purpose she advocates today. One can further argue that she stumbled on an opportunity to disrupt herself and be more than just a door-to-door salesperson and sales trainer at the office-supply company. In her celebratory speech in October 2021, after Blackstone valued the shapewear maker at $1.2 billion and agreed to purchase a major stake in Spanx, Blakey revealed the goal she wrote down on the whiteboard in the early days of Spanx. As she explained to her employees, Blakey simply wanted her company to reach a $20 million valuation. Her exact words were, "I said this company will one day be worth $20 million and everybody laughed at me, and you know, I said 'I really believed that.' So to stand here today and think about what we've been able to create, and what we've been able to do while being authentic, and kind, and delivering amazing products to women."

Clearly what motivated Blakey to keep going during the initial phase of Spanx was not the fulfilment of an audacious purpose; the kind that influencers so frequently talk about. Blakey had established a clear and significant personal goal and then she pursued it relentlessly. It is crystal clear that Blakey approaches her personal goal with zest.[14]

Our collective obsession with audacious purpose

Around the world, and aided by the reach of social media, we are seeing increased interest (bordering on obsession in some quarters) in finding one's purpose. Log into any social platform and you'll find countless influencers advocating their views on the necessity of finding one's purpose - and, in parallel, one's passion. Naturally, these power brokers offer a wide range of practical tips, many of which are profound and rich in substance. For those individuals who are lucky enough to have found their purpose, the messages from these influencers provides a sense of comfort. For those who are still seeking their purpose, these tips and messages motivate them to try harder and approach the voyage with a smarter outlook. The importance of these influencers lies in their ability to position themselves as experts, which they do skilfully by delivering exciting and enticing speeches. Yet, the depth of these messages sometimes don't stand up to scrutiny. They often don't provide all the answers that the audience is searching for and who continue to feel deeply frustrated because they haven't yet found an audacious purpose or those who feel that their old purpose no longer serves them.

This current flurry around the importance of passion and purpose has the potential to be a double-edged sword. We certainly believe that it is worthwhile putting in the effort to seek out your purpose and more importantly your audacious purpose, if you wish to do so. If your stumble upon the answers and solve these existential puzzles, we wholeheartedly cheer for you. If you are looking at finding your purpose, try to challenge yourself to explore various audacious possibilities instead.

But equally, if you have not yet found or unsure of your true audacious purpose, we still cheer wholeheartedly for you – maybe a little bit louder this time. It could mean that you are at the pre-activation phase of your self-disruption journey. At least, we suspect that could be one of the reasons why you picked up this book in the first place.

If you have not found your audacious purpose, or if you are uncertain about what happiness actually means to you, then let us assure you – resoundingly – that you are doing PERFECTLY well. Everything in its own time, as the folk band Indigo Girls once put it.[15]

Without dampening the merits attached to finding your purpose, it is important to note that we are living through a moment in time which borders on obsession with this illusive concept. If you do a Google search on the entry of these exact words, 'find your purpose', you will find close to 2.1 billion hits. Not millions. But billions.

The mainstream media is, not surprisingly, tapping into this conversation and driving this trend. Instead of following the crowd, our suggestion is to step away from the hype and ask if this makes sense to your individual context. Why not ponder the possibility that an alternative approach might exist, something that is equally – possibly more - powerful than the view we are currently being bombarded with?

In short, our recommendation is simple. Do not focus so heavily on finding your purpose. Keep the desire to find your purpose in your back pocket, just like Sara Blakely did.

Of course, this recommendation doesn't stop us from briefly wading into the 'purpose' debate by taking a longer look at what defines this sense of resolve and why the world is turning motivation into a veritable creed.

Purpose. Useful, but why the buzz?

Even if you've never read Greek philosophy you'll have heard of Aristotle (384-322 BC), one of the most admired scientists and thinkers in history. Aristotle used the term 'telos' to describe 'purpose'. Etymologically speaking 'telos' means 'the end, limit, goal, fulfilment, completion', it refers to the full potential or inherent purpose of a person, object or thing. So it's intrinsically part of who we are and why we exist. Aristotle even held that natural phenomena could occur for the sake of something, for a purpose. Consider, for a moment, a horse. You can describe a horse by the number of hands it measures from the ground to the top of its withers. Or you can add the colour and shininess of its coat, shape of its gaskin and other physical characteristics into your descriptions. For Aristotle, a horse is designated by nature to fulfil specific purposes: pulling a carriage, transporting passengers or goods, helping a soldier in battle, or ploughing a field. That is a horse's telos. Similarly, every human being has a telos. Based on this view, the argument is that we are at our happiest when we can uncover the purpose for which we were made, and fulfil that telos.

However, not everyone agreed with Aristotle's take on the telos concept. Epicurus of Samos (341-270 BC) is one.

For Epicurus, who flourished not long after Aristotle's death, pleasure is the telos. He believed that the telos of a human being lies in 'katastematic pleasure' – a state of being while performing an activity. This can take the form of quiet contentment or outright ecstasy, but it is pleasure nonetheless. Epicurus, who founded a school of philosophy that convened at his home and garden in Athens called 'the Garden', acknowledged that katastemic pleasure often followed kinetic pleasure – such as the satisfied pleasure after finishing a lavish meal. So, for Epicurus, the purpose of life was to seek out the pleasure which leads to happiness.[16]

A side step away from this more hedonistic view of purpose, the likes of Confucius (551-479 B), Mencius (372-289 BC), Laozi (around 600 BC) and other classical Chinese philosophers[17] espoused an eminently pragmatic philosophy, based on asking deceptively small questions such as: How are you living your daily life? They focused on the potential to achieve great change if you begin with the mundane and doable, if you stick to getting the fundamentals right.

Similarly, ancient African philosophers focused more on working towards the collective good, as is underscored by the philosophy of *Ubuntu* or working together to achieve common goals. This approach to collective humanity is quite a stark contrast from our modern-day, almost desperate need to define our individual purpose.[18]

So just what ignited this fire within us all to find our reason for being? We're not sure we have the exact answer. But if you take a quick glance through countless videoclips on 'finding purpose' on YouTube, it is very likely that you will come across a TED talk from Simon Sinek, an author and inspirational speaker, who spoke eloquently about how leaders can use his 'golden circle' concept to inspire action and create profitability.[19] The TED talk, entitled *How great leaders inspire action*, is well worth listening to as you attempt to get a handle on what purpose means and how some organisations and leaders are able to inspire, while others can't. Sinek tells us that it comes down to the why. The why requires us to interrogate "the purpose, the cause, the belief" which drives people and businesses.

Apple's place in the golden circle

Sinek is arguably one of the great influencers of our time. After his insightful TED Talk, he went on to publish a book called *Start With Why*[20] which quickly became a bestseller. Make no mistake, Sinek is a smart guy, but his insights don't just come from spending a substantial amount of time conducting research, they lie in his experience. It was working at leading advertising agencies Ogilvy & Mather and Euro RSCG that prepared him for his meteoric rise to fame. Some thought leaders have challenged the legitimacy of his ideas and stated that his actual content is flimsy, Sinek is adept at leveraging advertising principles to structure the tactics that help him to convey key messages and sell these ideas in the form of books, talks, and other engagements are remarkably effective[21]. He is definitely a guy whom aspirant influencers should learn from and, as authors and thinkers ourselves, we certainly take great pleasure in learning from him. But that doesn't mean we agree with everything he says.

In his numerous public engagements, Sinek asserts that finding one's purpose is the only path to success. We would like to challenge his view on this matter.

In his TED Talk Sinek attempts to attribute credibility to his golden circle model by using technology giant Apple as an example, stressing that Apple's success lies in it being purpose-led. He substantiates this point by suggesting this is the 'inner dialogue' in which Apple conducts its business. Donning his ad man hat he positions Apple's pitch as follows, "Everything we do, we believe in challenging the status quo. We believe in thinking differently. The way we challenge the status quo is by making our products beautifully designed, simple to use and user friendly. We just happen to make great computers. Want to buy one?"

Technically, there is nothing wrong with this pitch (even though some people have suggested that the first generation of Apple products weren't actually that great). Nevertheless, this self-centred version of inner organisational dialogue is not entirely correct when you start to unpack the building blocks which contributed to Apple's success.

We are not saying that having an organisational purpose is not a strategic imperative. In fact, it is highly recommended. In 2018 BlackRock Chairman and CEO Larry Fink wrote in his annual letter to CEOs that a company should have a purpose beyond profit. If it does not, it risks being ousted from BlackRock's investment portfolio. Why? Because organisational purpose is linked to long-term performance.[22]

Back to Apple. Today, we are most definitely talking about a company that is remarkable for being purpose driven. The benefits of this organisational purpose are evident in the fact that the company's market cap surpasses US$1 trillion – a clear indication of delivering on the promise of long-term performance.

But today's Apple is a different company to that just a few decades ago.

Exciting, creative and quirky. That was the Apple computer company founded in 1976 by Steve Jobs, Steve Wozniak and Ronald Wayne (yes, who? He dealt with the paperwork and sold his 10% share back to the two Steves 12 days after they co-founded Apple for US$800. He also signed away any right to future claims).

In a 2016 interview with BBC News, Wayne described his most famous co-founder as follows, "Jobs had this focus. Once he got an idea in his head, that was it. And you never wanted to be between him and where he wanted to go, or you'd wind up with footprints on your forehead."[23]

Jobs made Apple what it was, said Wayne, while Wozniak was the engineering expert. The problem was that neither man had experience running a company so, despite Jobs' aspirations to be CEO, John Sculley was appointed to the role in 1983. But it wasn't all smooth sailing. In 1985 Jobs resigned – although he consistently claimed he was fired – after being replaced as head of the Macintosh (Mac) division. This followed the release of 'Lisa', the first computer with a graphical user interface, which was a sales flop and the promising but less-than-stellar start for Mac as a competitor to rival IBM's PC stranglehold[24]. Yes, Jobs would return to the company in 1997 and would rekindle the Apple spark which evaporated when he left. He would, during those intervening years, create a new computer company called NeXT. NeXT didn't really shoot the lights out, but its operating system became the foundation for the Mac OS X.[25]

Apple decided to acquire NeXT for US$429 million in early 1997 and it was this move that brought back Jobs to the company, and sparked the start of a glorious era for Apple. In his first full year back at the company, the company turned a US$309 million profit after, in Jobs' words, being "90 days from being insolvent" on his return.[26]

Jobs' legacy looms large over the organisation as does his remarkable return, but what actually happened to Apple between 1985 and 1997?

Not long after Jobs' departure, Apple began to lose focus. They released the Newton MessagePad personal assistant, a handwriting recognition device, which didn't click with the market. Then they tried a new kind of processor called PowerPC, which cost Apple dearly and (by splitting the design focus) kept Mac prices sky high at a time when PCs were gaining popularity and coming down in cost. It was this decision which ultimately cost Sculley his job in 1993, as revenue tumbled by 30%.[27]

Given this synopsis, it is hard to say what exactly Apple's purpose was at the time. The closest incident that fits our discussion is probably the speech Jobs gave in response to an angry audience member during a rare Q&A session at the 1997 Worldwide Developers Conferences. Technology writer Austin Carr revisited the moment in an article for *FastCompany*, when he recorded Jobs' reaction as being, "We've tried to come up with a strategy and vision for Apple - it started with: 'What incredible benefits can we give the customer?' [And did] not start with: 'Let's sit down with the engineers, and figure out what awesome technology we have and then figure out how to market that'."[28]

What people don't generally focus on is this part of Jobs' speech, which started with the admission that "Apple suffered for several years from lousy engineering management." Jobs continued, "There were people that were going off in 18 different directions... What happened was that you looked at the farm that's been created with all these different animals going in all different directions, and it doesn't add up–the total is less than the sum of the parts. We had to decide: What are the fundamental directions we are going in? What makes sense and what doesn't? And there were a bunch of things that didn't."

Apple's turnaround was, in part, the result of great leadership which was meticulously aligned to everything the company tackled.

In a recent piece for Harvard Business Review, Joel M Podolny and Morten T Hansen, the Dean and faculty member of Apple University respectively, described how quickly Jobs reorganised things after his return to the company in 1997.[29] Apple had a conventional structure for a company of its size. General managers ran products, or 'business units', each with their own bottom lines. And, like in many large companies, those general managers often worked against each other, leading Apple to the brink of bankruptcy. "Believing that conventional management had stifled innovation, Jobs, in his first year returning as CEO, laid off the general managers of all the business units (in a single day), put the entire company under one P&L, and combined the disparate functional departments of the business units into one functional organization," wrote Podolny and Hansen.

Although some people have argued that this was just a powerplay by Jobs, and one designed to ensure that he would not be ousted again, the real Jobs' magic was in HOW he did things.

It is debatable if Apple actually talked through its purpose during Jobs' iconic big return that remarkably turned the company around. What is clear is that Jobs had a few clear strategic objectives. Apart from trimming operating costs, which included chopping back Apple's philanthropy initiatives, the main objectives in Jobs' mind were to turn the company back to profitability and make Apple a dominant force in the industry. Instead of focusing on shareholder needs (within reasons), Jobs focused strongly on increasing product-market fit by satisfying customers through innovation and attention to detail. Jobs' 'purpose' of "putting a dent in the universe"[30] had never left his mind, even during Apple's most challenging time.

Steve Jobs, as his biographer Walter Isaacson conveys so well, was a complex man, an exhausting man, a perfectionist. As a friend told Isaacson, "He had the uncanny capacity to know exactly what your weak point is, know what will make you feel small, to make you cringe."[31] He was a bully, but a brilliant bully. A problem solver who put his customers and their experiences first. This tough, demanding and uncompromising attitude paid off, as did his philosophy of putting customers at the centre of the business – a far cry from the somewhat self-absorbed message of 'we do this, and we do that' advocated by Sinek.

Let's be realistic for a moment, Apple did not become today's colossus enterprise by obsessing over their why. They succeeded because they focused on their customers' whys. They did this by interrogating what motivated their customers to do business with them. The iconic Harvard professor in innovation, the late Clayton Christensen, called this the 'job-to-be-done' (and no, this theory has nothing to do with Steve Jobs). Jobs-to-be-done is an approach for developing offerings based on understanding all aspects of a customer's rudimentary and ultimate goals, which Christensen termed as 'jobs'. We all have many 'jobs' in our lives which we need to tackle, some are small (renewing a car licence perhaps) and some are big (finding a meaningful career), others are unplanned (dealing with a family crisis) and others are predictable (getting your kids to school on time). Depending on the nature of the 'job', customers seek help by 'hiring' a company to help them complete the tasks at hand.[32]

In other words: If you understand the 'jobs' of your customers, you can tailor your products and services to meet their needs. Jobs understood this, but it was not the only factor that enabled him to turn Apple around. Apart from improving the company's product line, Jobs made a concerted effort to build up customer sentiment towards his company. He wanted to connect with the emotions of his customers, and not just focus on the products. Even though this approach is a norm of how businesses operate today, it was uncommon in the late 1990s.

Instead of going on and on about the technical specifications of the Apple product line, Jobs launched the iconic 'Think Different' campaign. The objective was simple: He wanted his products to resonate deeply with the identities of a sub-set of customers – the creatives, misfits, rebels, dreamers and game-changers – for whom owning a Mac said something about the off-the-wall people they aspired to be.

As a result, many customers did not buy an Apple simply because of the products on offer. They happily, proudly and enthusiastically purchased the products because they felt that their identities had been recognised. Jobs did not, therefore, focus on the 'why' of Apple. He began by focusing on a few key strategic objectives which included forging connections with customers by understanding their 'why'. He did not put Apple's 'why' at the centre. Instead, he put the 'whys' of specific segments of customers at the heart of Apple's approach, and the organisation innovated around this collection of needs.

Some may suggest that we are splitting hairs or using semantics to argue against Sinek's view. However, even though the differences between our take and Sinek's explanation appear to be small, the underlying ethos is profoundly different. Apple's great comeback should be attributed to how the company and its dynamic leader innovated the 'hows', which were anchored in addressing their customers' 'whys'. Sinek retrofitted Apple's success to fit his golden circle, giving particular emphasis to the inner component of the model – the why circle. The truth doesn't fit this model as easily or as simply as the golden circle implies. After all, evolution seldom follows a nice, neat pattern.

To truly understand the shift in Apple's focus we must remember that, until the 1990s, marketing concerned itself with consumer transactions. These were transactional in nature, focused on company profitability and the monetary value of customer relationships. But, over time, this changed and became more about relationship marketing, which highlighted the importance of building close, long-term ties with customers.[33] Almost all major enterprises at the time focused on giving their customers the best products to increase the sales – and their objectives (or, if you wish, their 'purpose') were not too different from that of Apple. The difference was that many of these companies did not focus on creating transformational relationships. They did not create hooks to connect to their customers' aspirations, which in turn build cult-like followers.

What personal lessons can we draw from this? Often your purpose does not lead to any gratifying outcome until you understand the needs of those you wish to contribute to and until you find meaningful ways in which they can contribute to you in turn. Instead of focusing on your purpose, you should rather focus on HOW to create reciprocal contributions; namely approaches which are mutually gratifying for both you and your stakeholders. Steve Jobs contributed to his customers' by satisfying their 'jobs-to-be-done', his customers contributed back to Apple with impressive sales figures which lead to remarkable profitability. Jobs' diversifying strategies – the launch of the iPod in 2001, iPhone in 2007 and iPad in 2010 – complemented this symbiotic relationship by taking an ecosystem view of doing business by creating amazing experiences for the company's customers. This was not really based on Apple's purpose, or Jobs' purpose - unless you argue that his purpose was to understand and satisfy his customers' purpose. Ultimately, Jobs cultivated and grew a cult-like customer base not only because of Apple's products and services, but because of their branding and marketing efforts.

Sinek argues that, "A purpose-driven organisation is a simple idea. It's an organisation of people who show up for the same reason, who work together to achieve something and will sacrifice so that the others may make it. Those are the great organisations, those are the organisations and the people that change the world."[34] Without blowing our own trumpets, the authors of this book are well-travelled global citizens. We have visited numerous stores around the world and have taken the time to ask frontline salespeople what they think Apple's purpose is. Not surprisingly, the opinions they gave varied from serving customers better, to being innovative, being cooler and making money. Some even suggested (perhaps a bit tongue in cheek) that Apple's purpose is to continue to outcompete other inferior products and achieve world dominance.

But let's not be too flippant. Having established a purpose can certainly help an organisation to increase its competitiveness. That is, if this purpose is crafted superbly, fits well with the lifecycle of the organisation, and can be executed effectively. Too often there is a disconnect between the top echelons and the staff at the frontline. But the magic still comes from the HOW.

An organisational purpose also changes as it evolves. In its early days, with a hyper-energetic, big-dreaming, 20-something Jobs as its co-founder, Apple worked according to the principle that "there is something very different that happens with one person, one computer. What we're trying to do is remove the barrier of having to learn to use a computer." Jobs aimed to 'domesticate" computers into the realm of day-to-day household appliances, like a dishwasher or microwave.[35]

Similarly, as an individual, uncovering your purpose can definitely add value to your life. However, is it always essential to have a purpose, especially a big hairy audacious one? No. It is perfectly alright, from time to time, not to have a clearly defined purpose. You will evolve towards an appropriate purpose as long as you know what value you are trying to create and have taken the time to strategically set goals to achieve this in an innovative manner.

The Wright brothers vs Langley

In the same TED talk, Simon Sinek also implied that the reason the Wright brothers outcompeted their rival, Samuel Pierpont Langley, during the race to invent the first man-controlled flight was due to the notion of 'begin with why'. In truth, many other influencers have attributed the edge which Orville and Wilbur brought to this race to self-belief and the ability to regard failure as a learning opportunity. However, these retrospective (and somewhat hero-worshipping) explanations are not entirely correct. We all love a good story, especially one where the underdogs win a competition (think of Kurt Russell in the 2004 real-life inspired ice hockey film *Miracle*[36]) or where an individual accomplishes a magnificent comeback which allows them to snatch victory from the jaws of defeat (Sylvester Stallone's *Rocky* film series springs to mind here[37]).

In many stories, including Sinek's take on the rivalry, Langley was villainised. Yet we don't believe this to be a fair and accurate portrait of the man. Langley also did not give up as easily as many influencers have suggested. He launched multiple versions of the Langley Aerodrome between 1892 to 1903. In 1903, the year the Wright brothers made the first man-controlled, sustained flight of a powered, heavier-than-air aircraft with the Wright Flyer on 17 December in Kitty Hawk, North Carolina,[38] Langley twice attempted to launch his Aerodrome by catapulting it from the roof of a houseboat on the Potomac River. Both attempts failed and the aircraft was destroyed after plunging into the Potomac. Langley, who died just three years after the Wright brothers conquered flight, was criticized extensively in the press for his efforts and lambasted by Congress for wasting money. He gave up, as Sinek says, after 1903.[39]

The majority of commentators on this historical rivalry fail to highlight three important points. Firstly, in 1896, Langley successfully flew an unmanned steam-powered fixed-wing model aircraft – which marked a significant advancement in the chronology of aeronautical technology. The *Smithsonian Magazine*, writing about a man who once held the role of secretary of that august institution, described the achievement thus, "On two fine days, one in May and one in November, the little planes, each about 16 feet long, soared away from their launching pad, a houseboat on the Potomac River. Small steam engines whiffling happily, they held a steady course on an even keel, one covering 3,300 feet, the other reaching 4,200 feet and a speed of 30 miles an hour."[40] What is funny is that this impressive achievement is hardly mentioned in the history books. Many other latecomers to the aeronautic innovation race built on Langley's numerous accomplishments.

Now let's take a closer look at Wilbur and Orville, who were born on 16 April 1867 and 19 August 1871 respectively. They were more than 30 years younger than Langley, who was born on 22 August 1834. In terms of energy levels, Langley was no match for the brothers. At the senior age of 69, facing mounting pressure from funders and policy-makers due to his failed attempts, Langley reluctantly stepped aside from the race. Less than three years later he died, on 27 February 1906. He was 71.

Let's put this into context. On 17 December 1903, when 36-year-old Wilbur and 32-year-old Orville succeeded in flying the first manned motor-operated aeroplane, Langley was a frail old man. Yet, none of the influencers and commentators have ever asked how this race might have turned out if these competitors were similar in age.

Thirdly, irrespective of the inspiring traits of the brothers, it is an innovation which the brothers stumbled upon that made such a difference. Langley was impressed by the light yet powerful engine built by Stephen Marius Balzer, a watchmaker at luxury jewellery retailer Tiffany's. Langley bet on Balzer to deliver the world's first 'aero engine' which, he hoped, would be light and powerful enough to power a manned aeroplane. However, Balzer just couldn't get the idea to work. Eventually Langley enlisted his assistant, Charles Matthews Manly, to deal with the project and when it didn't work Langley and Manly went in search of other alternatives and even travelled to Europe to seek out other options. By then Langley had already spent most of the US$50 000 grant he had received from Congress, which explains why the policy-makers were so disappointed when the Wright brothers pipped him to the post.

After a series of pivots and improvements, Langley seemed to be on the right track with a rebuilt engine, which was ready by March 1903. In a letter to Langley, Manly expressed his confidence on the performance of the engine and further stated that, "I am prepared to risk myself with it in actual flight."[41] And risk, he did.

On 7 October 1903 Manly climbed on their design and ran the engine full speed for the launch. The frame did not hold up under the windy conditions of the day and Manly plunged into the river. They went back to the drawing board on the design and on 8 December 1903 they tried again. Again Manly ended up in the icy river, almost drowning in the process. Nine days later the Wright brothers cracked it.

In the early stages of the race to fly, Langley took a chance on building a power engine. This would prove to be the wrong decision, and was compounded by the fact that his apparatus was disturbed by winds and the self-created mass of air swirling around the wings that reduced stability. But you can't accuse the man of not trying. Between 1887 and 1891, Langley's staff constructed more than 100 models. It should be noted that the radial engine, which would eventually power Charles Lindbergh's epic non-stop solo flight to Paris in 1927 as well as many bombers and fighter planes during the Second World War, was based on the engine improvements made by Langley and Manly.

What is important to recognise is that Langley lost the race to the Wright brothers predominantly because he took a different innovation approach. This is a pity, but it is not a shame. Let's think differently about it (pun totally intended) by circling back to the Apple example. Steve Jobs also produced many failed products. Yet few influencers dwell on his disastrous ventures.

Conversely, the Wright brothers focused on control. They designed a flyer with drooping wings, which would be less disrupted by cross winds, and they designed a system which put control in the hands of the pilot by building in the ability to roll the wings, pitch the nose up or down and yaw (or oscillate) the nose of the plane from side to side. These creative differences really set the two teams apart. The path the Wright brothers took, compared to Langley, made all the difference. By uncovering the right innovation, Orville and Wilbur passed into history as Langley passed away, demoralised despite having made significant contributions to the field of aeronautics and astronomy. In 1917 Langley's contributions were posthumously acknowledged when Langley Air Force Base in Virginia was named after him. The base would later become NASA's flight test centre.[42]

Recounting Langley's achievements in no way downplays the Wright brothers' impressive traits and their tireless work, innovation and world-changing success, notably made without any formal training in the subject. As the underdogs and the latecomers to this aeronautics game, their win was turned into an inspirational story, while Langley was unfairly portrayed as the money changing, hare-brained villain. In truth, Samuel Pierpont Langley was a successful inventor and a serious scholar with a background in mathematics, architecture and astronomy. He was highly scientific in his approach and extremely demanding of his staff, not unlike Steve Jobs. But ultimately, he lost the race because of the 'how' aspects of his innovation approach.

We would argue that Langley's failure had nothing to do with any lack of audacious 'purpose'.

Instead, it seems that influencers are happy to put a captivating spin on a classic underdog story in order to suit their own purposes and arguments. We all love a good story, and many of us wish to tell a captivating yarn through our own journeys, but in real-life it is the 'how' that makes the real difference.

Success springs from joy and intentionality

From Apple, a company that makes beautiful products, to another company that manufactures the most sought-after supercars, the prancing horse logo is definitely a symbol of luxury, edginess and a class-above the rest. It is hard to stop your heart from skipping a beat or two when you drive a Ferrari, ANY Ferrari.

On 5 October 1919, a young Italian car mechanic and engineer named Enzo Ferrari took part in his first car race, a hill climb in Parma, Italy. He finished fourth. Ten years after his first race, Enzo started his Scuderia (which means stable in Italian) Ferrari. It was 1929 and Enzo's initial intention was to produce road cars. He was not driven (at least at that stage) to create the greatest sports car in the world – a moniker that would last centuries. Instead, Enzo chose to make road cars simply because he realised that manufacturing road cars was an expedient way to finance his increasingly costly racing activities.

In the beginning, Scuderia Ferrari didn't even design its own cars. It was a racing team that had no problem using the models produced by other automakers, most notably Alfa Romeo, which outsourced its racing department to Enzo Ferrari in 1933. When, in 1938, Alfa Romeo brought racing under its banner again, creating the Milan-based Alfa Corse, they snatched up Enzo as the manager of their new racing department. Scuderia Ferrari disbanded.[43] But, as you know, that's not the whole story.

A year later, in 1939, Enzo left Alfa Romeo. There was, however, a catch to moving forward with the Ferrari dream: Alfa Romeo stipulated that he could not use the Ferrari name in the world of racing or on racing cars for at least four years. Undaunted, within days Enzo had founded Auto Avio Costruzioni, a company that produced machine tools and aircraft parts. Despite the trade ban, Enzo built his first Ferrari in 1940 but the real rollout would be deferred by the Second World War. It was only after World War II in 1947 that the first-ever Ferrari to carry the prancing horse was produced. It was the birth of an icon.

Enzo's empire was not built out of a larger-than-life purpose (as the influencers out there believe it should be). It took years from the time that Enzo was captivated by his first race at the age of 10 to the launch of the first Ferrari, 39 years in fact. From then on, doing things that involved cars and especially race cars, fuelled Enzo's passion and the zestfulness that comes with it. He made ends meet by working as a sports journalist and a racing driver. Not surprisingly for an Italian, he dreamt of becoming an opera singer and knew and revered the great Luciano Pavarotti.[44] His intentionality, it seemed, came from seeking joy in simplicity.

Of course, Ferrari isn't the only Italian supercar brand that captured the world's imagination. What about Lamborghini? What inspired the sleek-lines of the charging bull?

If you delve into the purpose that motivated Ferruccio Lamborghini to give up making tractors and start crafting supercars in 1963 you would most definitely hear about the famous disagreement between Ferruccio and Enzo.[45]

Ferruccio lived for cars, he loved them. In 1958, he went to Maranello to buy a Ferrari 250 GT to expand his collection of supercars. Ferruccio owned several Ferraris over the years. As the story goes, Ferruccio was hard on his cars and, as a result, often needed to replace the clutch of his cars at the local Ferrari factory. After yet another fitting, he decided to replace the part himself at his tractor factory. When they pulled out the Ferrari engine and transmission, he discovered that the clutch was identical to the ones fitted in his own Lamborghini tractors. Ferruccio was furious. He felt that Enzo's cars were equipped with clutches that were too small for use in a high-performance vehicle. Plus he knew he paid 10 lira for a tractor clutch and Ferrari charged him 1000 lira for the same part. When Ferruccio brought his views to the notoriously egotistical Enzo's attention, his concerns were met with mockery. According to Valentino Balboni, Lamborghini's former chief test driver, "Enzo Ferrari told him: 'You are a tractor driver, you are a farmer. You shouldn't complain driving my cars because they're the best cars in the world'."

Enraged by this exchange, Ferruccio decided to modify his Ferrari 250 GTs. He did such a good job that the modified vehicle outperformed Ferrari's stock models. But that wasn't enough. Ferruccio was determined to create a superior sports car that would outshine Enzo's Ferrari stable. Sure, it was hardly a noble objective, but it proved one that served Ferruccio well. The disrespect that was dished out to Ferruccio fuelled both the intensity and stamina of this intentionality.

The line between a purpose and an objective is blurry, isn't it? If you wish to argue that Ferruccio's intentionality served his ultimate purpose of beating Enzo, then you are also right. But this purpose is not as noble or awe-inspiring as the driving forces which are more often advocated for by the many influencers out there.

Despite the absence of a big hairy audacious purpose, many people continue to thrive in the profession they take on. Just to cement our point, and while not as fast-paced as the story of Ferrari and Lamborghini, here's another example to consider.

Chan Hon Meng, also known as Hawker Chan, started a small eatery stall named Liao Fan Soya Sauce Chicken Rice & Noodle in the Chinatown Complex Food Centre in Singapore in 2009. He would go on to become the first hawker to earn a prestige Michelin star, the hallmark of culinary quality and excellence.[46] When asked why he started his own business, Chan once responded that the idea of changing Hainanese-style chicken rice (which was almost regarded as the national dish of Singapore) appealed to him. Traditionally this recipe requires the chicken to be poached and chilled, but he chose to cook his chicken according to the Cantonese style of *siu mei*, where meats are usually roasted in a wood-burning rotisserie oven.[47] Chan went on to create his own signature dish, a soya sauce chicken rice. What makes this Michelin-starred chef so unique is that he set up his eatery near to his home, in Chinatown, where rentals were cheaper. This decision not only differentiated him from his competition but also created reciprocal benefits for both the food market and his profession.[48] Despite losing his Michelin Star in September 2021, Chan did not let this stop him from pursuing his passion. He continues upholding his intentionality of making simple, but delicious food that warms the soul.

The notion of the reciprocal contribution concept is also evident in the early years of Spanx. Blakely has told the world that she wanted to contribute something to women and ultimately, she created a business to contribute towards the lifestyle she had meticulously specified. In 2012, Forbes declared Sara Blakely to be the world's youngest self-made female billionaire, revelling in her inspiring rise from sometimes comic and door-to-door fax machine saleswoman to undergarment empire billionaire.[49] Although Blakely's purpose was to serve women by making better products, she had many other goals and purposes before that ah-ha moment that led to the inception of Spanx. She shares this type of journey with many successful business leaders, such as Vera Wang, Colonel Sanders and Jack Ma, as well as many other lesser known but equally courageous individuals who have taken the bold step of shifting their career trajectories. The brave transition embedded in these stories is what links them together. And that is something to be celebrated because it takes guts, instinct, self-belief and dogged determination – and above all, intentionality

While the media, in its search for clickbait headlines and content, could take some of the blame for mystifying and overhyping the 'finding your purpose' narrative - oftentimes with an undertone suggesting that purpose must be a larger-than-life audacious vision – the simple truth is that you do not have to follow the popular view or go with the crowd to propel your life to greater heights.

Subjectivity and the evolving nature of 'purpose'

Another mistake made by influencers who advocate the importance of finding purpose is that they don't spend enough time exploring how people evolve across different life-stages.

Many of us have no idea what our purpose might be whilst we are at high school. Perhaps we have some idea about what makes us happy at the time, such as sneaking a drinking, learning the ropes of dating, skipping classes, playing sports, but not all of these sources of happiness serve us well in the long run.

Some people continue to struggle to find their purpose in their 20s and 30s, and perhaps into their early 40s. They may also be puzzled when it comes to what make them truly happy. For those 'luckier' ones, somewhere between their late 20s and early 30s they might have determined their purpose. But it is not to say that life doesn't play with that certainty by throwing a few major curveballs into the mix from time to time. Often these life-changing moments which have us scrambling to revisit what we once, with conviction, thought our purpose was. Some of life's curveballs can be devastating, such as the loss of a family member, getting fired, battling illness, dealing with burnout, or going through a divorce. All of these moments can significantly affect how we define our purpose in life. Some of life's curveballs can also be exhilarating. Consider the impact of a new romance, parenthood, a career change, finding new hobbies, and many other wonderful opportunities out there which enable us to recreate ourselves.

Our inner constructs are always evolving, and on many occasions we are not even fully cognisant that we are changing. We are not always in tune with our inner constructs. For some people the pace of their evolution is faster; and sometimes even more ferocious. Whereas for others evolution takes place in a slower, more gentle fashion. As we evolve, our purpose and happiness often shifts in parallel with these internal changes.

Additionally, we all have multiple social roles which we fulfil in our lives. For example, a loving father of two young toddlers may also have a need to assume other roles such as being a responsible executive who is eager to contribute to his company and a caring son who needs to take time to support of his ageing parents. Sometimes, the purposes of these roles are not always fully aligned, which causes tension.

In short: One cannot simply look at purpose without taking into account the entire, multifaceted context of the situation and the foundation of who we are as a person.

LAGGING AND LEADING INDICATORS

'Purpose' can be a vague construct at times. While one can argue that purpose could serve as a precursor that governs what we do and how we behave, it is also possible to argue that having decided on a purpose is not enough. It is the value we create having found a purpose that counts. The value creation aligned to your purpose is a lagging indicator. So the power of having a purpose comes from how each of us shapes these leading indicators.

Let's back up a bit. What are the differences between a lagging indicator and a leading indicator?

In business, a lagging indicator measures production and performance, in other words, the output, outcome and impact. For example, Spanx will measure the total number of Spanx pantyhose produced in this year. It is, in effect, a record of what has passed.

Leading indicators are more predictive in nature, and they attest to inputs which might impact the results of the lagging indicators. For example, the managers of a factory should be examining how many machines and people are working optimally to produce their items.

So leading indicators provide the basis for business leaders to achieve the lagging indicators they desire.

The Ferrari company we have today clearly outlines its mission (not its purpose) on its corporate website. It goes like this, "We build cars, symbols of Italian excellence the world over, and we do so to win on both road and track. Unique creations that fuel the Prancing Horse legend and generate a 'World of Dreams and Emotions'." This is a powerful statement which outlines the group's strategic objective and how they wish to achieve this objective. In two concise sentences, the company has revealed both its leading and lagging indicators. Oftentimes, people focus so heavily on finding their purpose that they do not elaborate HOW they will act out their purpose.

If you have defined your purpose, are you intentional about setting up and carrying out both your leading and lagging indicators? Do ensure they are fully synchronised as you venture onwards and experience changes along your life's journey.

If you have found your purpose, have actively aligned your action to it and are hungry for more, then we salute you. But if you are still waiting for your purpose to surface, or if you are in transition between one purpose and a new yet-to-be-defined purpose, then we hope the stories and insights shared in this section give you the assurance and comfort to know that you will be all right. You've got this.

We believe that instead of focusing so hard on your purpose, there are other elements you should be thinking of. We call these elements the GPS (Global Positioning System) of enriched navigation and call upon you to formulate your unique GPS system that will work for your pursuit of an enriched life journey. But we will leave this important discussion to the very last chapter.

In the meantime, we will move on to exploring how to inject action into our audacious purpose in the next chapter.

Don't worry if you like many others, don't have an audacious (or any) purpose yet. Before you finally leave this chapter, we intend to get you started on your very own journey of self-mastery, help you find your motivations and identify what it will take to ignite your passion much like Jobs, Enzo Ferrari and Blakely.

Self-enrichment Exercises

Before you move into the next chapter, think about what motivates you. What are you passionate about? What makes you happy? Jot these down below.

_____

_____

_____

Based on your answers above, now start thinking about your goals, and what kind of reciprocal contributions these goals will create for you and your stakeholders. These goals could be about you advancing your career growth, uplifting your spirituality, improving your health and the like.

_____

_____

_____

Are these goals meaningful to you? If not, what would you need to change to make them more meaningful?

_____

_____

_____

Now, armed with what you consider to be meaningful goals, how do you feel about your purpose, even if you are still unsure about it? What emotions are you experiencing right now when you think about your purpose?

_____

_____

_____

We would like you to reflect on these emotions and get in touch with how you are really feeling. If you have anxiety or another negative feeling around your purpose or finding one, don't ignore it but reflect on how that is impacting you / your life. We suggest that where discomfort exists, there is value in investing energy in refining your goals so that you can generate reciprocal contributions. The clarity of your purpose will emerge in due course.

Remember we need you to be honest and raw.

Chapter 2
The Moment Two Stories Collide

The world's richest athlete.[50] TV gold. Arguably the greatest basketball player of all time. You don't have to be a sports fan or an NBA fanatic to know and appreciate the carefully crafted Michael Jordan brand. But looking beyond the multimillion-dollar sponsorships and celebrity appeal, Jordan has a thing or two to teach us all about life and seizing the moment. For us, as students of human behaviour, this is what truly defines the man.

But for now, let us take the spotlight off this legend of the Chicago Bulls and turn it directly onto you.

Before you lies a two-part challenge. To get the most out of this process and, quite frankly, this book as a whole it is important not to move to the second part of the exercise until you have completed the first element. Agreed?

Exercise: Examine your All-Star life

This exercise consists of two complementary parts for a very specific reason. So, let's crack on with Part One.

If you are old school in your tastes, then grab a piece of paper and a pen, a notebook, a journal, your Moleskine diary. If you're a digital native, or a keyboard philosopher, someone who prefers to reflect and save writings in electronic files, then charge up your laptop or your tablet and let's get started. Alternatively, if the idea of writing in this book doesn't make you squirm, then grab a pencil and simply write down your thoughts in the blank spaces provided over the next two pages.

This might feel a little foreign to some people, since most of us are not accustomed to referring to ourselves in the third person, but in this case we ask you to use the illeistic style of writing. For **Part One** of this exercise, please look onto your life and your achievements as a stranger might and, writing in the third person, take a few minutes to write a mini autobiography. For example, if your name is Jax, then pretend you are an author, a biographer, who has just been commissioned by Jax to write his life story. Instead of using personal pronouns like "I" and "Me", refer yourself by your first name.

Are you ready?

Part One: My short autobiography

_____
_____
_____
_____
_____
_____
_____
_____
_____
_____
_____
_____
_____
_____
_____
_____
_____
_____
_____
_____

All done? Ok, now you can turn the page. Good job.

This part of the exercise might be a little more challenging. Now turn to **Part Two** of this exercise – your short eulogy.

Without being macabre, let's assume that the next 6 months are your last on Earth. What would your short eulogy say about you? How would others pay tribute to you; especially the family members who you love so dearly or those work colleagues who interact with you frequently?

Again, writing in the third person like a biographer or newspaper columnist, or even better, someone who you deeply care about would, compose a short eulogy befitting of someone who will be genuinely mourned and missed.

Part Two: A short eulogy, to me.

_____

Nicely done. You can turn the page when you're finished.

Did you struggle with both components of the exercise? If so, don't worry. You are certainly not alone. During countless interactions with students, clients, colleagues and friends, and using our combined capacities as coach, lecturer, consultant, executive, chat-buddy and intellectual-sparring partner, we've found over time that the majority of people really battle with this exercise. In facilitated sessions, we've seen some people treat it as a joke and then decide to revisit the process again with a more serious focus. Some were so challenged that they even consulted their family members, friends and mentors for help. All responses and reactions are completely understandable. It is a difficult exercise. And it's meant to be. It's also not a one-off process. As co-authors of this book, we've tackled this particular exercise more than a few times and we can assure you that it never gets easier. After all, putting a magnifying glass to your life is never completely comfortable if you take the process seriously.

Right now you may be pondering the point of this exercise and why we've been so explicit in referring to it as an exercise with two parts, rather than just two exercises. If your curiosity is already all fired up, that's great.

Keeping your two-part exercise in mind – and we do hope you managed to write down something interesting for both tasks – let's circle back to Michael Jordan's story as we search for some hidden messages and meaning encapsulated in one particular moment in time.

Michael Jordan & THAT defining moment

Jordan was raised in Wilmington, North Carolina where he took to basketball, baseball and football (the American variety) in high school. He was good, but he wasn't great – famously failing to make the varsity team as a sophomore and instead playing junior varsity.[51] That's before he shot up, reaching his towering 1.98m, and fine-tuning his legendary work ethic. One quote really encapsulates the Jordan approach: "I've always believed that if you put in the work, the results will come. I don't do things half-heartedly. Because I know if I do, then I can expect half-hearted results."[52]

Netflix's *The Last Dance* takes us back to 14 June 1998 and Game Six of the 1998 NBA Finals. The visiting Chicago Bulls had travelled to take on the home side, the Utah Jazz, at the Delta Center in Salt Lake City. Thirty-five-year-old Jordan was playing his last game for the Bulls.

The atmosphere inside the arena was, to put it mildly, electric. The two very best basketball teams in USA for that year - arguably the two best teams in the world - were engaged in thrilling combat. The Utah Jazz players, widely admired for their mental resilience, were holding it together in superb fashion that evening. As the match restarted in the fourth quarter, Utah Jazz were leading the Chicago Bulls 66 to 61. What made matters worse for the Bulls in this critical game was that one of their star players, Scottie Pippen, had been in great pain since the opening basket, having aggravated a back injury while performing a slam dunk. As the result, he was practically inactive for the first half of the game. Despite receiving off-court treatment and returning to the court in the second half of the game, Pippen did not recover his usual sharpness on both ends of the court.

Each team had its own motivation for winning this particular game. Having lost to the Bulls during the 1996/1997 NBA season, a victory in Game Six of 1998 would give Jazz the chance to exact sweet revenge on the Bulls in Game Seven. The title was on the line. On 14 June, with precious home-court advantage on their side, Jazz was well-positioned to dethrone the Bulls.

The fuel enkindling the Bulls' drive was a different animal all together. Sure, the Bulls players did not want to play the seventh game in a hostile away stadium, but they had another entirely different reason that motivated them: Legacy.

This had been the team's motiving factor since the beginning of the 1997/1998 season. The unpopular Bulls General Manager, Jerome 'Jerry' Richard Krause, had already put the word out that he would be breaking up this team after the playoff. So for the incumbent Bulls players, this season really was their "last dance". They were determined to bag their sixth NBA championship title so they could end their formidable dynasty on a high note. No other Bulls team before them had ever pulled off one championship win, let alone the five shining Larry O'Brien Championship Trophies that were proudly displayed in their trophy cabinet at the time. Winning a sixth championship in Game Six of the season was, for the current crop of Bulls players, very likely to be their last opportunity to accomplish something remarkable in their profession.

As the referee blew the whistle to end the 20-second time-out called by Bulls, with eleven out of the twelve minutes in the final quarter of normal game time played, the two teams moved back to the court. That was the beginning of 60 nail-biting seconds which took fans on both sides on an emotional roller-coaster. Every second counted.

For those of you who aren't basketball fans, and who have never experienced the nail-biting drama of a world-class game, we encourage you to turn to YouTube and find the following video: *Last Minute of Game 6 1998 NBA Finals Jazz vs Bulls*[53] or this YouTube clip.[54] It's impossible not to be swept up in the intense energy, the tension, the anxiety, the hope, the fight and the raw human emotion of the moment.

As the time-out ended, despite looking visibly tired, Michael Jordan calmly walked to the penalty line and scored two consecutive penalty shots. The score was tied with 59.2 seconds remaining to the end of regular game time.

As the game resumed, John Stockton dribbled into left side of Bull's territory and passed to Karl Malone who occupied the low post position with 49.6 seconds to go – breaths were held as Stockton and Malone, one of the most feared duos in league history, showed off their well-tuned partnership of 18 years. Stockton took a u-shape run and positioned himself behind the three-point line on the opposite side of the court, diagonally across from where Malone was controlling the ball. It was a cleaver run, designed to expose the complacency of the Bulls' defence.

Stockton found himself totally unmarked. Of course, Malone was not going to miss this chance. Almost telepathically, Malone threw a stunning crosscourt pass to Stockton. This rare reversal of the roles between the two of them created a chance for the Stockton to net a three-pointer – a chance which the prolific point guard executed convincingly. With 41.9 seconds left in the match, Jazz was holding an 86–83 lead.

After another brief recess, Jordan took a beautiful layup and reduced the gap to one point with 37.1 second left on the game clock. As Jazz began to attack, Stockton once again dribbled the ball down into Bulls territory, except with a little less urgency this time. After all, Jazz was entitled to 24 seconds possession before the shot clock violation. Possession was all important. If they could take time to wind down the clock, perhaps sink a shot to increase the lead or regain the ball from a rebound, then a Game Seven playoff could well be a reality. At that point, and in the moment, Jazz looked like it had the edge.

Stockton once again found Malone in the low-post position and passed the ball to Malone with the clock showing these digits – 22.6. But Jordon, one of the smartest and most strong-minded athletes in basketball history, was resolute to try something different. Within one second of Stockton's successful pass to Malone, Jordon decided to take on a riskier approach by letting Jeff Hornacek wonder off unmarked. Hornacek, as a shooting guard, had been instrumental in helping the Jazz to reach NBA Finals in 1997 and 1998. It was a potentially dangerous move.

Instead of clearing off from his spot to shadow and pressurise Hornacek, Jordan made his move to strip the ball from the Malone by coming in from blindside of this 2,06m-tall giant. Jordan doubled-up with Dennis Rodman, who was marking Malone at the time. This risky move turned out to be a brilliant strategy and one that caught Malone by surprise. With 18.9 seconds left on the clock, Jordan managed to steal the ball from Malone and began to dribble down the court.

In response, and with the stakes reaching a crescendo, Jazz had to coordinate their best defensive. Bryon Russell was tasked by the coach to guard Jordan. To date, Russell is still considered by many experts as one of the Top 25 defensive players in the history of Utah Jazz. This was not a surprise tactic.

The tension in the stadium was almost unbearable.

After dribbling passed the halfway mark, Jordan bounced the ball in the same spot, a meter or so outside the three-point line, for close to ten seconds while contemplating the most opportune moment to make his attacking move. As the anxiety in the crowd mounted, and with 8.6 seconds remaining, Jordan accelerated, drove inside the three-point line then executed a rapid cross-over before he took off for the 18-foot jump shot. As the ball sunk in, Jordan's two-pointer gave the Bulls an 87–86 lead with only 5.2 seconds to spare for Jazz to orchestrate a comeback. In the end, that jump shot from Jordan was the last basket scored in the match as Stockton missed a three-point attempt at the buzzer.

That two-pointer was also the last shot Jordan would take while wearing the Bulls jersey. But it was also the shot that earned the Chicago Bulls a sixth NBA championship title. That basket remains one of the most legendary sports moments in history.

Just like countless other sporting contests before it, this particular game was not without controversy. But it was not just Game Six that made this championship title extraordinary. The 1997/1998 season was a memorable run for the Bulls' American supporters as well as the team's many fans around the world. This global appeal was the reason why ESPN Films and Netflix decided to capture the highlights of that season and co-produce *The Last Dance* documentary miniseries. Since airing on 19 April 2020, the ten-part series has been an overwhelming success.

The nail-biting dramatic event of Utah Jazz versus the Chicago Bulls, and Michael Jordan's breath-taking last shot to secure NBA title number six for the Bulls, encapsulates the sweat and the tears, and the sweet taste of victory which is backed into competitive sports of any form.

In Game Six of the 1997/1998 NBA Final, players from both teams had to keep looking forward throughout the night. Each time a player made a mistake or, in Pippen's case, suffered a distressing setback, they had to pick themselves up quickly, let go of the moment and rapidly learn from the error. Moreover, with Pippen's injury, every Bulls player had to accept the impact on the team and invite themselves to step up.[55] As Michael Jordan said, "You must expect great things of yourself before you can do them."

On that momentous night, each Bulls player was invited to set high self-expectations – a call magnified by the knowledge that the team would be no more after this season. Many of the players accepted that this could be their very last opportunity to show what they were made off and to elevate their greatness.

Yes, throughout the season, the Bulls players did look back to acknowledge their successes. And there is no doubt that they learned from their past experiences. They also welcomed constructive downtimes and even tolerated Dennis Rodman's "blow off some steam", "therapeutic" vacation in Las Vegas, slap bang during the NBA Finals. These actions all helped the team to keep polishing their tactics, and increase the energy to win. However, having grasped the inevitable demise of this team greatly propelled them to activate their respective version of best self. The mentality of "last dance" drove them to be hungrier and more determined to take that sixth championship title. The average retirement age for an NBA player is in the mid-thirties. Jordan was 35 when he took his last shot for the Bulls. Yet he still played 43 minutes and 41 seconds out of the 48 minutes of game time, giving of his best self in each second. Even though he was visibly tired, he gave every ounce of himself to the game. Even Pippen managed to active his best self and lifted himself up to play for 25 minutes and 43 seconds.

Each one of these gladiators gave themselves over to the moment. And, in that moment, they gave the best they had to offer.

Basketball, of course, has something else: It's a mirror of life. It reflects the speed with which life changes, the pressure that comes when every second counts, and the opportunities that come your way when you least expect it. There is a charming quote which pops up on social media feeds from time to time and is unattributed, but it goes like this, "Life is like a basketball. It just keeps bouncing up and down." That's life. It has it peaks and its troughs, but it keeps moving and, notably, the more energy you put into your dribbling motion, the higher the ball bounces.

Jordan, renowned for his legendary vertical controlled running jump, proved himself a master of taking his chances both on and off the court. Tenacity and a winner's attitude seemingly underpinned everything he did. As the man himself said in this 10-part Netflix documentary: "My mentality was to go out and win at any cost. If you don't want to live that regimented mentality, then you don't need to be alongside of me.[56]"

Jordan also wrote in his book, I Can't Accept Not Trying: Michael Jordan on the Pursuit of Excellence: "I approach everything step by step... I had always set short-term goals. As I look back, each one of the steps or successes led to the next one. When I got cut from the varsity team as a sophomore in high school, I learned something. I knew I never wanted to feel that bad again... So, I set a goal of becoming a starter on the varsity. That's what I focused on all summer. When I worked on my game, that's what I thought about. When it happened, I set another goal, a reasonable, manageable goal that I could realistically achieve if I worked hard enough.... I guess I approached it with the end in mind. I knew exactly where I wanted to go, and I focused on getting there. As I reached those goals, they built on one another. I gained a little confidence every time I came through." In other words, Jordan - arguably the greatest basketball player of all time - preferred to focus on setting reasonable, manageable strategic objectives and then dialling up his intentionality to work on the right leading indicators in order achieve these strategic objectives. Above all, Jordan's intentionality channelled his mind to recognise that every single moment on the court and during training was a moment to give his all.

Be in the moment

As human beings we are always at the precise moment of the past ending and the future beginning. These moments permeate our days and our nights, but – for many people around the world – these moments just evaporate away or fade into one another as we trudge forward on the same path, never taking the time to change our course, to examine our actions or refine our tactics.

But when we start to see that clock counting down, and we begin to embrace the belief that EVERYTHING in life is transitory, then we open the door to digging deeper into our potential. We give ourselves permission to take educated risks, elevate conviction and let go of the negativity associated with setbacks. After all, if life is transitory, then our setbacks will also be fleeting.

When we start to play the game of life by basketball rules, we start to appreciate its finite nature. We begin to appreciate that every second, every minute and every moment is precious.

If you think that mini autobiography you wrote previously doesn't seem as impressive as it should be, do remember that the Bulls were trailing when the fourth quarter started in Game Six. Even when the game clock showed there were only 37.1 seconds left to play, Jordan and his team-mates were one point behind. But their respective best self mentality knew they had to "be more". They knew there were chapters to their story which still had to be written.

Sure, it's impossible to know exactly what goes through the head of a Michael Jordon or a Lennox Lewis, the undisputed heavyweight champion of the world, or a Mia Hamm, arguably one of the greatest women soccer players of our time, during those do-or-die moments and in those final career appearances when they dialled up their performance for a big farewell. Imagine how you might feel. The moment you realise that the future is NOT infinite, a voice from deep inside your spirit kicks in, urging you to be curious; to be curious about how we can all contribute to one other, how we could possibly leave something of significance behind, how we might redefine ourselves or do whatsoever is possible to challenge the status quo, how we can be more than we are in the here and now. There is certainly empirical research to support these claims. Interestingly, the first piece of research is a sociopsychology study that has something to do with basketball players.

Empirical evidence

With his unassuming mannerisms and grey beard, Jeff Greenberg serves as the Regents Professor of sociopsychology in Psychology Department of the college of Science, University of Arizona. With 407 peer-reviewed articles under his belt, Greenberg is an outstanding researcher with an impressive H-Index of 122 at the time when this chapter was written. The H-Index is a rating commonly adopted across all scientific research communities to ascertain a researcher's individual scientific research output. It is arrived at by measuring both scientific productivity and the apparent scientific impact of the work. As the H-Index gets higher, it requires an increasing amount of effort for a researcher to increase it. For example, for Greenberg to move from an H-Index of 122 to 123, he has to have published at least 123 peer-reviewed articles and one of the articles must be cited 122 times by other peer reviewed articles. Jorge Eduardo Hirsch, the Argentinean-American professor of physics at the University of California who invented the H-Index measuring system, reckons that after twenty years of research, an H-Index of 40 puts a researcher in an outstanding category and any number beyond 60 is truly exceptional. Greenberg's H-Index of 122 is a striking achievement and one that solidifies his reputation in his field.

Greenberg has a few keen research interests, with one being the humanology of morality. For us mere mortals, one of Greenberg's areas of focus extends to how humans cope with concerns about our mortality and how we respond to this realisation by creating our respective "symbolic immortality"[57] – or the legacy we wish to leave behind after death.

In collaboration with three other colleagues, Colin Zestcott, Uri Lifshin and Peter Helm, the team found that reminding basketball players just before a match that their mortality was short and death was unavoidable created some surprising effects. The first study of their investigation discovered that after being reminded of this grim reality, each player's "one-on-one" basketball game performance improved by forty percent. In another study, the research introduced a subtle death prime to the participants, and the players who were exposed to this thinking ultimately took more shots and outperformed the scores of others taking part in a basketball shooting task by thirty percent.[58]

Social psychologist Zestcott, who assumed the role of the primary researcher for this study, suggested that even though this approach might not mirror the usual pep talk that a coach gives to inspire his or her team, this tactic was well-aligned with an established idea termed "terror management theory". This theory posits that human beings are naturally motivated to pursue self-esteem, meaning and symbolic immortality. Being more than you are now has been a fundamental desire for human beings since the days of early man. If we violate this desire, our energy feels trapped. You may often find that the laziest and most unmotivated of people, those who don't want to be more or do more, are often unhappy individuals. When you feel stagnant, you often feel jaded and miserable. One of the modern world's icons, Apple founder Steve Jobs, concurred with this sentiment and discussed the mortality-immortality paradox in his renowned 2005 Stanford University Commencement address. He stated, "Remembering that you are going to die is the best way I know to avoid the trap of thinking you have something to lose."[59]

In other words: Developing a healthy level of appreciation for the transitory nature of everything around us will liberate us and allow us to exercise natural credulous curiosity. And, yes, that's a good thing. It helps you to activate your best version of you if you are mindful about it.

There is another brilliant researcher whose work must be highlighted here: Professor Daniel M Cable, professor of organisational behaviour at London Business School. Apart from having published more than one hundred peer-reviewed papers and three popular books, Cable has worked with hundreds of multinationals and assisted tens of thousands of individuals to transform their personal and social circumstances through helping them to develop a new understanding and appreciation for a concept called "best self". In 2015, in collaboration with his colleagues Jooa Julia Lee, Francesca Gino and Bradley R. Staats, Cable published an article that discussed their research findings on a theoretical underpinning called "best self".[60]

The authors were intrigued by how one could activate one's best self, and also whether such activation would lead to both short- and long-term impact through, as they put it, "recursion, interaction, and subjective construal between the self-concept and the social system".[61] In order to test their hypotheses, they decided to conduct two laboratory experiments at the Harvard Decision Science Laboratory where 246 participants were paired up to go through a number of exercises. To increase the completeness, they also implemented more tests at a US-operated global consulting firm. The experiments and tests were, in essence, focused on offering the participants a chance to reflect on times during which they were at their best. In various reflection activities, they asked the participants to think about a number of potential triggers – including thinking about their eulogy – then they measured the biological and psychological responses of the participants.

Their findings showed that when participants reflected on past successes and achievements, when they tapped into best self moments and activated those memories, that all sorts of amazing improvements happened, from boosting creative problem solving and workplace relationships, to improved mood, better tolerance of stress and pressure and a greater resilience to burnout. What also became apparent was that best self activations had more firepower when they were supported by insights and reflections shared from the participant's social network, rather than only relying on personal reflections.

In the race called life, all of us are athletes. Some of us aspire to be the Most Valuable Player (MVP) by playing the field of business, healthcare, or science research. Some others thrive to be the Greatest of All Time (GOAT) in educating others, or full-time parenting. Irrespective of the game you play, it is scientifically proven that if you take the time to reflect on your journey and the successes you've racked up along the way to get here, you are more likely to live a better life, enjoy a more prosperous existence and have the benefit of tapping into a more mindful approach.

Your story. Your moment. Your legacy.
Be intentional and zestful about them.

Let's come back to the two tasks we set at the beginning of this section.

We are now going to answer the question of why these are two distinct, but linked tasks within a single exercise.

Your short autobiography captures the notable moments in different chapters of your life story to date. It invites you to celebrate, build self-efficacy, learn from past lessons, and provide a quick qualitative measurement of your life. Your autobiography invites you to take stock of the exclamation marks you have gathered so far in your life. If Part One of the exercise – your short autobiography – consists predominately of a description of the titles of all the jobs you've had over the years, the number of kids and siblings you have, and some other chronological events – it is time to question if you have a healthy understanding of your own magic? There must be something you have done right to get you to where you are today? Some spark or talent that helped you achieve all the things you have accomplished. Be intentional and zestful about your formula of success and take a moment to distil this down. Let the thoughts sink in. And, if you are compelled to do so, rewrite the short autobiography after you have finished this chapter.

Paradoxically, your short eulogy invites you to project the chapters that are still to be written. Your eulogy invites you to have an honest conversation with yourself about the key highlights in your future chapters. As such, it forces you to consider the aspects of your life that are in need of attention. Take some time to go through Part Two of this exercise. Is it sounding safe? Or does it consist of many reasonable, measurable but valuable goals or strategic objectives that you believe you can fulfil in the future? Do the sentences sound upbeat, courageous, and aspirational as if they are inviting you to do more and be more?

In life, we are ALWAYS in the flux between our autobiography and eulogy. We are always at that exact spot that permits us to see who we are and encourages us to visualise who we can still become.

We are always at the moment where the two stories meet. That moment can be defined as your moment to be more. Or even as your zone of self-disruption. What you do with the moment, is *the* question.

SIX PERTINENT QUESTIONS FOR SELF-DISRUPTION AND EXPONENTIAL GROWTH

Underpinning the desire to be your best self and live your best life is the innate human desire to "be more". After you've taken the time to reflect on the key points – and omissions - in your short autobiography and mini eulogy, be completely honest with yourself when you look at the accompanying graph as you determine where you would place yourself on your current trajectory

This mini-exercise draws on something known as basic innovation S-curve theory, which is a great way to illustrate innovation over time. We are going to use the S-curve to help you support and formulate the right tactics for self-disruption and exponential growth. The S-Curve of Innovation, which was first attributed to Richard Foster in his book The Attacker's Advantage and was elaborated on by Harvard Business School professor Clayton Christensen in his book Innovator's Dilemma, is a robust concept that can be used to describe various companies at their different stages and to explain their successes and failures. The S-curve tracks innovation from its slow early beginnings as the technology or process is developed, to an acceleration phase (a steeper line) as it matures. Inevitably, and despite becoming more and more competent along the length of the first S-curve, somewhere along the timeline the business environment changes and the rate of return on investment for growth starts diminishing. It is at this point that companies are compelled to disrupt themselves and start doing something new which they may not be as competent in or as comfortable with. This is the start of their second S-curve. Where the journey becomes tricky for many companies – and individuals, if we apply this approach to ourselves – is that we are required to fade away the old curve as we attach our fortunes to the new curve with gusto. It sounds simple enough on paper, but in reality this is not an easy feat.

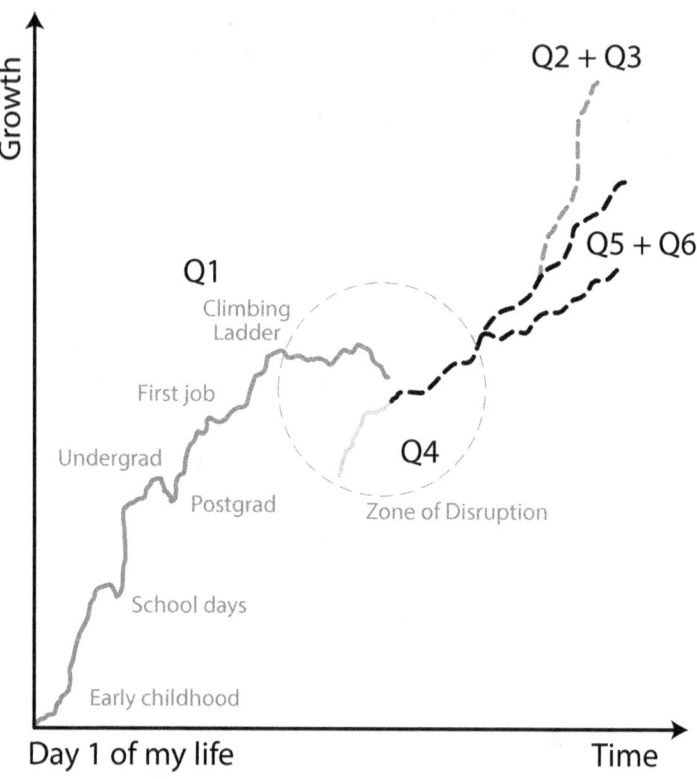

Q1: What is the current status of my growth trajectory?
Q2: What are the aspirations for my future self?
Q3: What attributes do I need to ensure the 'future me' can outcompete my competitors?
Q4: What are the right approaches and measurements to construct my zone of disruption?
Q5: What are my options as I immerse myself in the zone of disruption?
Q6: How many better options can I come up with?

Figure 2.1 Applying the double S curves concept to your self-disruption journey

To help you conceptualise these two S-curves, and understand where you lie on the axis, let's flick through the various stages in a bit more depth.

- Day 1 of your life. Well, that's your birthday, so that's an easy starting point.
- Your childhood and school years. For some of us easier than others, as we progress through the various stages of education and academia and life stages. Many of us may have gone on to study further at college or university, and even started a first job.
- Climbing the ladder. As we move up in our careers and begin to shape our lives, there comes a point where we may feel. Even if you are still enjoying the growth of the first S-curve, some aspects within this trajectory may need to change.
- The new you. So you must define a new growth curve and construct a zone to disrupt your old modus operndi and the mindset that no longer serves you. Can you do that to achieve maximum results from the 2nd S-curve but with minimal trade-offs and tensions as you phase off the first s-curve?

To help you analyse your own S-curve and determine where you are currently on your journey, we are going to pose *SIX* questions which are designed to disrupt your thinking and then spark growth. Here we go:

Start by examining questions one, two and three in combination. They are integrally linked, so you cannot deal with them in isolation.

Question One: What is my current status of my growth trajectory?

Be honest about who you are and where you are at this stage of your life. Be honest about your feelings. Are you growing at the right pace? Or are you tired of doing the same thing, but are gripped with fear when it comes to changing? If so, this anxiety will be holding you back from receiving greater things to come. It's time to start exploring ways to disrupt your thinking.

Similarly, if you are impatient and just want to jump ship without recognising that you are progressing reasonably well, your abrupt self-disruption may lead to some impediments to your growth. This scenario calls for self-disruption as well as redefining how you construe the meaning of some of the things that you dislike doing.

Question Two: What are the aspirations for my future self?

Explore if you are audacious enough to envision who and what you want to become. Question One will not give you much insight unless you evaluate the answer against Question Two. But this alone is not sufficient. It is not just about who and what you want to see yourself become in the near future as you set your goals or strategic objectives, it is integrally linked to Question Three, which asks us to focus our attention on being competitive in our chosen futures.

Question Three: What attributes do I need to ensure the 'future me' can outcompete my competitors?

What attributes and elements of this new version of you should you be focusing on? What will help you stand out from the pack? What will make you more assertive, or more empathetic? Being crystal clear about these specific attributes will enable you to take opportunities when they knock. Equally, this clarity will provide focus, so you know which doors to knock on to proactively create your own opportunities.

What these three questions all require is for you to issue an invitation to yourself to be courageous. We will explore more about this in Chapter Three: Courageous Invitation. Additionally, Chapter Four: Enlightened Selfishness will also provide you with some food for thought as you go about the task of unravelling these initial questions.

Moving on, Questions Four and Five should also be asked in combination.

Having clarified the first three questions, you now have a good idea of where you are now, where you want to go and what you need to standout. Building on these insights, keep the honesty levels on boil as you prepare to disrupt yourself and your growth trajectory.

Question Four: What are the right approaches and measurements to construct my zone of disruption?

Here we need you to start thinking about the outcomes you wish to target and based on these focus areas, the right processes that you need to establish to disrupt yourself. Do you need to stop being bureaucratic about your process? What about procrastinating unnecessarily? Can you shift unproductive routines? Should you take up an MBA, sign up a few relevant online open courses, or ringfence three hours every second night to gather information? Then how should you apply what you've learned and how can you measure what you have shifted?

Based on whatever these questions have stirred in you, spend some time formulating your input and outcome measurements both qualitatively and quantitatively. Often we find ourselves focusing so heavily on outcome measurements, for example: I want to lose 5kg in 12 months. We need to remember that outcome measurements are goals, and it is important to have good and established ambitions. However, complementary measurements should also be formulated. For examples, how many times I exercise a week, and what goes into my exercise session, from how many types of exercises I do, to how many repetitions and what mindset I adopt to approach every exercise session. This is just one set of the necessary input measurements. Others, like stretching muscles, diet and sleep must all be factored in if you are going to achieve your goal.

We shall explore the relevant constructs further in Chapter Five: Appoint Your Inner Advisors and Chapter Six, The Magic of Ampersand Thinking.

Question Five: What are my options as I immerse in the zone of disruption?

For example, what structure is right for me as I embark on this journey? Can you establish and leverage supporting groups, such as family, spouse, new mentors, lecturers, or people you know from LinkedIn or the social capital ecosystem?

You might look to starting small with a focus on consistency. How can you use small success to spin off bigger success? Sticking with the exercising goal from

Question Four, you might consider if you could slide in a few quick exercises while you are waiting for your bathtub to fill.

Question Six: How many better options can I come up with?

Often the initial or first ideas that pop up in our minds may seem plausible and helpful. But if we stop there, we may miss the chance to reframe our thinking or explore different thinking paths to come up with better options. Don't be fixated with your initial concepts or hold too tight with other people's suggestions. Spend just a little bit of time, but not too much, on questioning the ideas you have, and even questioning your questions. So deliberately park your original ideas on the side and force yourself to list down other ways to deliver the same value quicker, harder, and more efficiently. Refine and pivot. Creating smarter options can help you to lower the activation barriers or reduce the resistance you might feel during the initialisation stage, that is before your disruption habit has developed and matured. We shall incorporate more helpful constructs in Chapter Seven: It's Not About Fate, It's About Navigation And The Journey.

Armed with your responses to all these questions to drive your double-S-curve-like transition, it is imperative for you to activate your best self.

An invitation to 'be more'

From this moment forward, you should start to tune into the fact that there are many opportunities for you to be more than who you are right now. You can dream bigger, think smarter and take the shot with confidence. This book will offer you practical ways to do so.

As we go through this journey you may, from time to time, have to stop and remind yourself that you deserve an interesting autobiography and a great eulogy. But, to get to that point, you have to take more shots. You need to hear that basket whooshing each time a shot finds it mark. And, when it doesn't find its mark, you pick up the ball and try again.

We find it telling, to draw once again on Game Six of the 1997/1998 NBA Final, that media articles talking about how many shots Michael Jordan missed in that game were not readily available. As part of a research project into this phenomenon, we also noticed that very few articles focused on the mistakes made by other players in the Bulls and Jazz teams. When looking back, people recalled that each team gave its best. While different people remember the key moments of the game slightly differently, their common recollections always lean towards the feeling that these athletes had leveraged during that brief 48-minute game to be more than just basketball players. People remember these outstanding individuals for their concerted deliberateness, for giving every ounce of energy they had and for living through the game with such passion and dedication. They took their shots.

So, what's your excuses for not taking more shots?

Think about it: After passing your driver's licence test, how often have you been asked how many times you failed? Does anyone really care what mark you finished school with? As long as you know you can bounce back from the risks, unless your failures are catastrophic or highly immoral, most people only care about your achievements or how you bounced back from adversity and became more.

That's not to say that you should totally disrupt yourself and throw everything away just because a few aspects in your life aren't going right. In fact, the latter chapters of this book will help you to disrupt yourself more effectively and lower the mental resistance for change that may be obstructing your pursuit of more gratifying self-disruptions.

There is just one more thing we need to achieve in this chapter, before this book can continue to offer you more highly innovative, yet simple outlooks and practical recommendations to empower you to generate profound value for yourself and for those around you. We would like you to take a moment to ask yourself one more simple question: Are you prepared to issue a life-changing invitation to yourself, giving you the permission you need to '*be more*'?

Self-enrichment Exercises

Self-mastery begins by identifying, developing, and exploring your goals and most importantly how you will act out those goals to create the intentionality in your life, an essential ingredient for success. To get you started, we thought that a recap of the six questions would be useful.

Question One. What is my current status?

_____

_____

_____

_____

Question Two: What are the aspirations for my future self?

_____

_____

_____

_____

Question Three: What attributes do I need to ensure that the 'future me' is more competitive than my competitors?

_____

_____

_____

_____

Question Four: What are the right approaches and measurements when I construct my zone of disruption?

_____

_____

_____

Question Five: What are my options as I immerse in the zone of disruption?

_____

_____

_____

Question Six: How many other better options can I find?

_____

_____

_____

To incorporate our key propositions from this chapter, we would like to offer you a framework below (Figure 2.2) for your consideration. We call this framework, the "Best Self Goal Setting Canvas". This framework is intended to highlight the possible thought components which we believe underpin successful goal setting. Whilst we whole heartedly support self-reflection, contemplation, and perhaps even overactive imagination to encourage innovation and the identification of opportunities, we are also advocates of focus. This means that:

1. Goal setting should not be treated as a static process. It is an abductive process that can assist you to align all components involved in good goal setting. It is concentric in nature, requiring reflection, revisiting and circling back on initial and developing thoughts to delve deeper, to challenge ourselves, to build resolve and to focus on how those goals will be achieved. For some this may be daily, for others weekly and in some cases monthly or annually.

2. We believe that to achieve the level of focus required to create intentionality, you need to progressively record your goals (preferably in a journal) so that you can record the progress being made (based on the objectives set / actions taken), celebrate the wins, reflect on the challenges and document any changes to goals, what else you could be doing and / or what you could be doing differently to make them a reality.

3. Start small, but think big. Too many goals, too many things to focus on could become unmanageable. Your audacious purpose will come. Just give it time. There is no need to rush.

4. Don't forget about how your feel. That's right, your emotions as they will help to guide the achievement of your own personal alignment.

5. Revisit the answers you have come up with for the six self-disruption questions. Is there anything in this Best Self Goal Setting Canvas you would like to re-imagine, re-calibrate, and re-define?

Given the importance of this exercise on your journey, we encourage you to spend some time reflecting on your goals and to search deep within you to identify what you really want to achieve. Now record it in the first draft of your Best Self Goal Setting Canvas.

A digital version of the Best Self Goal Setting Canvas can be found on our website (www.courageousinvitations.com).

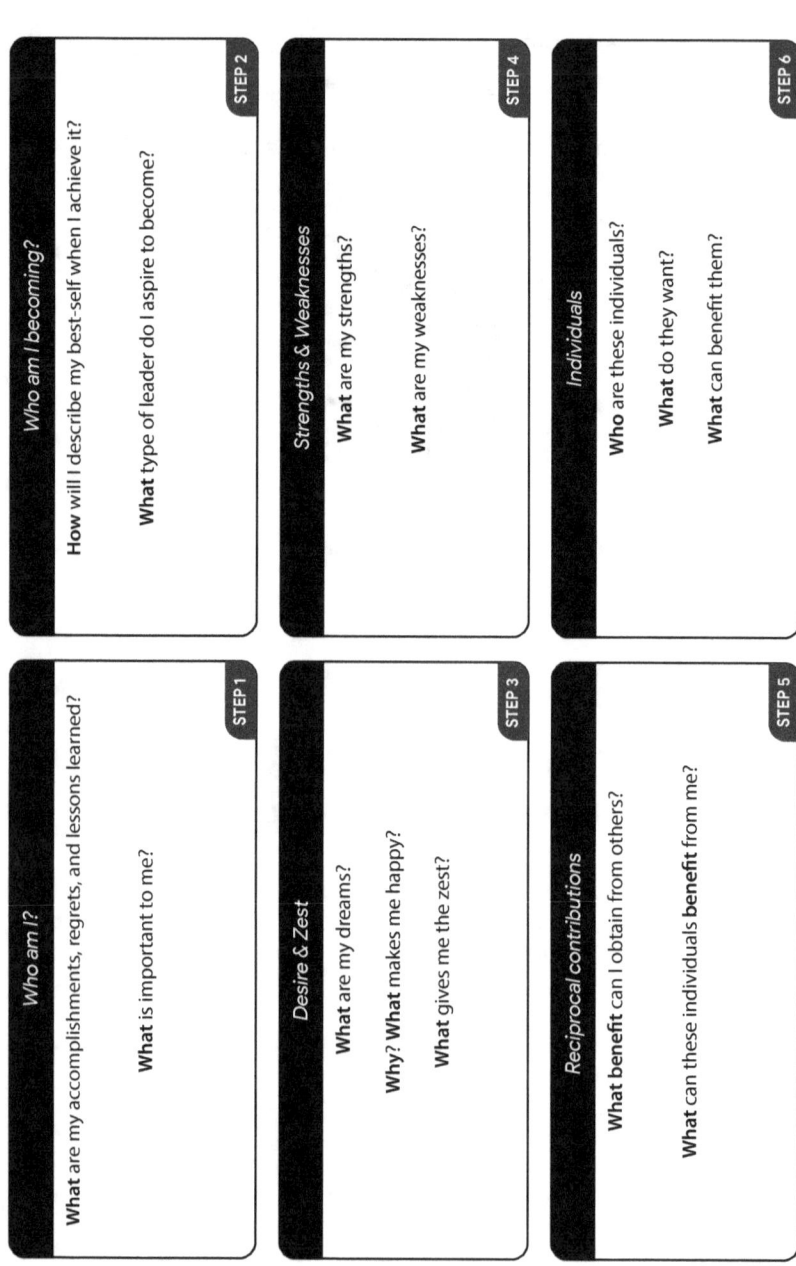

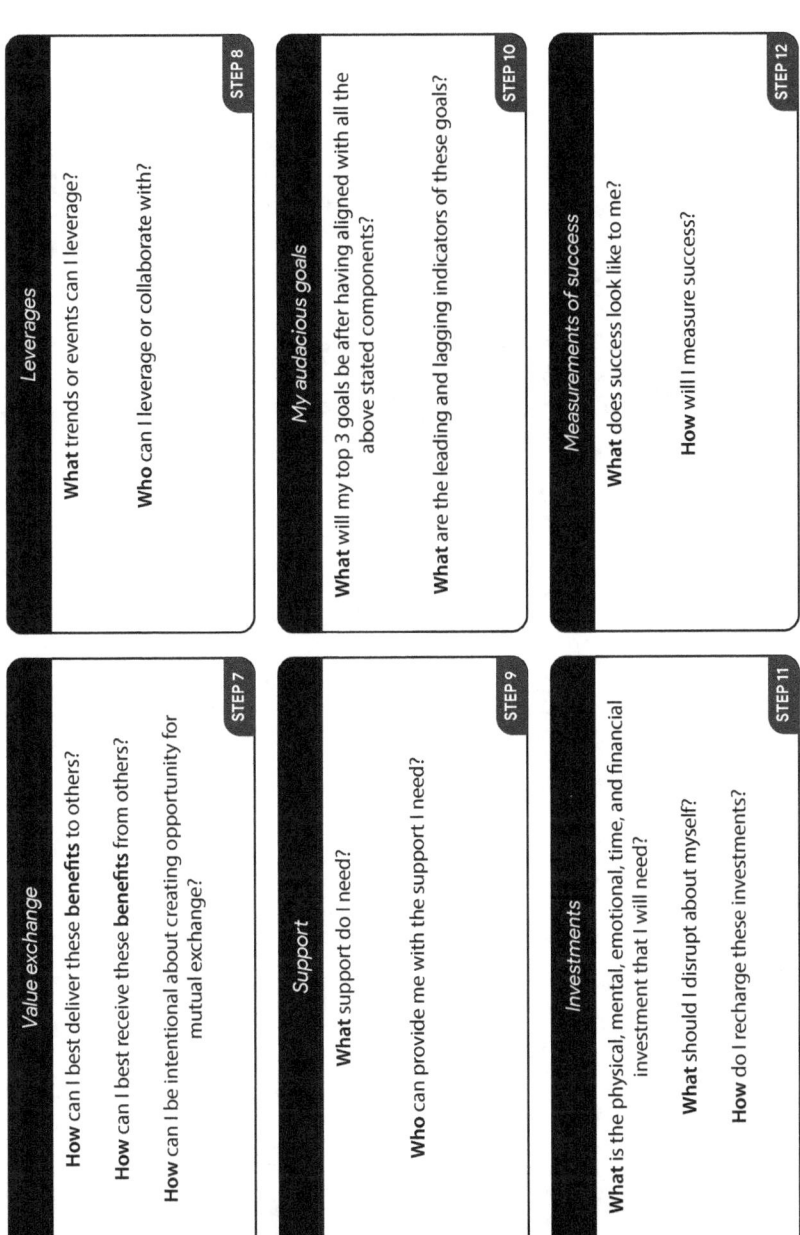

Figure 2.2 My Best Self Goal Setting Canvas

Chapter 3
Courageous Invitations

It's fitting that the oldest invitation known to mankind was written in Latin, the language to which we can trace the origins of the word. The Latin "invītāre" has two meanings: to entertain or offer shelter to, or - and here's where the etymology gets interesting – "to go after something, pursue with vigour and desire".[62] Bear that in mind as we travel back in time to the period during which Britain was living under Roman rule.

Today the ancient Roman fort of Vindolanda is a sprawling archaeological site and museum with UNESCO World Heritage credentials. Located in Northumberland, just south of Hadrian's Wall (which divides England from Scotland), the fort marked the strategically important, northern-most frontier for the Romans during their occupation of Britain from around 85 AD to 370 AD.[63] It's big. It's imposing. It's packed with history.

One of the most important discoveries on the site were the Vindolanda Tables, or Vindolanda Letters.

Archaeologists excavating this military site in 1973 uncovered a few pieces of spruce or larch wood. These pieces were about 0.3 to 0.5 centimetres in thickness, and about 10 by 15 centimetres in diameter. The surface of the wood had been treated and smoothed into 'writing paper' for the Roman soldiers garrisoned at the fort. The uses for these wafer-thin 'papers' ranged from recording the fort's official military matters, such as describing the interaction between the soldiers and the native Britons, to insights into the day-to-day workings of the fort. They were also used to capture personal communications to and from residents within Vindolanda. Whilst they aren't quite the oldest Roman writing tables ever unearthed in Britain – that title belongs to the waxed wooden Bloomberg Tablets discovered around 2010.[64] The Vindolanda Tablets are regarded as being the second-oldest surviving handwritten documents in the history of the island. They also hold the distinction of including among them the oldest surviving handwritten invitation known to mankind[65] and also the earliest Latin script written by a woman.

The tablet in question contains a birthday party invitation written by Claudia Severa, the wife of commander of Vindolanda fort, Aelius Brocchus, to her sister, Lepidina.[66] The writing style for the first part of the party invitation letter is rather formal, but it loosens up a bit towards the end. Experts have translated the Roman cursive writing to read as follows, "Claudia Severa to her Lepidina greetings. On 11 September, sister, for the day of the celebration of my birthday, I give you a warm invitation to make sure that you come to us, to make the day more enjoyable for me by your arrival, if you are present. Give my greetings to your Cerialis. My Aelius and my little son send him their greetings."

We may never know if Lepidina and her family made the trip to the Vindolanda fort to celebrate her sister's birthday, and her reply to her sister may be lost to history forever, but there is something deeply personal and human about glimpsing back in time and being privy to an intimate invitation of this nature.

Of course, throughout history individuals from different civilisations have been sending one another invitations for any number of reasons. Some were sent for the purpose of inviting others to share a joyful occasion or to partake in a memorable moment. While other invitations were sent with much more momentous intentions in mind.

Given the title of this chapter, you may well be wondering what constitutes a courageous invitation. Why do we specifically mention this plurality?

Courageous invitations are of particular importance to each of us during moments when we are poised to transition and transform ourselves, and when we are operating in the zone of disruption. As we get up close and personal with courageous invitations, we'll lay out our thinking and make practical recommendations about how to apply the courageous invitations concept in your own life. Hopefully, this section will trigger new thinking and inspire relevant questions.

Courage. A small word for a big construct

Before we start issuing invitations, a word on courage. How do you "see" courage in your mind's eye? Joan of Arc leading the French army to victory against the English at Orléans in 1429? Suffragette Emmeline Pankhurst leading a march of women to petition Britain's King George V on 22 May 1914, and being arrested outside Buckingham Palace? Or a single mother, holding down a job, paying her bills diligently, raising her children with care and holding her head up high?

One of the finest artistic depictions of courage in recent years is the bronze sculpture by Kristen Visbal, known as "Fearless Girl", which is now a permanent feature outside the New York Stock Exchange. A potent symbol of female empowerment, Fearless Girl first faced down Wall Street's "Charging Bull" sculpture in 2017 as part of an International Women's Day ad campaign run by the McCann advertising agency to highlight the lack of women on company boards. Such was the positive response to her defiance and courage that, in 2018, Fearless Girl was moved to a permanent spot in front of the bourse. Speaking at the time, Manhattan Democrat Carolyn Maloney observed, "Now, instead of staring down the bull, she's going to be staring down all of business right here in the centre and capital of business for America, here in New York

City." Maloney added that the statue had "started as a statement, and she completely changed it into a movement".[67]

This is how courage works.

In our daily lives, we often find courage is like dripping water into a pool. Allowing the first droplet to impact on the water is usually the hardest act. But when you let courage flow, it begins to generate a small ripple. As you continue to let more droplets of courage hit the water uninterrupted, and at the right frequency, soon the ripples become bigger, more expansive and wide-reaching. These droplets of courage ultimately generate waves with consistent rhythms – which we called habits. To switch elements for a second, the act of activating courage is like igniting a spark which has the potential to grow and absorb all in its path with its power and purpose.

For some reason, we don't always take the time to reflect upon the concept of courage, particularly when it relates to our own actions. Certainly, the majority of us do not often pause to reflect on the moments in our lives that were deserving of a little more courage, a bit more of a spark. Similarly, many – if not most of us - rarely take the time to prepare our future mind projects in order to galvanise ourselves towards courageousness in how we normally think and behave, but we should.

If you are determined to succeed, then it is not sufficient to give yourself permission to "be more", it is essential that you make it official – almost as if you are making a conscious declaration to yourself. Our heads are busy places, they juggle thousands of thoughts in a day, our dreams, our worries and our ambitions. Sometimes it necessary to help an intention stand out by doing something a little more special than just a cursory moment of acknowledgment. This is why we encourage you to issue an invitation to yourself, a call to action, putting this intention at the front of your "to do" list and giving it the prominence it deserves. If that means going old-school and writing out a formal invitation, using crisp stationery and a fancy font, then so be it. However, take the issuance of this invitation to yourself seriously, be bold about it. Be courageous.

It might also help and inspire you to be creative in how you frame and draw yourself in with this courageous invitation by hopping back in time with us as we pay homage to the history of the invitation and the importance of the moments to our humanity and how we understand what sparks a voyage of discovery.

Nelson Mandela: The road to forgiveness

One historic example concerns Nelson Rolihlahla Mandela, President of South Africa from 1994 to 1999 and a man considered to be one the greatest leaders of the 20th century.

Since becoming involved in the anti-apartheid movement in 1942, the same year in which he formally joined the African National Congress, Mandela had become an instrumental figure in the activism movements against the South African government's inhuman apartheid policies. This racist legislature legitimised and institutionalised ethnicity segregation, a controversial and widely-condemned policy which touched all aspects of life in South African between 1948 and 1994. During this atrocious phase of South Africa's history, black South Africans (and other race groups) were discriminated against and oppressed and were treated as second-class citizens to the white minority. The bitter aftermath of its divisive apartheid past still lingers in South Africa to this day.[68]

During the years of fighting against social injustice in South Africa, Mandela's personal courage created ripple effects across the nation, and the world. His ideology resonated with the majority of the country's citizens who were oppressed by the supremist government.

On 12 June 1964 Nelson Mandela and seven other men, known collectively as the Rivonia Trialists,[69] were sentenced to life imprisonment on charges of sabotage. Mandela served 27 years of this unjust sentence, including 18 years at the brutal Robben Island maximum security prison, living in a 2.4 metre by 2.1 metre cell and, alongside his fellow inmates, labouring day after day in the island's limestone quarries. The men undertook back-breaking work under the searing African sun, and often confronted with brutality from the prison guards, to mine the rock which was then used to surface the roads on the island.[70] Conditions inside the prison were harsh. Often inmates were not provided with shoes or sufficient clothing items – a move aimed to agonise and humiliate them – and they were frequently on the receiving end of various forms of physical and psychological ill treatment. Mandela's tiny cell had no plumbing and no bed.

Yet, after Mandela's release from Victor Verster prison in Cape Town on 11 February 1990, he did not encourage an approach of retribution and retaliation, but instead entered into a series of negotiations with the then South African President, FW de Klerk. These discussions ran from 1990 to 1993 and set the stage for the country's first democratic elections in 1994 and a peaceful transfer of power. In 1995, with the endorsement of then President Mandela, South Africa's newly-elected Parliament established The Truth and Reconciliation Commission[71] as an official body to hold formal hearings into apartheid-era atrocities and crimes, with the aim of healing and unifying the country through a process of restorative justice and conciliation. Having managed to terminate the apartheid regime peacefully, and lay the foundations for a new democratic South Africa, Mandela and De Klerk were named joint winners of the 1993 Nobel Peace Prize.

Nelson Mandela's life story is replete with examples of humility, wisdom, humanity and reconciliation. But one of the most profound and symbolic gestures of forgiveness on the part of the statesman came in the wake of his election as South African President in 1994 and three inauguration invitations he dispatched to attend the celebration.

Notable guests, seated in pride-of-place at that historic event on 10 May 1994, were James Gregory, Christo Brand and Jack Swart, three of Mandela's jailers on Robben Island.

Later, in 1995, Mandela would issue another grand gesture of forgiveness by inviting Dr Percy Yutar, the state prosecutor during the Rivonia Trial. The two would dine together over a Kosher lunch at the presidential mansion.[72]

As Mandela and Mandla Langa would go on to write in *Dare Not Linger: The Presidential Years*,[73] "Mandela believed that reconciliation and national unity were one side of the same coin, of which reconstruction and development were the other side – something that could be arrived at 'through a process of reciprocity' in which everyone should 'be part – and be seen to be part – of the task of reconstruction and transformation in our country'."

Or, as Mandela famously wrote in his autobiography *Long Walk to Freedom*, "No one is born hating another person because of the colour of his skin, or his background, or his religion. They must learn to hate, and if they can learn to hate, they can be taught to love, for love comes more naturally to the human heart than its opposite."

Daryl Davis: An unusual friendship

These often-cited words from a true African statesman also resonate strongly across the Atlantic Ocean in the United States; particularly with respect to the infamous Ku Klux Klan (KKK or Klan), a white supremacist hate group that has been committing horrific and violent crimes - predominately against African Americans - since late-1865, when it was founded in Tennessee by former Confederate soldiers and other Southerners.

The Klan emerged in the wake of the American Civil War, which raged from 1861 to 1865 and had at its core the issue of slavery – not necessarily, as some imagine, the morality of the abhorrent institution but rather the economics of the system and the political control it exerted.[74] During the so-called Reconstruction era, which ran post-war to 1877 and during which the remnants of slavery in the Confederate states were dismantled, the KKK was a violent and threatening presence across the Southern states of America. Ultimately the group was suppressed through federal intervention in the early 1870s,[75] but in the 1920s a new KKK emerged – less violent but equally virulent, according to historian Linda Gordon.[76] Today this truly equal-opportunity hate group continues to target individuals with different ethnicities, religious views and sexual orientations, as well as those perceived to be politically left-leaning.[77]

And yet, despite this despicable history of hatred, one African American man, Daryl Davis, made a name for himself by having a frequent presence at KKK rallies.[78]

It all started for Davis – a passionate advocate for addressing racism through education and communication - after an encounter with a KKK member in the 1980s. A professional musician known to turn his hand to all genres of music from jazz and blues to rock 'n roll, country, boogie-woogie, big band and swing, Davis had arrived at the Silver Dollar Lounge in Frederick, Maryland for a gig. It was 1983.[79] He had played this venue before, an establishment where black people were allowed but, in Davis's own words, "they were not welcome". After the band's set was finished, Davis was approached by a white man some 15 years his senior. There was nothing unusual about an audience member approaching a band member, but the man went on to comment that he had never seen a black man play the piano like Jerry Lee Lewis.

More curious than offended, Davis engaged the man in conversation. "Didn't this man know the origins of Jerry Lee's style?" Davis said in a 2017 TED Talk "I said to him – I wasn't trying to be facetious – where do you think Jerry Lee Lewis learnt how to play?" related Davis. "Jerry Lee learnt that style from the same place I did, from black blues and boogie-woogie piano players." The man countered that he'd never heard a black man play like that and refused to believe that Davis knew Lewis and had this information first hand, but he did offer to buy Davis a drink – and the musician used the invitation to have a friendly discussion. It was the first time, the man later disclosed, that he'd sat down and had a drink with a man of colour. Eventually, after some pressing, the man admitted he was a member of the Ku Klux Klan."[80]

Davis was surprised. The two shared contact details and every time Davis played the Silver Dollar Lounge he would let his drinking pal know and the man would bring other members of the Klan to watch Davis play. This gave birth to what was arguably the world's strangest side hustle: meeting with KKK members of various ranks and attending so-called cross lighting rallies.

After some arm twisting, Davis's contact reluctantly shared the details of the Klan leader for the state of Maryland, Grand Dragon Roger Kelly. After getting his secretary to set up a meeting with Kelly, under the guise of including him in a book about the KKK, Davis knew he was entering new and potentially dangerous territory. Kelly was unaware that Davis was black, so the grand reveal came as something of a surprise. Davis had no idea how Kelly would respond. When the time came and the door to his motel room opened, Davis greeted Kelly and his armed bodyguard, and they respectfully sat down to talk. A few tense hours of conversation followed before the men parted ways, but this would not be the end of their relationship. In time, Kelly started inviting Davis to his home. Then he invited him to Klan rallies during which ritualistic chants were intoned, giant crosses were burned, and beer and hot dogs were served. Kelly was completely open with Davis, even sharing the deeply racial stereotypes that underpinned the Klan's foundation. Davis listened, he asked questions and took notes. Slowly, bit by bit and through his actions, the Grammy Award-winning musician broke down one stereotype after another. As the gap narrowed, the two men became friends.

In time, Kelly would quit the Klan. He would close this hate-filled chapter in his life and symbolically hand his Klan robe over to Davis who, since then, has collected around 200 robes from former Klansmen. He keeps the robes at home, as a powerful reminder that through facilitating conversations it is possible to break down even the most entrenched of barriers. Davis continues to befriend members of the KKK.

"Hate stems from fear," Davis teaches. "Fear of the unknown. This is all across the board."[81]

So Davis issued an invitation to himself to open his own mind, to step out of fear and into understanding and to listen to the views of the Klan. This led Davis to the conclusion, "If you have an adversary, give that person a platform. Allow them to air their views. If you agree with them, fine, if you don't that's fine too. You challenge them politely and intelligently. Not rudely or violently. When you do things like that there is an excellent chance they will reciprocate and give you a platform to express your views. You make sure you do them intelligently and influentially."

Davis calls this a spark, which has the potential to become a flame. Philosophers and moralists such as Matt Ferkany have embarked on studies into the notion of open-mindedness and the willingness to engage with people whose moral ideas are strange or repugnant, possibly even on the very boundary of our own moral limit.[82] Whilst warning against moving too far away from your own beliefs in order to accommodate others, Ferkany does have this to say, "Open-minded engagement keeps conversations going, builds trust and, at its best, promises to break down divisions."

Issuing an invitation to engage open-mindedly with someone so fundamentally different from yourself, with such entrenched and potentially dangerous views, is courageous in the extreme. But it also helped to achieve the seemingly impossible: A closet packed with the discarded robes of 200 Klansman, housed in the home of a black musician who reached out his hand.

Courage brings mental freedom, even if the path ahead is treacherous

The stories of Daryl Davis and Nelson Mandela highlight the fact that to prevail in the face of obstacles, and to make a successful life transition, you cannot expect to issue a one-off invitation to be courageous. You need more than one drop of water to create a ripple and to sustain its rhythm. It is the persistence to choose courage time and time again that drives us towards success. Stop the droplets, or lose interest after generating just one spark of fire, and transformation, change and the attainment of your goals is likely to illude you.

Mandela had dedicated his life for the struggle of the African people. He served 27 years in prison in order to fulfil that dream; declining a number of offers from the apartheid-era government for a conditional release if he renounced violent protest as a means of bringing change to his country. Time and time again, he refused. He did so consistently, repeatably and courageously. Each defiance of his jailors was a small and powerful act of courage, together they are the stuff of legend.

We have many insights into how Mandela's thinking and journey towards freedom unfolded over the years, thanks to his books and countless interviews, but only the man himself would ever know what those individual acts of courage cost him. But this one quote tells us a great deal about how standing his ground, and leaving prison on his own terms, shaped the great man, "As I walked out of the door towards the gate that would lead to my freedom, I knew if I didn't leave my bitterness and hatred behind, I'd still be in prison."[83]

Yes, another courageous invitation. A clear and profound example of how courage sets the mind free from the fear and negative sentiments that trap our souls and weight down our spirits.

We spoke about activating your best self in the previous chapter, and how underpinning the desire to be your best self and to live your best life is our innate human drive to "be more". Our stories – our autobiographies and our eulogies – are testament to each time we have pushed ourselves to greatness and sought to change our current trajectory in search of something more.

We can only imagine what was going through Mandela's mind when he invited his jailors to attend his inauguration ceremony, during a time when racial tensions were running high in South Africa.[84] What we do know, thanks to insights which Mandela himself gave us into his life and his thinking through his numerous books and speeches, is that this incredibly mindful leader had a remarkable capacity for compassion. This empathy was a deliberate and conscious decision on his part and carried with it the aim of achieving a greater good. Time after time, Mandela invited himself to make peace with his country's bitter history of injustice, as well as cruelty imposed on him. He often achieved this by inviting his former enemies to collaborate. Above all, Mandela invited himself to step up when many of his fellow politicians doubted this reconciliatory approach. In his book, *Conversations With Myself*,[85] Mandela wrote that, "Success in politics demands that you must take your people into confidence about your views and state them very clearly, very politely, very calmly, but nevertheless, state them openly." Having set his vision, Mandela invited himself to be compassionate and to act in the best interests of his nation, in order to encourage healing and unity.

Where Mandela harnessed the power of compassion, Daryl Davis made curiosity his calling card. He managed to convince more than 200 white supremacists to leave and denounce their fellow Klansmen simply by inviting himself to be curious, and to listen with an open mind. How can you hate someone you've never met?[86] This was the question that drove Davis' curiosity and ultimately led to the publication of his book, *Klan-destine Relationships*, in 1998.[87] "Invite your enemies to sit down and join you. One small thing you say might give them food for thought, and you will learn," is the mantra underpinning his truly unique and open journey.[88] The Daryl Davis invitation is about trying to determine the source of the hate, rather than responding with hate.

From the outside looking in, the courage exercised by these modern-day icons appears larger than life. But remarkable individuals don't always start out that way. They begin like everyday champions. But everyday champions who know how to capitalise on every moment, and every micro-moment. They dig into their reserves and they pull out their inherent spirit of bravery. They prevail because they can sense the moments that call for courageous actions and, at each juncture, they invite themselves to make the best decision. Then they repeat this courage tirelessly, frequently and doggedly as the journey gets rougher and tougher. They prevail simply because they chose to take up the challenge posed by the countless courageous invitations they issued to themselves.

There are many books and articles written about individuals of this strength and calibre, and some of our personal favourites include Aruna Roy (1946-), the renowned Indian social activist who risked her life to fight corruption and promote government transparency,[89] and Benazir Bhutto, the 11th Prime Minister of Pakistan (1993-1996) and the first woman to head a Muslim state. Bhutto was a strong and visionary woman who ended a military dictatorship in her country and fought for women's rights. She was assassinated for her bravery and her desire to change her country for the better.[90]

Other examples, while they may not have made world news headlines, are by no means less compelling.

Dr Frank Magwegwe grew up in a disadvantaged community. He used to sleep rough in train stations, and sell vegetables on the street or do menial jobs to survive. But Magwegwe managed to enrich himself, find a job, and then work his way all the way up to the divisional CEO position of a large insurance company in South Africa. Later in his journey he would leave corporate life behind to pursue a career in lecturing.

Or consider the story of Kelly Cohen Navon, who was told by neurologists that she would not be able to function in higher cognitive level after a head-on car collision. Did that stop her? No. She went on to obtain an MBA degree from one of the Top 50 business schools in the world.

Or Antoinette van der Merwe, who was marginalised due to her sexual orientation but fought on to work her way up from floor cleaner to an executive managing a big, complex portfolio in the cleaning and hospitality industry.

The list goes on.

Magwegwe, Cohen Navon and Van der Merwe have one thing in common, they all chose 'courage over comfort'. We love this expression, which is the mental handiwork of *New York Times* bestselling author and University of Houston scholar, Dr Brené Brown. Brown is a vocal and passionate advocate for aligning her spirit, each and every day, to choosing courage and vulnerability over comfort and ease. As she says in her Netflix special *Brené Brown: The Call To Courage*, "Today I will choose courage over comfort. I can't make any promises for tomorrow, but today I will choose to be brave.[91]" *Ayoba*! ("Ayoba" is a South African slang which expresses delight, excitement, and approval when witnessed something interesting or awesome.)

Perhaps you are one of those everyday champions already? Maybe you just don't know it? Or perhaps you are one of those everyday champions in the making, but you've neglected to affirm your progress. Whatever your life stage, ask yourself if you have ever intentionally and mindfully invited yourself to be courageous for a particular challenge or opportunity. If you had, would your problem-solving and decision-making processes have been any different?

The origin of courage: Zest and bravery

The magnificent poet and activist Maya Angelou once stated that, "I am convinced that courage is the most important of all the virtues. Because without courage, you cannot practise any other virtue consistently."

Indeed, the critical role of courage in any epic voyage has been recognised and appreciated throughout history, dating back to the works of Greek philosophers Plato and Aristotle. It has been celebrated in myths and legends, from King Arthur's Knights of the Round Table to Johan Bunyan's 1678 allegory The Pilgrim's Progress and Dante Alighieri's poem Inferno. These earlier works often underscored the importance of showing immense courage in the face of extreme situations, such as death, war or disaster. These legends and celebrations of the extraordinary have elevated the concept of courage to something akin to a superhero comic book. However, increasingly we are starting to acknowledge that courage – in all its forms – is a daily action. A continuous and consistent characteristic which shows its face in every day interactions.[92] This understanding of courage holds even greater weight for us all at a time where rapid technological advancements are casting a pall over employment opportunities, where the global Covid-19 pandemic is threatening lives and livelihoods, and where fierce competition and political instability continue to throw us unknown curveballs when least expected.

The etymology of the word courage can be traced back to the 14th century, where it was derived from the French *corage*, which means heart or innermost feelings, or even temper. In turn, the word has a similar meaning in English, speaking also to the concept of heart being a state of mind or temperament. It draws as well on the Latin (*coraticum*), Italian *(coraggio)* and Spanish (*coraje*) – which have the Latin *cor* – or heart – as a common denominator. Thanks to Old and Middle English the word has come to be associated with bravery and confidence, inner strength, Zest, and pride.[93] Symbolically it's a pretty powerful world.

Over the centuries, scholars and deep thinkers have also provided different definitions of the word courage. Ernest Hemingway, the American novelist, described courage as "grace under pressure"; theologian Russell Haitch wrote, "Courage is two-sided: there is an aspect of standing firm or fighting, and an aspect of accepting intractable realities; courage is the psychic strength that enables the self to face danger and death." Psychologist Heinz Kohut surmised that courage sprung from opposing "the pressures exerted on them" and remaining "faithful to their ideals and themselves". While mental health specialist Deborah Finfgeld wrote: "Being courageous involves being fully aware of and accepting the threat of a long-term health concern, solving problems using discernment, and developing enhanced sensitivities to personal needs and the world in general. Courageous behaviour consists of taking responsibility and being productive."[94]

In recent years, as blogging and vlogging and social media have emerged as popular avenues for sharing and developing opinions, it's not surprising to see any number of options pop up if you enter the word "courage" in your search engine. The word also crops up increasingly in the realm of formal academic insights where we have seen a number of discussions, articles and papers published with an intention to understand the true nature of courage. We've seen clinical psychologists discussing the role of courage in how they deal with personal traumas, or how courage fits into the mix when achieving seemingly small feats. Industrial psychologists use the notion of courage in the context of explaining leadership or whistle-blowing. Researchers such as Matt Howard and Joshua Cogswell have even dug deeper by exploring the antecedents of courage, including the enabling role of leadership, personality types, age, culture and – to use the word explored by Angela Duckworth in her 2016 book – grit.[95] Certainly, more work needs to be done to understand these antecedents, something which James Detert and Evan Bruno[96] called for in their reflections on workplace courage.[97]

In their attempts to understand and measure courage, we've even seen the emergence of two valid measures which enable researchers to empirically study these traits. The Woodard Pury Courage Sacle-23 is one such measure as is Peter Norton and Brandon Weiss's 2009 Courage Measure, which is perhaps the most popular option currently available.[98]

How courage and fear are wired in our brains

Another thing icons and everyday champions have in common is their ability to overcome fear despite sensing the sentiment. As Rudyard Kipling (1865-1936), the English Nobel laureate, once put it, "If you can trust yourself when all men doubt you, but make allowance for their doubting too.[99]"

While any attempt to measure this trait is admirable, we also believe that irrespective of what sparks courage in any one of us – be it as the result of personality, environmental influences or any number of other factors – it is equally true that to completely understand courage, one needs a healthy appreciation for the motivation of fear. After all, courage is, at its core, the ability to carry out an action in pursuit of a goal despite experiencing fear. Nelson Mandela concurred with this view when he wrote, "I learned that courage was not the absence of fear, but the triumph over it. The brave man is not he who does not feel afraid, but he who conquers that fear."[100]

The fear-courage connection is well-founded from the neuroscience perspective.

Fear is your body's natural, biological response to external threats – usually regarded as emanating from a region of the brain known as the amygdala. For a tiny collection of cells situated at the base of the brain, the amygdala achieved a fair amount of notoriety in the 1990s when acclaimed behavioural scientist Daniel Goleman coined the term "amygdala hijack" in his book *Emotional Intelligence: Why It Can Matter More Than IQ*. According to Goleman, who was building on the research at the time, an amygdala hijack refers to an immediate and overwhelming personal, emotional response which is generally out of proportion with the actual stimulus. The reason? Because the stimulus has triggered a more significant and innate emotional threat.[101] But there's more to the amygdala than just this reactionary view, something which has certainly come to the fore in recent years.

The amygdala's role is certainly to detect threats. However, it would be strange – biologically speaking – to abdicate such a vital survival role to such a tiny portion of the brain, which is located in the anterior portion of the temporal lobe with one lobe on each hemisphere of the brain and comprises just under 0.3% of the volume of this remarkable organ.[102]

Instead, the amygdala forms, together with other brain regions such as the hypothalamus and stria terminalis, a neurocircuit that produces fear responses. It's really a complex circuit, or cluster of neurons, which are responsible for producing our thoughts[103] and emotions.[104] This, scientists tell us, means that the amygdala has a more universal function than simply responding to fear.[105] In 2018, a meta-analysis sampled a broader range of experiments measuring autonomic physiology – 223 studies in total and input from nearly 22 000 test subjects – and found a wealth of varied physiological responses for each emotion across different studies. Nothing seemed to give credence to the amygdala hijack theory or to the fact that these tiny lobes alone had their fingerprints all over our negative, fear-based emotions. Rather the lobes were activated by both pleasant and unpleasant stimuli.[106] In short, we can't pin our emotional responses on one portion of the brain alone, rather the amygdala works in concert with other areas; which makes more sense if you consider the interlinked nature of the human body.

Speaking of neural circuits, the fear circuitry has been commonly acknowledged to coordinate defence mechanisms in response to environmental threats. This circuitry has been suggested to be evolutionarily crucial to our survival as a species.[107] In 2018, a group of neuroscientists working with Professor Andrew Huberman of Stanford University School of Medicine uncovered some empirical findings which shed light on the interesting neurological circuitry relationship between fear and courage. The co-authors describing their experimental results in the highly acclaimed scientific journal 'Nature'.

The researchers identified two adjacent clusters of nerve cells in the brains of mice whose activity level upon seeing a visual threat spells the difference between a timid response and a bold or even fierce one.[108] *Using brain mapping, the Stanford researchers were able to monitor what happened in* a structure called the ventral midline thalamus (vMT) when receiving sensory information and then determine where the vMT sent this information. They determined that two main areas come into play when the vMT distributes the information it receives: the basolateral amygdala (which processes fear and aggression, among other emotions) and the medial prefrontal cortex (which modulates emotional responses).[109] Basically, you don't want your response getting bogged down in the amygdala.

Physiologically, a courageous individual prevents the signal of fear circuit from going haywire in response to a perceived threat. He or she reshapes the involuntary fear into courage, which is the foundation of courageous invitations. Huberman calls this interplay "the courage circuit". He explains the tendency to move towards, not away from, a perceived threat in this way, "... the reason we call it the courage circuit is that it triggers activation of the release of a neurochemical called dopamine, which of course, many people are familiar with for its role in reward. But dopamine is not only involved in making us feel good. And it has this element of reward and it's associated with reaching goals, but it also tends to reinforce, it changes the structure of those circuits so that we're more likely to engage in that behaviour again. In part, because it's desirable, but in part, because the circuit itself gets wired up in a way that it's more likely to get triggered in the future."[110]

But there is a catch. Isn't there always? You can indeed become more courageous, but for this to happen your "courage circuit" must make a connection to the medial prefrontal cortex – a region of the brain that does not store previously learned information which can, therefore, be misconstrued and tainted by past fears and previously negative experiences. If this is not the case, if this connection does not exist, then fear memory can merge with the current sensory and emotional signals to make our fear response even more accelerated.[111]

How this plays out in our lives is both good and bad news for those who, like best-selling author and Nobel Memorial Prize in Economic Sciences laureate Daniel Kahneman, have an appreciation for the different gears our brain is capable of operating in two different modes of thinking – System I, which is fast and autopilot based, and System II, which is slow and deliberate.[112] In order to issue the right courageous invitation and activate the courageous circuit in your brain, you need to reflect on the role both systems of thinking play in your mental processes. Do you have the tendency to use System I thinking? If so, when you experience fear, it is likely that your courage circuit will not spark readily. Even if your courage circuit tries to turn your fear into courage, it will not help you to rise up against the occasion if your prior System II thinking is bogged down with pre-existing biases and generated illogical interpretations. This is likely to spark more fear, and not liberate you to issue a courageous invitation.

These sorts of insights are invaluable in our quest to understand our own reactions and responses, but let's be clear: to date, scientists have yet to fully comprehend how human brains really work. So our best bet is to keep learning, and keep exploring new insights into the facets of the brain that are involved in the acts of bravery and risk-taking. If you are interested in exploring the neuroscience of courage, then we suggest you look into *oriens lacunosum-moleculare interneurons*, or OLM cells,[113] or watch some of Huberman's YouTube videoclips, including the ones we have cited in the list references, which are also available on the Huberman Lab web page at hubermanla.com.

Alternatively, you can leave the homework behind you and just regard your psychophysiological responses to fear as simple biochemical responses, and try to amplify your courage by undertaking activities that generate serotonin, oxytocin and dopamine; as well as those that can help you to boost testosterone and reduce cortisol, when your find the process of transitioning yourself derailed by fear.[114]

In short, your brain is like an orchestra and the different regions resemble skilled musicians, all accomplished at playing particular instruments. When you feel emotion what you are sensing is the full orchestra of the brain united in playing a symphony. Sometimes, the symphony is aggressive or melancholy, while other times it is soothing and even jovial. In certain circumstances, different groups of musicians don't get along and might be playing totally different symphonies concurrently. It is totally possible for you to pick up the conductor's baton and gain control of how your brain musicians should be harmonising with each other and in what sequence. You can also determine which group of musicians in this orchestra should rise to a crescendo, and which should fade with diminuendo. In order to be a good conductor, you can rely on the interplay between two psychological constructs: self-regulation and self-certainty.

Self-regulation meets self-certainty

Apart from rewiring at the neurological level, we can also rewire our minds at the psychological level. Self-regulation is an extremely important skill that allows us to recognise the amygdala activation - or fear response - that is blocking us from achieving our potential. This mindfulness allows us to regulate the amygdala activation so we can save ourselves from the paralyzing impact of fear.

Yes, it is possible to develop this mindfulness and change your fear response, which in turn will allow you to find comfort, even joy in action and courage.

Again, you achieve this through small changes which, over time, help to shift mindsets and make it easier for us to self-regulate how we feel when confronted with a new task or a new invitation. Professor of social work and psychology Dr Daphna Oyserman of the University of Southern California has researched this phenomenon extensively and has come to the conclusion that ineffective self-regulation increases the likelihood that we wander off our goal-focused trajectory. As a result, this disengagement from our dreams can lead to feelings of inadequacy and unworthiness. Conversely, she tells us that if you learn to regulate your throughs and actions better around the perceived courage benefits and perceived courage risks involved in a specific decision, then it is possible to become better at generating and accepting courageous invitations.[115]

We see this self-regulation phenomenon at work among musicians, who Australian researcher and musician Leon de Bruin studied using the lens of improvisation. He found that creative curiosity and self-analysis were heightened if the six elite musicians he studied were able to self-regulate their behaviour beyond fear and into courage; this led to more creative solutions to problems and better creative outcomes.[116]

Sure, you might say, I'm not an acclaimed musician or a world-renowned neuroscientist. Fortunately, it's possible to tap into this type of thinking in a way that benefits us all.

Elevate one's own self-regulation emotional regulator will generate even more impact, if you decided to ground your decision making on 'self-certainty'.[117] A Stanford University study actually validated "attitude certainty" as type of psychological safety net that keeps fear in check in the midst of uncertainty and anxiety, something which is important to consider when we embark on the process of issuing courageous invitations. If, for example, you've taken the time to consider (even better, to write down) the positives you possess and which could help you on your life transition journey, such as your values, strengths and resources, then you'll have the in-built self-certainty and belief when the time comes to take yourself up on those invitations.

Albert Camus, the French philosopher who won the 1957 Nobel Prize in Literature at just 44, once wrote, "In the midst of winter I finally learned that within me was an invisible summer."[118] In short: Connect to that part of you that is not buffeted by the outer conditions of your life. This will give you the strength, in the midst of life's storms, to dive inside yourself and find the certainty you seek.

The interplay between self-regulation and self-certainty enables you to rise to the occasion when you need to respond with courage. But this dynamic duo are by no means the only ingredients in this recipe. You can use other factors – such as posture,[119] breathing,[120] mediation,[121] diet, and even the words you use (which we will be discussing in Chapter 5) to help you to elevate a self-diminishing frame of mind into a self-empowering psychological state.

More of that later, but right now, and as far as this life transition experience goes pause for a second while we affirm something for you: Yes, you've got this. You are moving up and looking good.

Own your fear to help you craft courageous invitations

As psychology professor Abigail Marsh puts it, "Fear is the brain's best tool for keeping us safe from harm. It helps us learn to avoid danger, or to escape it when avoidance is impossible".[122] If harnessed, fear can be a marvellous motivator – we know this from an evolutionary perspective and from sheer self-preservation. Consider the involuntary, reactive fear you might feel if a snake gets into your house. In that moment you are called upon to dial up your courage and act. Of course, oftentimes we might not be skilled in harnessing a constructive level of fear, and we might not be willing to examine the plausible consequences. Perhaps we would rather avoid confronting an aspect of our lives, simply because we lack the guiding power of a healthy dosage of fear.

Broadly speaking we all share similar fears. Dr Karl Albrecht, an executive management consultant, coach and scholar, rates our levels of fear according to his "feararchy", a five-point hierarchy[123] which pinpoints the five basic fears we all share:

- **Extinction** — the fear of ceasing to exist.
- **Mutilation**—the fear of losing any part of our precious bodily structure.
- **Loss of Autonomy**—the fear of losing control.
- **Separation**—the fear of abandonment, rejection or loss of connectedness.
- **Ego-death**—the fear of humiliation, shame, or any other

mechanism of profound self-disapproval that threatens the loss of integrity of the self.

Under normal circumstances, we believe the best way to help formulate the right courageous invitation is by giving voice to the fears occupying your headspace. It's possible to categorise various types of fear as shown in Figure 3.1 below. After you have understood what the fear is and why you are experiencing a certain magnitude of fear during this transition phase of your life, then you can begin to design the right courageous invitations to suit your context and the ambitions you have to launch a better version of you. Therefore, it may be useful to spend some time examining the "Fear Classification Summary". Try to identify past moments in your own life and identify which type – or types - of fear you experienced most often and most intently.

We would like to point out that for some individuals, particularly those battling with phobias and psychological disorders or challenging personal circumstances, coming to grips with those fears might require more than just a spot of self-reflection. Such types of fears are beyond the scope of this book. It may, at times, be important for some people to seek help from a professional therapist to guide them on this journey. While this is not the scope of this book, as authors we know that accepting help from psychologists, mentors and coaches can be immensely helpful or even prudent, to act as one's own trusted advisor.

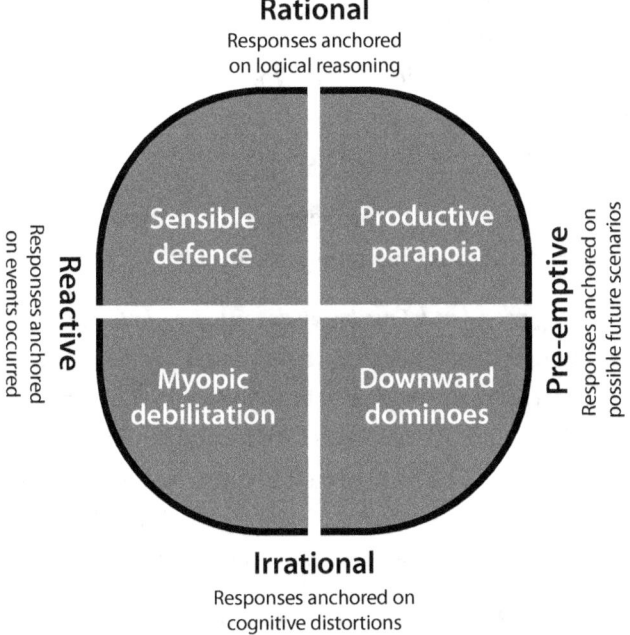

Source: Author's own, with acknowledgment to Jim Collins

Figure 3.1. Fear Classification Summary

We're going to spend a bit of time on this summary, quite simply because it is so important to validate if you have labelled your fear correctly. Once your fears have been correctly categorised and labelled (even if there is a mixture of different categories of fears), you can harness or channel your efforts differently in the face of challenges. We are not advocating that your approach the issuance of courageous invitations in a haphazard fashion. Rather, we believe in facing fears strategically and taking educated risks.

So, with that in mind, let's drill down into these four categories of fears in a bit more depth.

Sensible Defence: Objective threats occur where there is a real or imminent threat, such as the response you might feel if both front tyres on your car burst in the middle of nowhere, on a cold winter's night when your cellphone battery is dead. This type of response may also include some elements of primal fear, which is defined as an innate fear that is programmed into our brains to protect us.

If you are dealing with the Sensible Defence response, then you might consider courageous invitations of this ilk:

- *I am sensing fear, but let me break down why I am truly afraid? What part of the fear should I address first to create the most value-return for my effort?* Break down your fears to isolate the parts that are sensible. Sometimes, when fears step in, our hearts and heads operate under stress. We may end up to being fearful about doing the wrong things or solving the incorrect problem. Remember that fear gives you tunnel vision, so expand your horizon.

- *Let me accept the situation so I can dedicate concerted effort to moving forward.* Accept that there are aspects of the situation you probably cannot change. Stop wasting time using downward counter-factual thinking to keep wishing that the situation did not happen. Stop dwelling on aspects of the past and how you could have done better.

- *If the worst comes, and as long as I am alive, I can bounce back.* Approach the worst-case scenario optimistically and generate potential options to advance your position. Be positive and work backwards from the future to explore how bad the specific situation could actually be, thereby enabling you to give the situation a fair and balanced evaluation instead of being skewed by negative biases. For example, is this really rock bottom? Or can I still climb out of this situation? If all is not lost, then invite yourself to ask, "What resources can I channel into solving this challenge at this point in time?"

Myopic Debilitation: These are irrational fears that might not make logical sense. They are subjective in nature and vary from person to person. For example, as a youngster you might have worried about a monster under your bed after watching a horror movie, while others were completely unaffected. Or sometimes, as grown-ups, your impostor syndrome hijacks your self-confidence. Often our response to such situations switches on negative thoughts which can make situations seem worse than they are. Myopic debilitation is often disguised as a sensible defence. In fact, many people who are inclined to this category of fear will believe that their fears are rational and logical. Sometimes they will stubbornly hold to this belief, no matter what.

If Myopic Debilitation is your dominant response to fear, then consider the following courageous invitations:

- *Can I minimise the magnitude of my fear by thinking differently?* First distinguish if your response is, in fact, a myopic debilitation. Then ask which part of the fear, however small, is rooted in the myopic interpretation of the circumstances at hand.

- *Let me set up a ritual that can help me to shift how I think. Am I willing to choose bravery and courage?* For this to work you need to prioritise "bravery-building" rituals. Enlarge your comfort zone by setting up some useful rituals. Listen to music that can uplift your spirits or read quotes out loud that will refuel your soul. Stare into the mirror to psych yourself up. Try deep belly beathing. Sometimes, even inviting a confidant for a coffee session will help. Experiment until you find the right ritual for you.

- *If I am acting out of fear for now, will I regret this later?* Overcome your loss aversion mindset. Loss aversion relates to how humans would rather avoid a loss than receive any sort of gain, even when the magnitude of the loss and gain are the same. Do take a moment to let this sink in: The opportunity lost will yield a sense of regret.

Regret does not come when you have taken a step forward, any step. But it will haunt you forever if you realize you should have taken a different approach, rather than letting fear paralyse you.

- *I have analysed the whole situation. It is likely that I will achieve more if I pivot my pursuit.* Yes, it's ok to give up. In fact, sometimes, you are not actually giving up on your dream. You are just pivoting towards something a lot better. If you keep going at something only because you believe other people will regard you in a negative light if you fold, then it really is time for you to consider if your fear is correctly placed. Oftentimes, the negativity you assume others will heap on you just isn't true. Even if it is, does it really matter what a few individuals think of you?

Productive Paranoia: In this case, fear is sparked as the result of well-analysed rationales. Productive Paranoia is a concept developed in the book Great by Choice written by Jim Collins and Morten Hansen.[124] Collins, in particular, is an interesting case study: a teacher, author and student of business who was named by Forbes magazine in 2017 as one of the 100 Greatest Living Business Minds. In Great by Choice the term refers to a "what if" attitude that assumes that change and disruption are around the corner. The term is about contingency setting, it's about idea doubt, which is a healthy form of doubt that doesn't detract from the person's sense of self confidence in their abilities. Rather it's a fear response that embraces the idea of challenging our biases and reasoning inadequacies with both zest and vigour. In the process this has the potential to spur on the creation of helpful insights and constructive emotions that can propel us forward to making courageous decisions.

How does Productive Paranoia work in practice? Well, as long as you have diligently analysed the trends and have total certainty that what you are experiencing is not the result of a downward dominoes of fear, then you may want to issue courageous invitations such as these to yourself:

- *Let me stop worrying about the myriad things I still need to change and rather focus on one or two of the most important things and change them well.* Sometimes you will get overwhelmed by thinking about how much more work you still need to do to keep up with the trend of change swirling around you. While this reality may be true, you will only overwhelm yourself by dwelling on how far behind you are in your plans. In the early stage of change, the progress is typically slow. But oftentimes, change comes a lot faster as you get stuck in and as you get over the initial hurdles.

- *I can always evaluate my growth as I change and pivot my direction if I need to.* You could feel confused and uncertain about what the future may bring and, as a result, you might hesitate or prevaricate about the right path to take. This indecision just increases anxiety and fear. Rather have faith in your ability to adapt, this way not all the investments you've already made will be lost. Even though changing direction in your pursuit of growth is not ideal, this approach will still allow you to leverage some of the experience and learnings you've made, adding to your toolbox in the face of similar situations in the future. Just because you've started doesn't mean you can't pivot. There are always options and new paths that open up.

- *Let me work on not overplaying my Productive Paranoia.* We often find that once people have acquired a few solid skills (and, yes, we'll go into some of these later in this book) they have the tools to navigate this fear response, even in the face of the ever-changing nature of the future business landscape.

Downward Dominoes: In Chinese culture, there is Chengyu (the Mandarin word for idiom) known as 杞人忧天 (qǐ rén yōu tiān) which speaks to a fearful or fragile person who is absorbed by groundless fears. The literal meaning is "a man in the ancient Qi State fears the sky falling", which is a pretty clear way of describing someone who worries for the sake of worrying".[125] Often this level of anxiety is accompanied by self-doubt and false beliefs which exaggerate existing inadequacies or deficits and hold us back from experiencing joy in the moment. Psychologists regard this "worst-case scenario" thinking, a state which is all consuming and can lead to entrenched and unproductive worry patterns.[126]

Again, let's put a practical tilt on how you might invite yourself to courageously change this fear response by highlighting a few examples:

- *Tell yourself that, rationally speaking, the probability of this worst case happening is small. Therefore, it would be a waste of effort to linger in this thinking and allow it to absorb your energy.* It is always important to reel in fear-casting behaviours. The more out of control you feel, the more likely that your forecasts will morph into fear-casts. It may be a good idea to ask yourself the probability that such a scenario will actually happen.

- *Parts of this problem look a lot like issues I've successfully resolved before. Therefore, I should be fine if I can draw on the lessons I learned previously.* You may well get overwhelmed by having assigned too much emphasis to the portion of the problem at hand which you fear the most. But if you break down the problem and find similarities between this current conundrum and past experiences, then you can boost your confidence in your ability to devise plausible and workable solutions.

- *I am going to focus on this moment and appreciate the opportunity. So, let me drop my baggage from past experiences.* Supressing the negative sentiments that are occupying your mind will feel a bit like you are trying to stop a runway train. Instead of supressing the negative sentiments that arise from an unpleasant situation, be a bit more intentional in your efforts to redirect the momentum of this locomotive that is carrying these undesirable feelings. This is the best way to lead yourself towards gratifying outcomes. Practise savouring the moment and the ensuant gratitude will give you inner peace. When caught in downward dominoes, why not take a split second to appreciate the moment, to see the positive opportunity before you and to pat yourself on the back for past successes on your journey.

- ***Let me talk to my friends and mentors to learn from ways they've handled similar situations in the past.*** Studies show that our preferences and threshold for risk-taking or risk-averse behaviours begin to reflect those of our peers or the people we observe. This is known as the contagion effect.[127] Watching others overcome their fears and triumph can, to some extent, help us to reduce our own fears.

Apart from the above-stated courageous invitations, there are many more powerful ones that you can formulate accordingly to suit your unique context. But it is important for you to be honest with yourself first, before you issue courageous invitations to yourself. As Professor Carl R Rogers, an esteemed psychologist who founded person-centred psychology and popularised humanism in psychology, one wrote, "The curious paradox is that when I accept myself just as I am, then I can change."[128] In other words, the process of acknowledging and elucidating your fear can be highly liberating. Once you have recognised your fear patterns and evaluated the triggers, then you can tame these responses, leverage them and, ultimately, prevail.

Each of these wins, moments where you prevail over a fearful situation, are in themselves moments of potential and profound learning. So it is important to immediately interrogate what you learned from the situation. By jumping into self-analysis swiftly, you can effectively analyse the situation and use this insight to potentially break your fear triggers by re-assigning new meaning to these activations. Conversely, if your fear is well-founded, then you can draw lessons from what you have conquered, extrapolate the learnings to solve similar issues in the future or, at the very least, build confidence.

The big take away is, therefore, not to wait. Reflect immediately but do so by leveraging positive psychology. As soon as you have managed to overcome fear, or created value despite feeling fear, then stop and honestly consider what you learned in every milestone.

Small courageous invitations cultivate profound differences

Drafting your courageous invitations, be they immense and audacious or small and shorter in duration, can be tough for all of us, predominantly due to the doubt and fear that taints our convictions and constantly suppresses our desire to shine. But bravery doesn't always have to be on a grand scale to reap life-changing rewards. Growth is not the preservation of dramatic gestures recorded in newspaper headlines, so we argue that it is less daunting to design smaller courageous invitations than big, bold, and audacious invitations. This incremental approach also means that you are likely to experience less fear and face fewer challenges along the way.

Small, seemingly ordinary but repeated acts of courage are more than likely to pave the foundation for your success. A fact that is also borne out by biology. How? Well, let's get into that for a moment.

Each time you celebrate a victory, no matter how small, your body releases a small dose of testosterone – both in men and in women. This hormone makes us feel powerful and potent. But this is not the only physical response through which our bodies "reward" courage. Another hormone, oxytocin, is widely associated with positive emotions such as falling in love. Recently, scientists have determined that oxytocin is also released when we've been through something fearful which tested our emotional reserves and physical capability – effectively oxytocin increases the level of fear we experience, thereby cementing the event into our memories. By enhancing the memory of the event, this neurotransmitter helps us to draw out (and later draw on) the valuable lessons inherent in navigating a stressful event[129]. This way we build our own internal encyclopaedia of bravery, assembled courtesy of our small victories and the neurobiological response which makes it easier to enjoy being courageous in the future. Another affirmation of the power of issuing small courageous invitations that can stir and sustain our can-do spirit and build confidence in our abilities.

Huberman's research also tells us that using the courage-fear dopamine system intelligently, by rewarding small wins and victories on the road to achieving our goals, allows the brain to register those moments and celebrate them, making it easier to ignite courage circuits again in the future.[130] In other words, if you aren't courageous yet you can train yourself to be. However, one of the first steps is to get over the idea that small victories don't count, or the belief that these minor wins don't play an important role in our grander scheme of advancement and transformation. The simple truth is that small victories are the bricks and mortar of successes.

In the world of business, it's a common mistake to only associate disruptive innovations with massive transformative leaps. This is most certainly not the case. Disruption, or radical change, comes from being able to spot a goal that can deliver better value in a different way to your competitors – just think about Apple founder Steve Jobs and Lego's Jørgen Vig Knudstorp. This was their approach to disruption, along with an openness to attaining goals using habitual discipline and adaptivity. This confirms the benefits of a perpetual, sustained approach rather than a one-off big bang. Similarly, when it comes to the personal self-disruption and transition which you may currently be undergoing, a grand approach often falls flat in comparison to a consistent effort based on crafting and carefully executing small courageous invitations on a regular basis. It also keeps your neurotransmitters and hormones busy.

Savouring the sweetness of life

Courageous invitations, and the pursuance thereof, lie at the very core of what make us happy. They challenge us to be daring, encouraging us to try new things and unlock the many hidden emotions that life wants us to experience on our way to designing a full and rich life. If you think about it, these are the significant moments that make up the memorable fabric of our life.

Courageous invitations allow us to hold ourselves accountable as we strive to be our best selves. They remind us of our responsibility to wow, to live our lives in awe and humility. They offer the promise of achieving eudaimonia (to borrow from the Greek sage Aristotle's take on the happiness achieved in the pursuit of excellence).[131]

Every single day, countless numbers of people around the world are seeking to improve their lives or find innovative ways to achieve life-changing breakthroughs. Often, we already know the areas in need of work: Some of us should focus on the relationship with our family, or need the courage to quit our jobs, change our friends, be more at peace with ourselves, or find unique ways to up our game, shape our dreams and ignite the inner passion and drive to accomplish our goals.

If you know you should be focusing on one of these goals – or have your own audacious goal lurking in the back of your head just waiting to jump into the chronology of your life – then now is the time to send yourself a series of small, yet complementary courageous invitations.

Saying yes opens the door to a level of growth that is more gratifying and will generate more momentum throughout your life. Saying yes is your invitation to yourself to "be more". When combing this philosophy with the other principles that we will elaborate on in later chapters, you may find yourself navigating uncharted waters with greater efficacy.

Alternatively, perhaps you should ask yourself whether an existence in which you never have to be courageous or stretch yourself can ever be a truly beautiful life. Without occasions that require us to draw upon courage, can we ever really envisage our "best self"? Without courage, visions become narrower, hearts grow smaller, and dreams become stagnant. Or as Anais Nin, the French-Cuban-American novelist, once declared, "Life shrinks or expands in proportion to one's courage."[132]

If you are still uncertain about how to frame your courageous invitation and where to begin your journey, then we invite you now to consider the following avenues:

Courageously invite yourself to *re-envision* elements of your life, interrogate your current modus operandi and identify what aspects of your current approach are holding you back from achieving your full potential. You may well have goals in play, but by staying on the same trajectory are you ultimately short-changing yourself? Try to outline hairy-audacious promises to yourself, do so wisely but courageously.

Courageously invite yourself to *withstand the feeling of being ridiculed*. Making the shift isn't an easy process, it requires you to step out of your comfort zone. Often, you will find your actions seem ridiculous, but this is because you are forming a new habit and a new way of solving problems using rational thinking. Mastering new behaviours takes time, so it inevitable that you will experience setbacks and, sure, you may look ridiculous from time to time in the eyes of yourself and, possibly, others who find your growth uncomfortable. Take this as a sign that you are on the right path.

Courageously invite yourself to **persevere**. Only if you are determined to see this journey through do you have any hope of making it to the finishing line without dropping out early. Invite yourself to activate the strengths that can help you exercise your will and face adversity. Fall in love with your audacious goals by treating them with respect, nurturing the potential and focusing on a future when this reality is in play. When you have wobbles or doubts, refocus yourself and reharness your courage.

Courageously invite yourself to **be kind** to others, and above all, **to yourself.** For many of us being kind to others is the easy part, we support and encourage others and give where necessary and worry about the feelings and needs of those we love. But do we do so for ourselves? Do we do so without being labelled self-obsessed or selfish? It may sound trite, but being your "best self" is the best and in fact, the only way to be of service to others. Being kind to yourself, being supportive of your dreams makes you a better person, a happier person and a more fulfilled person. That, in turn, is a kindness to those around you and the world in general.

Courageously invite yourself to **drop your unconstructive ego.** With ego muddling your thought-process it will be hard to exercise vulnerability and without vulnerability it is hard to be honest. Without embracing honesty, you may be blinded to the disconnects around you and you will inevitably ignore the elements of your life that no longer serve you well. The problem is that sweeping problems under the carpet is no solution. Without being honest, without acknowledging your own magic and the magic around you, you may also fail to spot the illusive opportunities that await you. Professor Carl Roger, the eminent American psychotherapist and one of the founders of the humanistic approach to psychology, once said, "The curious paradox is that when I accept myself just as I am, then I change."[133] Accepting the circumstances, without necessarily being satisfied by these circumstances, is the first step towards making a shift. In the world of business, we call this "intellectual bravery", and it's considered a spur for organisations to foster innovation.[134] In order to cultivate such intellectual bravery, leaders themselves need to treat their unhealthy egos as the enemy. The same ethos applies when leaders want to foster their own personal innovation; we sometimes need to get out of our own way.

Courageously invite yourself to **take risks,** but at the same time **trust** your process after you have meticulously designed it. This may seem counterintuitive, but remember that risk-taking by self-regulating our fear response is the kick-start which courage needs to take over. But it's not sufficient to take up the invitation, we need to trust that this is both the right direction to follow and that our ideas and planning to achieve our goal will hold up to scrutiny and doubt. If you don't trust yourself, then now is the time to start.

We've been privileged enough to see courageous invitations of this nature issued by our students, colleagues, clients and friends, and we've been delighted over the years to see the positive results of these bold strides forward. In the pages that follow we'll take the time to get to know some dynamic people. Their stories will, we hope, inspire you and put an increasingly human face on the issues we raise and the theory we share along the way. Their journeys will no doubt trigger your own thoughts, helping you to formulate and implement effective courageous invitations for yourself more judiciously and habitually. They will share practical insights which we will also explain in more detail, to help you craft your own courageous invitations. We are grateful to them for allowing us to relate their stories.

To wrap up this chapter, we are turning to the following words which we believe were first used by Gary Earl Johnson, an American businessman, author and politician, who served as the 29th governor of New Mexico from 1995 to 2003. It is believed that Johnson once said, "Life's a party. Invite yourself." Isn't that the truth. Life is indeed a great party. So issue yourself that invitation. Accept the invitation. Give yourself permission to invite you onto the dance floor to boogie until your soul is filled. Then invite others to issue themselves a similar invitation.

Now it is time for a little self-reflection.

Self-enrichment Exercises

Looking back at your goals that you developed in Chapter 2, are there any areas in which you may be held back in achieving those goals by your fears? Have you honestly reflected on your fears and identified where they may be holding you back?

_____

_____

COURAGEOUS INVITATIONS

_____

_____

Thinking through your fears relative to your goals in the following manner, may assist you to identify where courageous invitations may be useful in your life. To help you on your journey, we have provided you with the following questions to support the development of your thinking about your fears, and how you can use courageous invitations to achieve your goals and promote a better best self. Have a go at the questions below.

What are my biggest fears that may impact achievement of goals in the Best Self Goal Setting Canvas? How may these fears hold me back? List as many as possible.

_____

_____

_____

_____

Now, go back and classify these fears. Are they logical? Are they helpful? Are they leaning more towards 'Sensible Defence' and/or 'Productive Paranoia'? Or are they more in the categories of 'Myopic Debilitation' and/or 'Downward Dominoes'.

_____

_____

_____

_____

What courageous invitations can I issue to leverage the rational fears more effectively? What and who can I tap into so I can accomplish these courageous invitations more resourcefully, effortlessly, and successfully?

_____

_____

_____

_____

_____

What courageous invitations must I issue to address the irrational fears more effectively? What and who can I tap into so I can accomplish these courageous invitations more resourcefully, effortlessly, and successfully?

_____

_____

_____

_____

_____

Before we leave this chapter, we suggest that you now update your Best Self Goal Setting Canvas from Chapter 2. Explore if your best self is indeed the best possible version of yourself. Also consider what changes you can make to enhance the impact of the areas included in the Best Self Goal Setting Canvas. Update your Best Self Goal Setting Canvas accordingly.

Chapter 4
Strategic Selfishness

You may have turned the page on our Courageous Invitation conversation feeling a little off-centre. That's completely normal. After all it's not every day that you are being asked – no, actively encouraged – to re-envisage your life, to take risks, to potentially line yourself up for ridicule, to be kind to yourself and to persevere on this trajectory. There may be a nagging little voice in the back of your mind reminding you of your responsibilities and casting doubt about the wisdom of being, well, selfish. So let's linger here a little and concentrate on the ins and outs of Strategic Selfishness – and why it is an important construct when you are undergoing this transition phase in your life.

To do this, we are going to turn to social media – that microcosm of human nature, memes and self-assertion. Let's start by paying a visit to Karen and Ken.

It's all about 'me' ... and the Karens

The 'Karen' and 'Ken' labels, which emerged on social media platforms about a decade or so ago, are the pejorative terms for women and men who act out their entitled attitude and make ridiculous demands which are beyond the scope of what is normal. There are countless memes and videoclips capturing these individuals as they carry out their aggressive self-centredness, blithely pushing forward with little or no respect for the feelings of others around them. Worst of all, in all their puffed-up self-righteousness and shamelessness, they seem to revel in going against the common good of the society. Their selfishness seems to know no bounds.

The internet is awash with memes and quips about 'Ken and Karens', such as the gun-toting couple from St Louis in the United States who pointed guns at Black Lives Matter protestors in 2020,[135] but it's the term Karen which has really been the butt of online memes. The exact origins of these labels are unclear, but perhaps the finest urban dictionary definition of what it really means to be a 'Karen' came from Dane Cook, an American stand-up comedian, who put forward this theory and popularised the use of the name during a comedy special which aired in 2005. "Every group has a Karen, and she is always a bag of douche," Cook said in the routine. "And when she's not around, you just look at each other and say, 'God, Karen, she's such a douchebag!'"[136] Since Cook had people in stitches with his description, the cult of self-centred people has propagated across the globe. Recently, fuelled by incidents such as the St Louis standoff highlighted above and encouraged by Twitter hashtags such as #AndThenKarenSnapped, the Karen meme has become more mainstream,[137] even featuring in a Domino's Pizza promotion in New Zealand, where the pizza franchise offered free pizza to 'nice Karens'. The offer was quickly withdrawn after a backlash.[138]

The rise of the self-centred Karen and Kens of this world – fuelled in part by a parallel uptick in baseless conspiracy theories and biased sentiments, ill-founded frustrations and nasty behaviours – is also part of a worldwide increase in individualism[139] over collectivism. Based on 51 years of data and assessing the individualistic practices and values present in 78 countries, researchers from the University of Waterloo and Arizona State University noted a rise in behaviours which are "self-directed, autonomous and separate from others", as opposed to collectivism, which "fosters an interconnected view of the self as overlapping with close others, such as one's thoughts, feelings and behaviours are embedded in social contexts". In other words, scholars believe that one of the downsides of this social psychological shift is that individuals are becoming more selfish.

What is fascinating to observe is that many individuals find it hard to detect self-centredness and selfishness in themselves. In 2020, the reputable journal Nature Communications[140] carried the results of a study carried out by psychologists and economists from Yale University in the United States and the University of Zurich in Switzerland determined that selfish people wilfully "misremember" their selfishness, adapting their memories to protect themselves from feeling bad about their self-centred behaviours. The study showed that people tended to recall themselves being better to others than they were in practice. Why? In order to protect and defend their self-image as being moral individuals. After all, confronted with the reality of regarding yourself in one way but acting in another creates a tension, so our brains opt for self-preservation by jiggling with the facts.

As one of the study's co-authors, Yale neuroscientist Dr Molly Crockett, told Yale News: "When people behave in ways that fall short of their personal standards, one way they maintain their moral self-image is by misremembering their ethical lapses."[141]

When it comes to a person's moral self-image,[142] or the way we view our own morality, the Karens and Kens of this world often interact with their surroundings with a firm belief that what they are doing serves a greater purpose and with a notably heavy dose of self-serving bias. In other words, they puff themselves up and take credit for positive outcomes but tend to blame anything negative on external factors.[143]

What is becoming increasingly clear is that these are not limited behaviour traits; this self-centredness and tendency to point fingers at external factors instead of taking time to examine their dominant logics, occurs far more widely across populations than many of us realise. Combine this realisation with the identification of a new personality construct, identified by four Israeli researchers and explored in a 2020 journal article,[144] and some pretty interesting personality traits spring up. The new construct, dubbed Tendency for Interpersonal Victimhood (TIV), supports a tendency to identify the self as being a victim. This is not reserved for certain situations in life, but tends to be a dominant response. According to the Israeli researchers, there are four dimensions to TIV: a need for recognition, moral elitism, a lack of empathy and rumination over past wrongs committed against them. These behaviours could, in turn, trigger a range of negative sentiments and counterproductive behaviours,[145] such as the selfishness and self-centredness on display by many individuals around the world in response to the Covid-19 pandemic.[146]

If you are looking for more examples of highly selfish individuals in action, you need only look to the worlds of politics and business, where leaders from both spheres have, in recent years, begun to appear more self-centred than ever. Perhaps this observation is driven by the polarisation created by social media platforms and exacerbated by the lack of honesty and accountability of certain media houses. Given that news in the digital era travels faster than ever before, especially the bad and controversial stories, it is understandable that we are hearing more stories of leaders who have made decisions based on their selfish point of view. As an example, Brazilian President Jair Bolsonaro has been tagged with the selfish label due to two major incidents in recent years: the devastating wildfires which ravaged the Amazon in 2019[147] and his handling of the Covid-19 crisis.[148] Look around and you'll find an abundance of other examples, which may leave you wondering if leadership is somehow a breeding ground for these behaviours. Well, there might be something to your observation. In a peer-reviewed article published in 2010 in Psychological Science, Joris Lammers, Diederik Stapel and Adam Galinsky conducted five social psychological experiments which suggest that that the attainment of power really can change people for the worse.[149] According to the authors, "… irrespective of how power was manipulated, or hypocrisy was measured, we found strong evidence that the powerful are more likely to engage in moral hypocrisy than are people who lack power."

The self-centeredness of leaders propels them to disregard the wellbeing of others, the overall common good of mankind and, above all, their own integrity. Yet, many of these leaders seem to be gaining more momentum and are consolidating their empires. Their behaviours are often tolerated, or even supported, by their stakeholders thereby enabling them to continue to behave in offensive ways. Tech founders and CEOs get away with making outrageous and insensitive comments by generating profitability and creating edgy innovation.[150] Whereas some politicians consolidate their powers, while hiding their own greed, by praying on their followers' discontent or by offering up outlandish conspiracies to provoke negative sentiments and cause division in society. Either way, at a glance, the traditional belief that selfishness begets self-destruction seems only to hold true if one does not have some form of power to back up these negative behaviours. These days, it feels as if these leaders are not only primed for survival, but that they are also thriving.[151]

This opening salvo has probably got you skimming through your phone contacts and remembering old bosses and relationships, perhaps recollecting an incident or two. But before we continue further, and before you get too wrapped up in labels, let's take the time to clearly define self-centredness and selfishness based on common beliefs.

A key difference: Where self-centredness and selfishness diverge

For those of us who don't traverse the world with a Thesaurus in hand, the notion of self-centredness and selfishness may appear to be pretty similar. But there are subtle differences between the two.

We turned to the Cambridge Dictionary[152] for clarity. Here we learnt two things, that being self-centred means you are "only interested in yourself and your own activities" and that selfishness is defined as "the quality of thinking only of your own advantage".

Let's expand upon these two definitions a bit, by unwrapping the views of three well-known psychologists.

Michaël Dambrun, a professor at University Clermont Auvergne in France, and Matthieu Ricard, whose business card bears the eclectic 'Buddhist monk, humanitarian, author and photographer' moniker, believe that self-centeredness comes down to attributing an exaggerated sense of importance to the self.[153] Ever heard the old saying that the world revolves around someone? Well, this is fundamentally what Dambrun and Ricard are talking about when they explain that being self-centred means putting the self at the centre – from how we think and feel and process thoughts, to our outwards displays of behaviour. "The exaggerated importance given to the self emerges mainly from self-centeredness and refers to the increased degree with which the individual considers that his own condition is more important than that of others and this takes unquestionable priority," they explain.

A selfish person, in contrast, only thinks about his or her needs. To be fair, most of us probably live somewhere on a sliding scale where we edge between selfless to selfish moments – a reality which accords with the views of psychotherapists such as F. Diane Barth who define selfishness as comprising two primary pillars. The first give away is, Barth explains, "being concerned excessively or exclusively with oneself". The second revolves around "having no regard for the needs or feelings of others".[154] So quite a wide continuum, and something to bear in mind when – a little later in this section - we refer back to these points and argue that there is a type of selfishness that is actually good for you. That said, this type of selfishness has to take the needs and perspectives of others into account.

But we are jumping ahead. For now, at least, let's agree that based on common beliefs and despite the subtle differences that the end result of both self-centredness and selfishness can lead to behaviours which can be termed selfish.

Are we inherently selfish?

Throw the word selfish out there and you are bound to hit a few speed bumps. It's often – or inevitably – not well received, which is why the publication of *The Selfish Gene* in 1976 caused such a stir. More than four decades after British zoologist Richard Dawkins' famous book hit the shelves, it still causes controversy based on his argument that biologically we are inherently selfish[155] and that human behaviour is driven by selfish genes. However, despite its best-seller credentials and relatively simplistic argument, Dawkin's argument is at its essence based on philosophy and not scientific fact.[156] But Dawkins was not the first to posit this theory, and no doubt he won't be the last.

The concept of selfish genetic elements, or selfish DNA, dates back to the earliest days of genetics research. In essence the idea is that certain genes effectively manipulate the genetic transmission process to ensure their survival, selfishly pushing their own genetic agenda at the expense of the overall health and fitness of the organism in question.[157] Back in 1928, Russian geneticist Sergey Gershenson noted a sex-ratio abnormality in the Drosophila obscura, a European species of fruit fly. The tendency, among a small collection of captive fruit flies, was towards males largely siring daughters. The X chromosome was dominating.[158]

Swedish botanist and cytogeneticist Gunnar Östergren contributed fresh insights into how chromosomes spread in a population because of their "parasitic" nature back in 1945, observing that some chromosomes being passed on from generation to generation did not serve any actual useful function for the species, but often pushed other genetic options aside in order to advance their own agenda of survival.[159] Richard Dawkins' work built on these early foundations, as did the 2006 book

Genes in Conflict by Austin Burt and Robert Trivers which argued that: "The existence of selfish genetic elements has been known since the birth of genetics more than 100 years ago, but their selfish nature has been appreciated only more recently. What began as a trickle of information is now a flood."[160]

Nature offers us a wealth of examples which underscore the notion that living creatures can be both selfish and manipulative. The common cuckoo lays its eggs in the nests of other birds, often in colours similar to that of the unwitting foster parents. A cheeky habit, to be sure, but also potentially dangerous to the host and its offspring as freshly hatched cuckoo chicks sometimes push host eggs out of the nest. This has earned the cuckoo the label "obligate brood parasite".[161]

There are any number of other examples of selfish behaviours among different species, some parasitic and some symbiotic, such as the oxpecker bird which both protects Africa's buffalo from parasites by cleaning the host's skin, but which also pokes at open wounds to feed on the buffalo's blood.[162] That's relatively mild as far as selfish behaviours go, while others are darn right Machiavellian, such as the tale of the fork-tailed drongo, a small yet deceitful African bird which secures about 20% of its food by conning other species out of their prey, from other birds to the small, mongoose-type "meerkats" prevalent in the region. Researchers who travelled to Southern Africa to study the cunning techniques of the drongo established that some birds had a repertoire of some 30 alarm calls, some their own and others imitations of those used by other species. By mixing it up with a range of fake calls, real calls, vague calls and their own calls, the drongo is able to consistently mimic itself to some fine dining by keeping its neighbours guessing while it stirs trouble.[163]

While it might be easy to label the drongo's behaviour as selfish, the world of genetics is a complex and multi-layered, which is why the building blocks of life are often so hard to fathom. As we see from the animal kingdom, sometimes actions that are easily deemed selfish and self-serving might actually prove altruistic in the long run. Consider the simple honeybee. If you've ever been stung by a bee and earned a swollen and aching welt as a result, then you'll know that the culprit's punishment for stinging is death. But a bee doesn't sting just because it has taken a personal dislike to your laugh or the colour of your shirt, it does so because it feels threatened, confused or at risk. The ultimate selfish and selfless act, you might think, since how does dying ultimately serve the benefits of the species? But there is something deeper going on here, since a honeybee stings to protect its queen. And this is what makes the act altruistic, because the fallen bee is genetically linked to its queen so protecting the breeding queen ultimately ensures that the bee's genes will survive.

This behaviour might not have gone down too well with the likes of Ayn Rand, the philosopher whose system of objectivism is neatly encapsulated by the following observation: "Collectivism is the tribal premise of primordial savages who, unable to conceive of individual rights, believed that the tribe is a supreme, omnipotent ruler, that it owns the lives of its members and may sacrifice them whenever it pleases."[164] We'll delve more into Rand's philosophy as well as more recent neuroscience research evidence uncovered by Hiroyuki Nakahara and his colleagues at the RIKEN Center for Brain Studies in Japan a little later in this section. But sufficed to say that the likes of Rand have come under fire for extoling the virtues of selfishness, which she once wrote had become a word synonymous with evil. "The image it conjures is of a murderous brute who tramples over piles of corpses to achieve his own ends ... and pursues nothing but the gratification of the mindless whims of any immediate moment."[165]

Certainly, a quick Google search will unearth any number of famous quotes which equate selfishness with negative sentiments, ugliness and shame. British comedian David James Stuart Mitchell once noted that, "In an individual, selfishness uglifies the soul; for the human species, selfishness is extinction." William Ewart Gladstone, statesman and four-time prime minister of Great Britain (1868–74, 1880–85, 1886, 1892–94) considered, selfishness to be "the greatest curse of the human race". Former US first lady, Barbara Bush, lambasted then President Donald Trump (2017-2021) in her biography using three words designed to cut deep: Greed. Selfishness. Ugly.[166]

Psychologically speaking, it fair to say that many individuals continue to regard the word "selfishness" as a reference to an ugly and shameful trait which makes it harder for the perpetrator to distinguish themselves from animals.

If you broaden this word association to a sociological perspective, and without a doubt civilisations, political parties and world religions have constantly reinforced the notion that true happiness only comes from serving others. Sometimes the popular dominant logic in the tribes and communities to which we belong are designed to make us feel shame if we are seen to be placing self-interest ahead of serving others. However, if we dig deeply into the underlying motives for calling out certain individualistic behaviours as "selfish" then we might be struck by a sudden clarity as to why community, religious, business, economic or political leaders advocate so tirelessly for others to put the needs of their party, religious organisation or community ahead of their own. Is it to foster selflessness and genuine altruism, or is it simply a ploy designed to advance the self-interests of these self-same leaders and provide a means of hanging onto power?

The relative vagueness with which we regard selfishness is also not helped by the absence of standardised research and recognised personality trait tests for selfishness – in other words, some sort of recognised assessment instrument to gauge the level of selfishness, much like you might take a Myers Briggs personality test online to figure out if you are an Advocate, a Defender or something in between. Not too long ago steps towards this were made by two researchers from the University of Pennsylvania, Adrian Raine and Stepheni Uh, who developed an instrument to assess selfishness.[167] The research resulted in the creation of a quick test – which would take about two or three minutes to complete and enable individuals to assess where they fitted in based on three selfishness subtypes: egocentric, adaptive, and pathological. Even though this assessment appears to be a successful one with high academic credibility, the very nature of the questionnaire's design already enforces the widely-held view that selfishness is a negative behaviour.

While selfishness is undoubtedly a double-edged sword, which does have a beneficial side – just ask the African drongo bird – in general, the word "selfishness" continues to receive bad reviews, and in some cases perhaps rightly so. However, if the notion of selfishness is correctly expressed, it can lead to desirable outcomes. It can generate enormous value for all stakeholders. It can lead to individual happiness and collective happiness.

Not convinced? Then join us as we journey up to the very north of western Europe, to Norden.

The happy (selfish) Vikings

What springs to your mind when you think of Finland, Denmark, Iceland, Sweden or Norway? The majesty of the fjords? Pickled herring and meatballs? Danish open-faced sandwiches called smørrebrød or the notoriously smelling Swedish delicacy of surströmming (fermented herring)? Or is it the perception of a functioning and educated society?

According to the World Happiness Report the big differentiator between the Nordic countries – as these five are collectively known – and the rest of the world is happiness. For the fourth year in a row Finland took the title of the world's happiest nation in 2021, in spite of the unfolding global pandemic and the economic pressures the contagion has wrought around the globe.[168] Sure, happiness is a subjective construct, so the researchers behind the report don't just focus on confidence in public institutions, income equality, gross domestic product (GDP), life expectancy and trust in the system, but they also look at well-being and quality of life – including the freedom and mood of society, urban living environments and settings and the protections and appreciation in place around the natural environment. In 2020, the report also rated capital cities for happiness for the first time and guess which city came in first? You got it, the Finnish capital, Helsinki.

Not to be outdone, Denmark came in second, followed by Switzerland, Iceland and the Netherlands. Norway and Sweden took sixth and seventh spot, respectively. The question is, why? What do the Nordic countries have that sets them apart in terms of happiness?

Most of the potential explanatory factors for Nordic happiness are highly correlated with each other and often also mutually reinforcing, like standard of living links to income equality and GDP per person. This can make it challenging to untangle cause from effect. A common viewpoint seems to rest on the importance of Nordic institutional quality, equality, freedom to make life choices, trust in other people and social cohesion. These, we are told, are some of the main reasons why our Nordic brothers and sisters are happier than so many other people around the world – in spite of the surströmming.

But the Nordic happiness can also be attributed to philosophy which, on the surface, may seem somewhat paradoxical.

Take a step back and consider for a moment that temperatures across the Scandinavian peninsula are often brutal. If your first idea of paradise is a tropical island then a long, dark and harsh Nordic winter will certainly challenge that notion of happiness. Ironically, this challenging environment might have everything to do with this happiness quotient because it encourages – even demands – that the people of this region take care of themselves first, ahead of others. The ripple down effect of this type of survivalist behaviour – which has been honed over generations and generations - is that it highlights how personally destructive it can be to impose limits on ourselves and neglect our ability to live life to the fullest. As a result, it has become an accepted norm in Nordic societies to be 'selfish' in moderation.

Coupled with this sentiment of self-preservation is another notable social philosophy which permeates the Nordic mindset: The Law of Jante (Danish: Janteloven). Jante Law describes a set of cultural norms common in Nordic countries which emphasise collective well-being and group accomplishments, and offers a hearty disapproval of individuals blowing their own horns and promoting their victories. The idea was first outlined in a 1933 book by Aksel Sandemose, called A Fugitive Crosses His Tracks, in which the main character outlines and explores these universal laws.[169]

The notion of Janteloven in no way implies that the Nordic people lack ambition or drive. But by putting society ahead of self, by not boasting about their own accomplishments, and not being jealous of others, individuals in this region give in to fewer negative competitions and foster less uncooperative behaviours.

Of course, the question on who decides common good is another debateable topic. Selling the idea of upholding common good is easier to some communities than others. But what we do know is that many countries walk a fine line between individual rights, minority rights and the collective good; some more successfully than others.[170]

It's worth remembering that our understanding of the common good should be linked to the long term, indirect impact of individual actions on the collective. Having just navigated our way as a global society through the Covid-19 pandemic, most of us can attest to the fact that we dutifully wore our masks to prevent ourselves from getting the virus or from spreading the virus to others. A purely selfish motivation. The thing is that if everyone in the society thought selfishly like this, rather than throwing a tantrum or seeking immediate gratification and self-centredness, then this collective selfishness would have profoundly reduced the spread of the Covid-19 virus. Of course, it is a bit hard to exercise selfishness collectively if a selected few don't believe the existence of the virus, believe they are immune or figure that divine intervention will insulate them from harm. Which underlines the point that not all selfishness is good, or logical.

Which brings us back to Janteloven and the idea that the act of sacrificing a little bit of one's self-interest for the common good might actually translate into a whole range of additional perks. After all, if the majority of citizens prefer to live in a harmonious, joyful and positive environment, it means there is a higher chance that others will refrain from antagonising or disrupting your way of life. People in the Nordic region appear to grasp the trade-off of forgoing some self-interest in order to enjoy the benefits that come with additional self-interest in return. By putting self-interest at the ultimate heart of this philosophy it could be construed as being selfish, but in the end everyone benefits.

So the concept of Janteloven is a more nuanced notion of self-interest as part of the common good than the hive mentality depicted by The Borg alien race in the Star Trek sci-fi series. You don't have to be assimilated into a cybernetic 'collective' like The Borg and block out all personal interest or ambition, but there is an advantage and strength to be had in having one other's backs. As the Finnish example tells us, a combination of Janteloven collective harmony linked with an appreciation for selective selfishness might just be the key.

While this requires a careful personal and social balance, there are other philosophies – such as the objectivism posited by Ayn Rand – which are a lot more to the point. Rand seemed to go to the other extreme of The Borg assimilation with her controversial view that deemed selfishness to be a virtue.

Ayn Rand and objectivism

On 22 January 1905, just days before Alisa Zinovyevna Rosenbaum came into the world on 2 February, her birthplace of St Petersburg in Russia witnessed the massacre of unarmed demonstrators by the Imperial

Guard, setting in motion the events which would ultimately lead to the country's First Russian Revolution in 1905. Tsar Nicholas II's officials downplayed the death toll from 'Bloody Sunday', while a report in The Manchester Guardian the following day stated, 'The total casualties are still uncertain, but it is given as the official police report that 2 000 have been killed and 5 000 wounded. The wildest estimate is 24 000."[171]

This was the brutal and politically divided world of anti-Semitism, insurrection, and mayhem into which the young Ayn Rand was born. Intelligent, captivated by the written word since the age of six, when she taught herself to read, and absorbed by the romance and poetry of authors such as Victor Hugo, Rand – who changed her name in 1926, after leaving the Soviet Union on the pretext of visiting relatives in the United States – sought refuge from the fatalistic Russian mindset in the world of fiction.[172] She went on to study philosophy and history at the University of Petrograd and the State Institute for Cinema Arts, where she studied screenwriting. It was the claim of studying film making in the United States which saw her moving first to Chicago and then to Hollywood in 1925.

In late 1925, Rosenbaum obtained permission to leave the Soviet Union to visit relatives in the United States, on the pretext of learning the American film business. She landed a job with Cecil B DeMille, the famous director on his epic film of the life and death of Jesus Christ, The King of Kings. She met her future husband, actor Frank O'Connor, while working on the film. They were married in 1929 and remained so until his death in 1959. Famously, Rand once explained why she supported her husband financially when he left acting to pursuing a career in painting, an action which on the surface seemed remarkably unselfish. Rand explained her rationale to journalist Mike Wallace in a 1959 interview, "… you see, I am in love with him selfishly. It is to my own interest to help him if he needed it. I do not call that a sacrifice because I take selfish pleasure in it."[173]

Rand's philosophy of Objectivism hinged on one thing: self-interest.[174]

She held little truck with the idea of altruism, arguing that even when helping others the giver's own need was being satisfied. She held that it was each person's moral duty to ensure their own wellbeing. So, if selfishness was a necessary tool to ensure the attainment of moral value, then it was a virtue.

Rand is best-known for her two best-selling novels, The Fountainhead and Atlas Shrugged, she also penned a provocative book with Nathaniel Branden in 1964 entitled The Virtue of Selfishness: A New Concept of Egoism, in which she set out to challenge the notion of selfishness being negative and evil. She rejected the idea that to be selfish was immoral and that sacrificing our own values to satisfy the needs of others was to be applauded. But she also didn't buy into the idea of selfishness being an open invitation to do what you want, when you want and how you want – asserting that moral principles are universal and not a matter of personal opinion. However, within the realm of morality, it's up to each individual to identify the actions which best benefit them.[175]

She regarded this ethos of reasoning 'rational selfishness' and argued that it gave rise to a new concept of self, which ensured that the 'self' was satisfied. Her ideas found fertile ground among writers, politicians and artists, from former Chairman of the United States Federal Reserve, Alan Greenspan, to Star Trek creator Gene Roddenberry and the founder of the gonzo journalism movement, Hunter S Thompson. The famous musician Duke Ellington certainly reflected Rand's views in this comment, "Selfishness can be a virtue. Selfishness is essential to survival, and without survival we cannot protect those whom we love more than ourselves."[176]

Remember the legendary Michael Jordan from the start of this book? He once uttered something very Ayn Rand-esque but with a touch of Janteloven for good measure, "To be successful you have to be selfish, or else you never achieve. And once you get to your highest level, then you have to be unselfish. Stay reachable. Stay in touch. Don't isolate."[177]

In other words, once you've made it, once your name is in lights and you've achieved your goals, you can afford to be a little more self-less. Although, of course, Rand would argue that such actions would continue to feed one's selfish appetite.

Based on the new research we alluded to earlier, coming out of Japan's well-respected private research foundation, the RIKEN Center for Brain Studies, Rand's view may indeed be right.

Japanese society is renowned for its selflessness and its regard for self-sacrifice. This mindset is embodied in the word *omotenashi* (おもてなし) or 'the spirit of selfless hospitality', which was summoned forth by the Tokyo Olympic bid committee as the country vied to host the mega sporting event in 2013. It's the exact opposite of another word, *jikochuu* (ジコチュー), a common Japanese slang word for a person who thinks he or she is the most important person in the world and who doesn't care at all about other people. *Omotenashi* is something to aspire to in Japanese culture. While *jikochuu* has no redeeming features.

We raise this because there is something ironic in scientific confirmation around the value of selfishness emanating from such a majestic Japanese research institution. But that's exactly what Hiroyuki Nakahara and his team of researchers have done by examining what happens in the brain when a person is giving a widely regarded selfless action. Using functional magnetic resonance imaging (fMRI) and a computational modelling method called a connectivity analysis to see which parts of the brain fire up when the subject considers giving rewards to others, Nakahara and his team examined 36 healthy volunteers between the ages of 20 and 32 years. They wired up these volunteers and then mapped the brain's activations when the potential for a financial reward was offered to themselves and, conversely, when a reward – in this case to popular charities – was up for consideration.

The result? Volunteers who had a pro-social mindset (leaning towards generous behaviour) versus an individualistic approach (having a tendency towards selfish behaviour) showed different neural processes during the act of giving.[178] In other words, pro-social subjects used a similar brain process for other-bonus and self-bonus choices based on activity recorded in the left dorsolateral prefrontal cortex to medial prefrontal cortex pathway. The brains of individualistic subjects responded differently during their process of weighing up the decision to give a reward.

This led the researchers to determine that how we rationalise giving doesn't just come down to issues of selfishness and generosity, but rather perceptions of value. Instead of being awash with altruistic feelings, generous pro-social subjects may rather perceive more value in social contributions or they might be more likely to feel aversion or guilt. Nakahara and his team dubbed this process of deciding to give to others 'social value conversion', hypothesising that it might be linked to a primitive computation in the brain. What it also means is that some of us may simply be wired differently when it comes to giving, and this could also call into consideration cultural and religious learnings, as well as accepted social behaviours in different countries or regions which shape our internalised view of social value.

Imagine, for example, that you grew up in Southern Africa and internalised the notion of *Ubuntu*[179] – a phrase which, roughly, translates to 'I am because of who we all are.' This cultural and social construct would have a profound impact on communities and individuals and how they regard social value compared to our Nordic cousins, and their acceptance of being 'selfish' in moderation. In short, we are motivated by how we perceive the value generated from the actions that can serve us best.

The RIKEN Center's work reignites interest in Ayn Rand's philosophy and belief in each human being's motivation being grounded in self-interest and asks us to reframe how we view 'selfishness'. By understanding the inner workings of the brain just a little better we begin to see that the traditional framing of selfishness might not always be a case of immorality, or right and wrong. Almost four decades after her death, Rand's view of reason and logic underlining our more selfish instincts, might actually be confirmed by science. This has important implications for how we view 'selfishness', and how we begin to apply selfishness in a more strategic way in our own lives as we see to create more value in our own lives.

A new, strategic approach to selfishness

On 5 May 2020, Nienke Feenstra an active blogger and activist for adding value in healthcare (who also happens to be General Manager of pharmaceutical group Takeda Poland) posed a new personal blog. She delved into the impact of Covid-19 on what she termed 'my strategic acts of selfishness'.[180] Other than our own focus on what we refer to as the concept of 'strategic selfishness', Feenstra is the only other writer to make this of this terminology. Her understanding of strategic selfishness differs from ours, however.

In a 2017 LinkedIn post, Feenstra defined her concept as "putting my own needs first".[181] However, we believe that our take on strategic selfishness raises the discourse to a new level by taking into account the recent neuroscience research our of Japan, in tandem with Rand's work on objectivism.

For us, we regard strategic selfishness as a philosophy that advocates for putting the benefits for one's best self at the forefront of the decision. What strategic selfishness is not, and never will be, is the act of indulging in all-consuming, self-centred type of behaviours, such as pursuing career advancement at the expense of family time, or becoming addicted to certain activities while sacrificing different forms of wellbeing. These are instances of pure selfishness that we definitely caution you against, but they are far removed from what we are advocating in this chapter.

Strategic selfishness is a matter of adjusting value perception to create more value. By putting our own interests at the centre, and aligning these with the interests of others, more value can be generated. If you consider any action from the perspective of elevating the end value of the action to positively impact you and maximise value for you, then the potential to creatively activate your best self will anchor any decision.

When furthering the interests of others, be it an individual, group or groups, strategic selfishness asks us to consider the implications for our self-interest. Exercising strategic selfishness is a highly rational approach and highly self-directed. It requires each of us to exercise cause-and-effect systems thinking (which considers the interaction of all parts of a system or environment),[182] and reframe how we see and re-envision the potential for any and all projects to yield maximum benefit and value for us. We all have limited resources, be they time, assets, social capital or even happiness, and the goal for us all should be to extract the maximum from these reservoirs of value. After all, when you make an investment don't you always desire the best value-return?

This value may not be immediate, it may well take time to pay dividends, and it may require us to fine-tune our response along the way, making other choices and decisions as the project unfolds, but this golden thread of self-interest is implicit in the strategic selfishness approach.

Getting to grips with the philosophy of strategic selfishness in action is helped by asking – in the heat of the decision-making process - these two simple question clusters:

1. The I Lead, You Follow approach.
    - What action should I carry out to benefit myself right now?
    - As the result of allowing myself to benefit from this action, others will benefit too. Will this open doors that will allow me to benefit from the advantages given to others?

2. The Delayed Gratification approach.
    - What strategic actions should I carry out right now to benefit others?
    - After others have felt the benefits of my contributions, and as they make further progress, will this create opportunities for me to benefit from their progress?

Let's examine the I Lead, You Follow approach in a bit more depth. By taking care of your own needs first – depending on the circumstances in play, of course – you potentially create the space to be more impactful in the future. This type of selfishness is purposeful. It can even be deemed courageous at times. The benefit to the group or society as a whole from this approach is a possible by-product of taking care of yourself first.

In the second, Delayed Gratification approach, by taking care of someone else's needs first and assisting these individuals to advance their positions, you stand to benefit in the future as they progress. This means access to new opportunities and value, but down the line. You have to wait for this investment to mature. In this case, the benefit you stand to reap is a possible by-product. However, by carefully analysing the situation and reconsidering the nature of your action thoroughly, it is likely that you can maximize the chances available to you to extract value. Of course, there is a bit more risk in this approach, to adopt some investment lingo, but the profits could prove attractive in the end.

There is, of course, a catch. For strategic selfishness to create real value it needs to align with the nature of our courageous invitations. The two cannot be at odds. To create maximum value return when you interact with others requires you to embrace one of the Four Dimensions of Strategic Selfishness:

- Dimension One: Even superheroes get the blues.
- Dimension Two: Betting wisely by giving now to gain more later.
- Dimension Three: Everyone has some value to offer (just draw out the mutual benefits).
- Dimension Four: Establish multiple niche tribes.

Used these simple levels to guide your strategic selfishness based on a particular situation. They are simple, quick and easy to apply, and they will help to keep you – and your thinking – on track at all times.

Dimension One: Even superheroes get the blues

The first dimension represents the foundation level of strategic selfishness, so it's likely to be the example that first springs to mind when you think of the concept strategic selfishness. It is also closely aligned to the approach adopted by our Poland-based blogger Feenstra.

Since the best way to learn is often through storytelling, let's explore a real-life example.

Since graduating from university, Cindy Smith[183] had been working for a large hospital chain in South Africa. Owing to her ambition and diligence, she had been climbing the corporate ladder steadily and rapidly. Within a short space of time, she was able to capitalise on her smarts and hard work to move up from an intern role to a middle manager position. Despite her diligence, her line manager of two-and-a-half years seldom gave her the recognitions she deserved. At least, that was Cindy's reading of the situation.

Cindy could not help but compare her current situation with the motivation and support meted out by her former boss, who took an active interest in her on a weekly basis. In contrast, her new boss appeared very hands-off and disengaged. This lack of recognition from her new boss caused Cindy to doubt her abilities. Battling a minor episode of mid-life crisis (or as some author prefer to call it, mid-life self-discovery) didn't help matters. So Cindy started to question if her company was the right fit for her, despite the fact that she continued to love the work and her peers. It should be noted that Cindy had only worked for her former boss for 13 months.

The tension was compounded by Cindy's firm view that it was not 'her job' to discuss her need for more recognition with her current boss. Her boss should see her worth of his own accord and come to the realisation that Cindy was a great asset to the company by himself, she felt. Despite feeling neglected and despondent, Cindy was adamant she was not going to 'kiss arses to get recognition' (her words, not ours).

Time ticked on and what started life as a minor dissatisfaction grew into a fully-fledged anger over her failure to be recognised. The onset of Covid-19 in 2020 compounded the situation as the team began to work remotely, further reducing her interactions with her line manager and making it even harder to build a relationship.

So Cindy decided to hire a coach. After three coaching sessions she came to the realisation that external validation was not the secret, instead she needed to incentivise herself based on intrinsic motivation (the ability to do something for the inherent satisfaction, rather than the external consequence).[184] She came to realise her intrinsic motivation and self-efficacy needed to improve. So Cindy asked her coach to extend their coaching sessions so they could work on her 'neediness'.

Unfortunately, by suppressing her inner need, Cindy's happiness steadily deteriorated. She felt less engaged and committed to doing her best. Sometimes she found herself pulling herself back, telling herself there really was no point to working harder. However, internally, she was conflicted and began to hate the person she had become. Cindy knew that giving her work less than her best was destroying her soul. Yet, her coach continued to guide her to search for intrinsic motivation, and they began to discuss ways in which she could find other opportunities within the company or seek employment somewhere.

Then Cindy met Chen, one of the co-authors of this book. About 30 minutes into their chat she brought up the topic, filling Chen in on her internal conflict.

"I really don't know how to suppress this neediness," a despondent Cindy said.

"I can emphasize. It must be hard, especially during this Covid time, to build a relationship," said Chen, before gently inquiring, "Why do you call it 'neediness'? Why do you believe that sharing this 'neediness' ... well, actually, no ... let's rather call it, 'feedback', with your new boss is not a feasible way forward?"

Cindy provided a firm response, "It is just not how things are done."

Chen smiled and responded, "How about you add the word 'because' at the end of your previous sentence, then finish the sentence? If need be, add in another 'because' and another 'because' and another. Shall we give it a try?"

Cindy dug in her heels. "It is just not how things are done because I am not here to seek praises, and because it is wrong to be boastful," she said.

So Chen probed further. "But is it true that you desire a healthy level of recognition or praise to do better work? And that when you do better work, do both your boss and your company reap the benefits from a re-vitalised best form of yourself?"

Cindy nodded her head, but her facial expression showed that she was still not in full agreement.

"Could you say that if you are a bit 'selfish', maybe by taking care of your needs in a healthy way, that in the end everyone stands to benefit?"

Cindy agreed but not without protesting slightly. "All right. Maybe, should I say ... it is just not how things are done because my boss is supposed to notice my work."

Chen responded simply, "Do you think that because your line manager has the title of a senior manager that he should suddenly become a flawless superhuman and that he doesn't have a gap in his leadership style? Let's say you agree that your line manager is still human, now is it ok – as a good follower - to tell him what your needs are? Don't you think that would actually help him to lead you more effectively? Remember there is no great leadership without great followership."

As Cindy exhaled with a small sign of relief, she brough back her dominant logic once again and asked, "But it is just not how things are done. We were taught right from a young age that we are not supposed to seek praises and brag about our work. Because a strong individual operates based on intrinsic motivation. Isn't that what we learn from magazines, blogs and YouTube, like those TED talks?"

Chen asked, "Your husband, your family members and friends, do they think you are an excessively needy person?"

Chirping back with a smile, Cindy replied with a resounding 'no'. "Even though I'm the youngest of three siblings, I don't ever recall them thinking I was the needy one."

"Would you mind telling me about your siblings, and also about your parents, or whoever raised you?" asked Chen, following Cindy's lead as an opportunity to probe a bit deeper.

Cindy went on to share a few stories about her upbringing. During the next 20 minutes of the conversation, she spoke about her happy childhood, how successful her older siblings were, how her mother was always very competitive, and how her father still set such high standards for himself; even with retirement less than 30 months away.

This glimpse into her past raised some questions for Chen. "I was just wondering, could your need for recognition actually come from the fact that you no longer have much clarity on whether you are doing well? And that this lack of clarity prevents you from knowing how to be competitive, because you don't have a clear benchmark?"

As Cindy's face began to light-up, Chen added, "... since you come from a competitive family and you have great ambitions, maybe not knowing if you are doing good work, or great work, is causing some tension inside your head?"

As Cindy took a few seconds to think about these words, her eyes began to sparkle. She physically relaxed as she exhaled. Only this time, there was a gusto to her breath.

Watching the signs, Chen continued down the same path. "While it may be a good thing to keep working on your intrinsic motivation, would you also consider exercising a bit of selfishness mixed with vulnerability from time to time? And, under the auspice of great followership, help your line manager to give you what you need to do better work? Maybe you can just think along the ethos of guiding your line manager to be a better leader, instead of thinking it is actually for you? Possible?"

Cindy agreed and added, "In my family, we don't ask for help. We are happy to help others. But we do NOT like to be helped."

Chen joked, "Seeing that you are not asking for help, that you are merely helping your line manager to be a better leader, I guess it is ok, right?"

"I think I can agree with that," laughed Cindy. "I guess I can help him a little bit."

Cindy eventually sat down with her line manager to discuss the issue. The conversation went well. By exercising a combination of selfishness and vulnerability, in a gentle but courageous way, her line manager also decided to share his perspectives. Having been moved from another division into his current post, it turned out that her new boss was struggling to get to grips with some work-related processes. The Covid pandemic had also put a strain on his marriage. His wife, chief financial officer for a large division of a local bank, was similarly ambitious and focused on climbing the corporate ladder. Between looking after three kids and trying to achieve at work, they were both under inordinate pressure. Another issue had also arisen for her line manager, just six months into his new role, when he realised that his world view was diametrically opposed to that of his own boss. That was hard to stomach. Faced with these challenges, Cindy's boss – believing her to be a competent manager – had elected to be very hands-off with her, so he could spend time focusing on his current challenges.

During the conversation, Cindy's boss also acknowledged (in an indirect way without using the following words) that he often forgot to acknowledge the good work of others or to empathise with his subordinates when they were having a tough time. Even in his marriage, they seldom recognised one another's achievements. He implied that Cindy's help in managing this aspect of his leadership style would be helpful from time to time.

Triggered by Cindy's selfishness, the outcome of the conversation benefited both parties. As the result, Cindy felt recharged and less disoriented. She decided to do her best to cover her line manager's back and, as a result, her motivation levels soared.

So let's circle back to the idea behind Dimension One: Even superheroes get the blues. Sometimes even those we regard as being highly resilient, talented and dynamic need to rest or recharge. We all have needs, even the high-performers of this world, and yet we often battle to ask for help or to prioritise our needs and our time when we are crying out to fill our tank. By shifting the focus, and in the name of benefiting others, we can unlock ways to take care of ourselves and put our needs first.

In a world that over glorifies being busy, running on empty could lead to devastating results. This is something that former CEO of toymaker Lego, Jørgen Vig Knudstorp, has been vocal about, advocating for the courage to put personal needs first (providing that your list of personal needs is concise and not ridiculously lengthy). This from a man who rescued the company from the brink of collapse and transformed it into a highly profitable enterprise. But, in order to achieve this remarkable feat, Vig Knudstorp sometimes had to prioritise his needs over business matters.

In an interview with business collaboration platform *Meet the Boss*,

Vig Knudstorp shared his approach. "You have to build your defences. I have periods that I don't get disturbed by phone calls. I don't get disturbed by emails. That means sometimes there is a long log of things that are fairly important, some of them may even be urgent, that I am not touching because I want to make sure that I have rooms for the not urgent, but extremely important stuff." He added, "… you need to carve out that time, and it is hard. Because you will say no to things that you were thinking, ah shoot, I actually should be doing this. But you don't."[185]

Short and to the point: Even Superman has to turn his super hearing off, from time to time.

Dimension Two: Betting wisely by giving now to gain more later

When 'selfishness' is applied strategically, being 'generous' is often a very good first step. In fact, researchers such as Sweden's Kimmo Eriksson tell us that generosity really does pay. Eriksson's work, which uses the markers of higher yearly income and number of biological children as an indicator of success, conducted research in 2018[186] and determined that people with a selfless attitude and behaviours actually scored higher on these traditional measures of success than people deemed to be more selfish.[187]

Of course this works on the assumption that having children of your own and enjoying a healthy bank balance define your view of success, rather than taking into account other motivations such as personal fulfilment or contributions to society. But let's take Eriksson et al's research at face value and assume that generosity does, indeed, pay.

They question is: Does this generosity bring any benefits down the line? And does this research actually contradict the messages being conveyed in this section. Well, maybe not.

Let's discuss this by drawing in the concept of social exchange theory. American sociologist George Homans gave flight to this thinking back in the late 1950s when he created a framework which merged behaviourism and basic economics.[188] Over the years other studies have expanded on his initial thinking to create a concept which equates human interactions to a cost-benefit analysis that measures the effort an individual might put into a one-on-one relationship based on the risks and rewards which might emerge. Obviously, each of us brings our own expectations to a relationship and our own needs and wants, but one thing is clear: if we find that the costs of a relationship outweigh the benefits then often that relationship has had its chips.[189]

This brings us to the issue of reciprocity. As Carroll Quigley, an American historian and theorist on the evolution of civilizations, once said, "The basis of social relationships is reciprocity: if you cooperate with others, others will cooperate with you."[190]

Under the phenomenon of social exchange, reciprocity is elemental to human social psychology. This concept could be traced as far back as the time of Hammurabi, the sixth King of Babylon of Mesopotamia and, by all ancient accounts, a just and fair ruler. Hammurabi's eponymous Hammurabi's Code (c. 1894 to 1595 B.C) is one of the earliest written legal codes and consists of a collection of 282 laws and standards, which set fines and punishments for transgressing.[191] Listed as rule 196 is: "If a man put out the eye of another man, his eye shall be put out." Or, in modern lingo, the 'eye for an eye' principle. (For the record, rule 200 equates to 'a tooth for a tooth', which may seem rather tautologous, but you get the gist.)[192]

Psychologists argue that trust and reciprocity are cornerstones of human nature, and are interwoven into both our relationships and our societal structures. Researchers can even point to neurobehavioral mechanisms which support reciprocity in human beings[193] and point to instances where trust and reciprocity can break down. So, along with the tender issue of trust, reciprocity is a delicate requirement in any relationship.

It is pretty much strategic selfishness in the world of social networks, and its being applied by young generations with notable success of social media platforms. A recent study tells us that students with higher marks are leveraging their social networks to create reciprocity more effectively and more selectively than their lesser-performing counterparts.[194] We may be entering a new digital world, but the game, it seems, is still the same.

In the popular self-help book *The Seven Habits of Highly Effective People*, which was first published in 1989, author Stephen R. Covey outlines as Habit Four the concept of 'think win/win'.[195] Win-win, he said, was a balance between courage and consideration, empathy, and bravery. When the balance slips, you lose the win-win and descend into win-lose, and that comes with resentment and distrust. Certainly the balance between win-win doesn't have to be the same constantly, it can and should ebb and flow, but when the benefits are all flowing one way you have a problem.

Chronologically speaking, it's not essential to experience 'wins' instantaneously; you can also bank these for the future. As Albert Einstein famously observed about compound interest being the "eighth wonder of the world", so too does helping someone in the present have the potential to achieve exponential growth.

If you apply this logic, by proactively helping 10 people – even if only three of them return the favour in the future – you still have three more people contributing towards your growth than you had initially. If you are smart at reading people and can foretell their potential, by courageously investing your effort to help others you stand to benefit from the seed you sow. This is through the lens of an angel investor making investments in start-up ventures. But, of course, just like an angel investor, you must first establish a clear investment rubric to help you to identify and filter out those worthy of your investment of time and energy. This is win-win thinking over time, rather than in the here and now. Both parties benefit, even if one has to wait a little longer to reap their reward.

One point though, it is always advisable to ensure than anyone you help remembers you. By playing an open card upfront - utilising what are known as social exchange principles and telling them that you will be asking them for help one day down the line, you increase your chance of having a favour returned.

To adopt this 'betting wisely' type of investment mindset, Chen invites anyone attending one of his classes to meet him for a coffee session, which he terms an 'intellectual sparring session'. Not only does Chen love coffee and never misses an opportunity to treat himself to a cup, but he also knows full well that those students who contact him to take up on the offer really have something to offer him - their enthusiasm and positive attitude are often most infectious.

In early February 2019, as Chen concluded his lecture in corporate innovation to one of the MBA cohorts, one of the students approached him. Nicol Mullins, in his gentle and respectful voice, politely inquired, "Dr Chen, may I take up that offer on that intellectual sparring coffee session?"

"For sure, but only if you drop the Dr Chen this and Dr Chen that business. Call me by my first name please", Chen joked.

Chen was delighted that Mullins invited himself to create an opportunity for a one-on-one conversation. Having witnessed Mullins' conscientiousness and brainpower in the class, Chen immediately believed this student would flourish into an impressive leader in his own right.

"When would it be good for you?" Mullins asked. But in his eyes, there were shades of anxiety and sadness. Despite Mullins not intentionally revealing his feeling, Chen could sense something was weighing him down.

"How much of what you wish to chat about is bothering you? If the answer is a lot, then we better do it now, or as close to now as possible." Chen responded positively. "I am sensing that it's more of a 'let's chat now' type of topic?"

"Right now is great!" Mullin responded with a smile.

The two walked to the coffee shop and sat down for a long conversation.

During the chat, Mullins expressed a desire to leave his current employer because the company's modus operandi was incongruent with this personal values. The conversation then dug deeper into Mullins' misconstrued loyalty to his employer and his false guilt. Eventually the reflective thoughts being generated flowed into a moment where Mullins courageously invited himself to resign from the company.

Over the years following that first 'intellectual sparring session' the two continued to meet from time to time. Chen was delighted when Mullins started his own firm. Ever since that initial mindset shift and leap of faith, Mullins had made a remarkable transformation in how he saw the world and how he engaged with his career. Mullins regarded starting his new firm as a means to set up his own 'experimental laboratory'. He wanted to test out the learnings he'd gained during his MBA, believing that a failure to experiment in this fashion would be quite a waste of his time and financial investment. One of the perks of running his own business, rather than staying employed as a domain specialist at his previous company, was that he had the luxury of putting his learnings into practice.

At the time of writing, Mullins was not only earning more than twenty-fold more than he did as an employee, but he enjoyed the peace of knowing that his strong work ethic was aligned with that of his company. He was also enjoying the autonomy of being able to decide what work to take on, as well as the privilege he had to prioritise time with his wonderful children and loving wife. He continued to challenge himself by mentoring students from his alma mater.

Although running his own business, and overseeing its expansion into greater Africa as well as selected countries in Europe, is not without challenges and headaches, Mullins feels more in control of his destiny.

For Chen, Mullins' story is an important illustration of when strategic selfishness works out well. From that first cup of coffee, Chen was betting on Mullins and his potential, and was there to help him make a life-changing shift. As the result, Mullins is always keen to collaborate with Chen, be it as a guest speaker during academic lectures or by sponsoring business challenges. The two have also partnered to undertake advisory work together.

Dimension Three: Everyone has some value to offer (just draw out the mutual benefits)

By all intents and purposes, the Chinese philosopher and politician Confucius (551 BC to 479 BC) was a modest man, who might have been somewhat bemused by the popularity nowadays of his pithy epigrams. Among his many famous statements, Confucius once said, "三人行必有我師" (or in simplified Chinese, 三人行必有我师; pronounced as Sān rén xíng bì yǒu wǒ shī). The direct literal translation of this phrase is "(where) three people walk, (there) must be my teacher (among them)". The figurative meaning is simply that when you observe the people around you carefully, you can always learn something.

In other words, if you apply an abundance mindset to courageously explore the nascent greatness lurking in all of us, and if you help this person to give expression to their greatness, one day they might become your teacher and change your life in untold ways.

The concept of an abundance mindset can also be traced back to Stephen Covey. It refers to a mindset of plenty and of limitless opportunities, as opposed to a narrow view of scarcity. Individuals who can tap into this abundant view of life choose to focus on the positive things in order to propel them forward, instead of dwelling heavily on negative things. That doesn't mean they exist in rainbow Utopia, happily oblivious to the wrongdoings or challenges around them. Rather these individuals focus their effort on imagining the possibilities that might occur in the future and envisioning how this might play out to enhance their own lives. There is a growing interest in understanding this capacity for what is termed episodic future thinking in both the spheres of cognitive neuroscience and psychology, and how we can harness this mind power to our personal advantage.[196] Without a doubt more gems will come to the fore as researchers keep digging into this area of study but, for now, the answer is remarkably simple: If you come across a person whose hidden greatness is aligned to your courageous invitations, and you can give them a leg up by investing your time and effort in their success, then you probably stand to benefit from this association down the line.

Chen's keen interest in meeting people for coffee also firmly embraces the 'value extraction' ethos. He believes everyone has some value to offer him, if only he asks the right questions. Chen's 'intellectual sparring' partners comprise his former students, consulting clients, coachees, executives and young talent he meets along the way, all of whom offer him value-return in the form of knowledge. Many of the conversations that emerge from these discussions have helped Chen to learn new things and gather new insights. Even if the conversation did not help him to acquire new knowledge, it may still have confirmed a stance or understanding which enables Chen to lecture, deliver motivational speech, consult and coach with a higher level of confidence. On other occasions, the outcome of a coffee session could result in the broadening and strengthening of social capital through direct relationship building or by leading to a valuable new referral. From time to time, the discussion can even unlock new opportunities.

It's important to note that it is perfectly OK if some people you have helped along the way don't return the favour. Irrespective of what long-term value that person can potentially bring to your life, while you are in the process of helping them it is also possible to extract value for yourself out of the process. Getting this right comes down to how you exercise your abundance thinking, and how you define all forms of value associated with this relationship.

You may find yourself, for example, at a stage in your life and career where you elect to help someone in order to practise your leadership skills, exercise a new form of innovative thinking, contest your problem-solving ability, or challenge your patience. Sometimes, you may just be interested in gaining a better understanding of why this person's thinking patterns have steered them into a rut. These insights may help you to assist other people, even yourself, more effectively in the future. Naturally, it comes in handy when the people you help return the favour, but sometimes the value you generate for yourself isn't direct, it may come indirectly through a referral to a new connection or the expansion of your social capital. As long as the value exceeds the input cost - be it spending your time engaging with this person instead of investing your time on another activity that potentially has a more gratifying return – then you should consider offering that helping hand.

Sometimes, and this is important, you may just want to help to uplift your own spirit. To feed your soul. As long as the balance between the value gained and the investment output is equitable, and you've applied strategic selfishness to your deliberation process, then go ahead and give flight to your abundant mindset.

Dimension Four: Establish multiple niche tribes

For Dimension Four, let's roll out the time machine and head back to the time of the Mesopotamian tribes and the Phoenicians and the Babylonians, all the way back to around 6000 B.C. when people used the barter system rather than the monetary system we know today. Even today, tribes from the Sukma region of Chhattisgarh in India make use of a system akin to the ancient barter system to exchange forest product like sesame and tamarind seeds, oranges, or dry Mahua flowers (a sweet-tasting flower used to make various fermented food products and also traditional medicines),[197] for rice and iodized salt. The majority of goods are traded by women who gather as part of the trial 'shady', or market.[198]

The tribes of the Sukma region offer a glimpse into how our ancestors traded and how these smaller groups worked, both in terms of internal structure and responsibility and in their interactions with other tribes as they exchanged goods and services. This system was also prevalent in post-war Britain when a scarcity of clothes and food gave rise to a system of using coupons and ration tickets, which were traded – bartered – among people to fulfil certain needs. As the author A.A. Milne, the creator of the Winnie the Pooh books, explained the phenomenon in a 1946 article in *The New York Times*, "Today England is a land of barter. Buying and selling – retail trade – is too difficult. Coupons, queues, permits, priorities, 'export only' are hurdles which few of us have time or ability to negotiate. Barter is the short-cut which brings satisfaction to both sides."[199]

Today, while we have a deeply embedded and formalised monetary system, bartering is not lost as a means of exchange. In the midst of the Covid-19 pandemic, the barter system kicked in around the world with people formalising barter groups to trade everything from masks to eggs and even services, such a spot of landscaping in exchange for a dentist's appointment.[200]

Swapping favours and leveraging off your network is, therefore, nothing new in terms of human trade and interaction. Dating back to the 18th century, when Scottish philosopher Adam Smith published *The Wealth of Nations*, the idea was spawned that the barter system was inconvenient and less effective than the monetary system. After all, if you didn't have something of worth to trade, then no exchange could be made.[201] Well, ethnographic studies increasingly tell us that rather than being some sort of precursor to our current system of monetary exchange, bartering was inter-personal and gift-giving in nature.

The late David Graeber, anthropologist and self-professed anarchist who helped kickstart the Occupy Wall Street movement, explained the concept in terms of the Iroquois Native Americans and other traditional communities which rely on 'gift economies'. Rather than a straight swap – your apples for your neighbour's oranges – the two ladies of the house might casually chat. One could mention that a pair of shoes are worn through, the other might disclose that she is two eggs short to bake her son's birthday cake. They would help one another out by enlisting the skills and resources at their disposal.[202] Even if a straight swap took place, Graeber argued, the trade would be framed as a gift. Making it a highly personal exchange.

Viewing the age-old concept of bartering from this personal perspective, we believe the approach can be incorporated neatly into the philosophy of strategic selfishness.

If you can form a few tribes, with each tribe made up of individuals with niche skills and invaluable resources, it is likely that members in the tribe can look out for each other using the 'gift economy' approach. In other words, Dimension Four builds on Dimension Three's outlook that 'everyone has some value to add' and takes it a step further by grouping people into tribes.

How does it work? Well, when someone owes you a favour, but you don't need to take up the favour at that time or their skills aren't really in line with your courageous invitations, then you could offer the 'favour debt' to other members of your tribe. This keeps the tribe tight-knit as the members look out for each other. As a tribe member openly expresses his or her 'selfish' needs to other members of the tribe and collectively encourage one another to share 'favour debts' within the tribe, the pursuit of everyone's courageous invitations gets a boost. Now the entire tribe has access to a wider source of assets from individuals outside the tribe. And so the system of gift-giving perpetuates and the line between 'selfishness' and 'otherness' blurs.

What each of these Dimensions highlights is that strategic selfishness does not take the form of the self-obsessed, negative and disconnected evil-doer that we've come to associate with the world. Like most things in life, selfishness is nuanced. By applying the concept strategically, selfishness has the potential to offer bounty to individuals and communities alike. But there is a secret, a potential crystal of Kryptonite in the application of strategic selfishness. The logic which underpins this approach depends on a rational reframing of how we measure, create and capture value. To get this right we sometimes need a little help, so that's our next port of call, we explore how to appoint the inner advisors who can help us in our recalibration.

Self-enrichment Exercises

As you start making a transition, and go in search of a new direction, you will no doubt start experiencing a range of emotions, many (or most) of which are likely to be negative. Anxiousness, confusion, restlessness, lost, anger or possibly loneliness will all bubble to the surface. It is perfectly all right to reveal these feelings to the stakeholders who can help you through this challenging time. Above all, it is very important for you to acknowledge these negative sentiments instead of just trying to supress them. Channel them for your benefit. Take time to rest or slow down the pace if necessary. Remember that putting unnecessary pressure on yourself will not help.

During the transition from the old chapter of your life to the new, exciting, and yet to be written ones, being intentional about selecting the right individuals to assist you can generate multiple benefits. Let's run through some here – as we do, be sure to jot down the names and ideas that spring to mind in support of your unfolding journey. Apply intentionality to these questions:

- What can you do to take your mind away from this perplexing phase of your life?

_____

_____

_____

- Have you been placing your own needs last way too often and forgetting that all superheroes need time to recharge?

___

- How can an act of giving help you to create new or more value? How do you feel when you see how those you have helped make a breakthrough?

___

- Can you conceive how, somewhere down the line, the person you have helped might offer you resources, opportunities or energy?

___

- Can you think of how people you have exchanged values within the past might now be able to help you to clear your roadblocks?

___

- Have you managed to establish multiple niche tribes that can help you to sense and seize opportunities as you redirect your own journey?

Do you see the value emerging? If so, can you commit to continually challenging yourself to adopt the philosophy of strategic selfishness to re-imagine, re-calibrate, and re-define your goals?

We now encourage you to sit down and revisit your goals and reflect on the concept of strategic selfishness. Write down what tangible steps you will take with respect to the Four Dimensions (as we have discussed in this chapter) so that you can empower your best self to be more and do more.

Dimension One: Even superheroes get the blues.

_____
_____
_____
_____

Dimension Two: Betting wisely by giving now to gain more later.

_____
_____
_____
_____

Dimension Three: Everyone has some value to offer (just draw out the mutual benefits).

_____
_____
_____
_____

Dimension Four: Establish multiple niche tribes.

_____
_____
_____
_____

Now that you have completed the exercises, are any significant changes required to your Best Self Goal Setting Canvas? At this point, it would be useful to update your Best Self Goal Setting Canvas if there are any changes before we move to the next chapter.

Chapter 5
Appoint Your Inner Advisors

We are going to start this chapter with a little poetry, the words of 17th century English poet and priest John Donne (1572-1631) to be precise. One of Donne's most famous works, No Man is an Island, starts something like this: "No man is an island entire of itself; every man is a piece of the continent, a part of the main."[203] Cutting through Donne's delightful prose, the message is quite simply that human beings do better when they are part of a community, when they don't isolate themselves or when they know when to ask for help and guidance.

On your journey to be your best self, knowing when and who to appoint as an essential inner advisor is an important step. It is also a mental leap with which many people battle – after all modern-day life lauds self-reliance above learning how to put our egos to one side and reach out to another human being. Many of us don't like to ask for help. Some of us actively avoid feeling reliant on another. So we're going to spend quite a bit of time understanding the value of appointing a trusted inner advisor. We will also explore techniques and theories which can help us break through our personal barriers in order to issue what is an extremely personal and vital courageous invitation.

Lessons from a scrawny boy

It was shortly after 7am in late October and the morning traffic had been buzzing around the Shilin District in Taipei for some time already; after all peak traffic hours over weekdays typically started at a crisp 6am.

A scrawny 12-year-old boy, wearing a pair of thick spectacles and a school uniform indistinguishable from those worn by most public primary school learners, was waiting for the pedestrian light to turn green as he made his way to school. It was autumn (or fall if you are American) and as the season was changing the air had notably cooled from the intense summer heat. Apart from the exhaust fumes from the traffic, it was a pleasant morning, at least by Taipei city standards.

The scrawny boy's body posture was poor. He stood, hunched on the pavement, as he patiently waited with both of his shoulders up by his ears. In part this was due to the big and heavy school backpack he had over his shoulders and heavy duffle bag he was holding. The backpack carried all the books and notebooks he needed for that day's lessons. Lockers were not suited to the Taiwanese education style back in the 1980s, since learners were typically loaded with homework which meant that books and learning paraphernalia had to be mobile. Digital wasn't an option, since the internet was seldom found in the average household. Instead, lugging books to and from school was the common practice. Into the duffle bag, the scrawny boy's loving mother had carefully packed his physical education kit along with a pack of geometry models and two meal-boxes, so he wouldn't go hungry for lunch and dinner. When school finished at 4pm or so, the boy would stay behind at the school for a brief hour of self-study followed by an extra lesson at 5:30pm, which it was hoped would pull up his disappointing grades.

Primary school days were not smooth sailing for this Taiwanese boy. His grades appeared to deteriorate with each and every year-end exam. Having moved two different schools already during the two years prior (in part owing to his parents' failed business) he had to start all over again at a new school on the final year of primary school. Despite the challenging circumstances at home, his wonderful father wanted the best for him. The scrawny boy's dad had somehow managed to plead with the headmaster to accept his boy into the homeroom class under the watchful eye of an exceedingly reputable teacher. Back in those days, and even to some extent in these modern days, Taiwanese teachers enjoy a relatively high occupational prestige and social status. Some teachers back then would even regard themselves as the saviours of the nation which, in some ways, was not wrong. Given this status it wasn't unthinkable that, on occasion, some teachers would develop a rather strong mindset of unfounded arrogance.

Our scrawny boy was far from charismatic. Nor did he have the bearing of a dynamic individual with the potential to become a future leader. He was definitely a student who was on the lower end of the intelligent spectrum in class, at least that was the firm view held by his homeroom teacher.

When the traffic light turned green our young man rushed across the road. He couldn't risk getting punished for being late and, quite frankly, patience wasn't a strong suite (actually it still isn't, and he's in his 40s now). It was quite common for his homeroom teacher to dish out humiliating punishments to those learners in her class who were deemed "incapable of being responsible for themselves" and who had "shamed the class". Typically students who were late received bad marks from tests, did poorly on assignments or committed other offenses that would be considered to be minor infractions in many other cultures. A favourite punishment was to take one shoe away from the perpetrator, for a morning or a whole day. Another was to instruct the class captain and vice-captain to slap the faces of each "shameful" individual - between 10 to 500 times depending on magnitude of the "wrongdoings". After receiving their slapping punishment these individuals still had to thank the teacher for helping them to improve.

Given these potential punishments, you can imagine the boy's urgency in crossing the road. But, on this occasion as he rushed across the road, the scrawny lad was narrowly missed by a car rushing through the red traffic light. Luckily only the duffle bag was hit and, apart from damaging one of the meal boxes and couple of geometry models, the young man was unharmed. Shaken by the near miss, the youngster's gate and posture after this episode was even more tentative and awkward than usual as he entered the school gates, so much so that his homeroom teacher noticed. Her response? To mock him in front of more than 50 homeroom students by imitating and exaggerating his bad posture.

Later that afternoon the same homeroom teacher had a meeting with the young man and his dad.

"Mr Chen, Yu-Jen is a polite boy. But I don't think you should expect much out of him when he grows up," she said. "If he is lucky enough to graduate from a skill-based senior high school and get a menial job, you should consider that a job well done."

The sacrifices Chen's parents made to help him achieve a better life hung unsaid in the air after that comment and they lingered in Chen's head for many years thereafter. He only managed to break free from this mental trap in his late 30s. Today, that scrawny boy is one of the authors of this book.

Perhaps you can relate to this story? Perhaps you experienced something similar? Or worse? Maybe you were mentally and emotionally scarred by a domineering authoritative figure who only knew how to express love using harsh words? Possibly a judgemental or nosy family member took joy in dishing out unfair criticisms? Or a friend and confident broke your trust and then gaslighted you to reassign blame?

In the timeline of our lives, many of us have been on the receiving end of an unintentionally or mean-spiritedly comment, or a highly offensive remark that caused feelings of inadequacy. These messages get stuck in our minds, playing over and over like a bad broken record. Well, it's time to change the message.

Become your own bandleader

If you are unsure about how to switch this record, then settle back and enjoy the story of Les Brown, the American DJ, motivational speaker, politician and afficionado of the courageous invitation. While others played an important role in supporting Brown's success, it was ultimately his internal dialogue that motivated him to change his mindset, take chances and achieve profound personal and professional success.

If you've ever seen Brown in full flight, it's a sight to behold. Words flow out of him like a river, inspiring and motivating, but all the time delivered with the gentleness and determination of someone who understands the hurdles of life and what is required to overcome them.

The adopted son – along with his twin brother, Wes – of a Miami kitchen worker and maid, Mamie Brown, Les Brown grew up in a poverty-stricken neighbourhood on the rough side of town. According to his early school teachers, Brown was a lousy student, who battled with concentration and reading, so his teachers labelled him "educable mentally retarded" and repeatedly told him he was slow and incapable. The negative perception of him held by some teachers resulted in him being stuck in special education classes for the learning disabled.[204] What made matters worse is that Brown heard these negative messages so many times that even he began to believe he was a lost case.

Fortunately, these labels never stopped Brown from dreaming and fantasizing about one day being on a stage and holding the attention of crowds of people with his words. Even these dreams of greatness were constantly under attack, with one psychiatrist even telling a young Brown that he suffered from delusions of grandeur. Brown's inimitable response to this negative comment was, apparently, "Is that a bad thing?"[205]

It took one teacher to offer young Brown the encouragement he needed to turn his dreams into reality. LeRoy Washington was a high school drama teacher whose words resonated with the Brown when he told him, "Someone's opinion of you does not have to become your reality."[206] Washington did not condone malicious self-talk. He added his voice to that of Brown's mother, Mamie, who inspired the young man to fuel his hunger and pursue his dreams.

After graduating, Brown became a city sanitation worker in Miami Beach. However, he kept his dream of being a disc jockey alive by studying the patter of the local jive-talking DJs and working on his own style and approach – all the while chattering through his hairbrush 'microphone' to his sea of imaginary listeners.

While he was still refining his approach and his banter, Brown applied for a job as a DJ at a local radio station in Miami Beach. With no broadcast background and no journalistic experience, the answer was a resounding no. But Washington encouraged Brown to go back, telling him that most people are so negative they "have to say no seven times before they say yes".[207] Brown went back, again and again until the station manager hired him as an errand boy. He earned nothing for fetching and carrying for the DJs, but he soaked up the experience, watched and learnt, and studied how the station talent handled the control panel. At night he'd practice the moves, preparing himself for the day he would be in the hot seat.

That day came on a fantastic Saturday afternoon when the DJ in the booth, Rock, was drinking on air. Brown was asked to call in a replacement DJ. He never did, telling the general manager 20 minutes later that nobody was available – having alerted his mother and girlfriend to tune in to hear him take to the air. Asked if he knew how to work the controls in the studio, Brown was able to confidently answer yes. He got his shot and he grabbed it with both hands.

As Brown's fellow motivator, Ty Bennett, tells the story, "Les darted into the booth, gently moved Rock aside and sat down at the turntable. He was ready. He was hungry. He flipped on the microphone switch and said, "Look out! This is me LB, triple P – Les Brown, Your Platter Playing Poppa. There were none before me and there will be none after me. Therefore, that makes me the one and only. Young and single and love to mingle. Certified, bona fide, indubitably qualified to bring you satisfaction, a whole lot of action. Look out, baby, I'm your lo-o-ove man."[208]

Brown didn't just issue himself with an invitation to achieve greatness and to be his best self, he was constantly speaking to himself; engaged in bold, big, sassy, hungry and passionate self-talk that was filled with possibilities and positivity. With this self-motivating attitude, combined with talent and hard work, his words wowed the radio station's audience. He won over his general manager. He used that moment to launch a successful career in broadcasting, politics, public speaking and television. To this day, Brown is a big believer of the power of thought self-leadership – conceptualised as a process of influencing or leading ourselves through the purposeful control of our own thoughts[209] – and how our personal internal dialogue can impact our own growth.

In later years Brown would admit that it was difficult to pick himself up each and every day when he was pursuing his dreams. Oftentimes when he started questioning and doubting himself, his hesitation would be met with a clear and steady inside voice, "You are the one. Don't give up on your dream."

Brown shared more about his positive self-talk during a podcast interview in 2020. "Early on in my career, my ex-fiancée's friends asked me, 'What do you do young man?' I said, 'I'm a motivational speaker'. She asked me who I spoke for, and I said, 'No one yet, but I'm going to speak for major corporations all over the country and around world'."[210]

Today when Brown addresses those crowds he envisaged in his youth, he is replete with anecdotal wisdom and practical and profound insights – many of which are drawn from the positive self-talk he employed as a young man, when the name Les Brown was unknown to most people.

Of course, Brown's story doesn't end when he switched the record of his life in that radio booth. He went on to reinvent himself and change the song of his life on more than one occasion. In the late 1960s, he moved to Columbus, Ohio to work for WVKO Radio, and at this point in his life he became active in the community. His political activism in

Columbus won him a seat with the 29th House District of the Ohio State Legislature. In his first year, Brown passed more legislature than any other freshman representative in Ohio State legislative history. In his third term, Brown served as chair of the Human Resources Committee.[211]

In 1981, Brown left the Ohio State House of Representatives to care for his ailing mother back in Florida. While in Miami, he continued to focus on social issues by developing a youth training programme. In 1986, he began public speaking on a full-time basis and formed Les Brown Enterprises Inc. In 1989, he received the National Speakers Association's highest award, the Council of Peers Award of Excellence. In 1990, he recorded the Emmy Award-winning series of speeches entitled You Deserve, which became the lead fundraising programme of its kind for pledges to PBS stations nationwide. In 1991, Toastmasters International selected Brown as one of the world's best speakers and awarded him the Golden Gavel Award. Not too bad going for a kid who was labelled by teacher and himself to be the "educable mentally retarded".

Today Brown inspires others to run towards their dreams; especially those big and daring long shots. "Don't stop. Don't stop running towards your dream," he says. Don't stop.

Les Brown's courageous invitation was distinctly and gloriously personal. Guided by his teacher, LeRoy Washington, he began to tell himself that he could "be more". This propelled him to make a habit out of issuing bold and ambitious dialogues with himself as he continued to feed his hunger for success. Brown conditioned his intrapersonal communications and nudged himself closer towards this dream every single day, step by step.

Your thoughts shape your world

Les Brown is an inspiring example of a leader. He's a man people innately follow and he's used this skill to profoundly change the world.

Oftentimes we talk about leadership from a business or career advancement perspective, where it is most certainly an indispensable skill. But that's not the whole story. Scholars have identified a number of layers and types of leadership, from transactional and transformation, to contextual, facilitative and autocratic. What is important to note is that irrespective of how you regard your own leadership behaviour, an important aspect of the discussion lies in unpacking self-leadership, particularly thought self-leadership. This is because all leadership behaviours ultimately manifest from your relationship with ourselves and whether our identity generates contrasting or well-aligned thoughts.

In Chapter 2, we discussed the transition of autobiography to eulogy as the preparation to activate your best self. We also deliberated on the importance of creating powerful courageous invitations as the bookmark for the moment when autobiography and eulogy meet to constantly remind you to thrive to be your best self. Now for the next step.

None of these early intentions can create the profound impact we are seeking if you do not appoint the right inner advisors to your intrapersonal communication advisory board. Give this grouping of people the gravitas associated with the board of a company. They are that important to your journey. If these appointed inner advisors do not align to your courageous invitations, they cannot initiate and create discourse that is helpful to your growth.

Let's elaborate what the above statement means by going through this approach step by step.

Throughout the years, many thought leaders have discussed the importance of thought self-leadership at length. Marcus Aurelius Antoninus, who ruled from 161 to 180 AD and was known as the last great Roman emperor, was among this number. He was a staunch follower of Stoicism, a form of philosophy that emphasises personal ethics and highlights positive emotions over negative ones. Aurelius reflected on these views in a series of private musings which were eventually published under the name Meditations. Broken down into 12 sections, Meditations offers a glimpse into different, formative periods in Aurelius's life and highlights his profound wisdom and straightforward approach in the face of bloody battles and intense challenges, such as watching millions of his people perish during a smallpox outbreak. Many of the thoughts are personal reminders of how to rise above adversity and channel personal growth and transformation out of loss.[212]

One of Aurelius's more well-known observations goes as follows, "Our life is what our thoughts make it. The happiness of your life depends upon the quality of your thoughts: therefore, guard accordingly, and take care that you entertain no notions unsuitable to virtue and reasonable nature."

This view went on to influence a number of philosophers, including the 'Father of American psychology', William James (1842–1910), who clearly embraced Aurelius's tenet when he develop pragmaticism, which centres on the workability of ideas in practice and not in theory.[213] Within the epistemology of pragmatism, James makes statements such as this one, "The greatest discovery of my generation is that a human being can alter his life by altering his attitudes of mind."[214] Sound familiar?

Just over 800 years after Aurelius ended his impressive reign, and more than 8 000 kilometres away from the capital of the Roman Empire, the great Chinese 'master teacher' Confucius interpreted thought self-leadership based on the principles of 'self-cultivation'. This cognitive development notion is exactly as it sounds: a concerted effort to develop personal mental capacities by nurturing their growth in a clear and integrated way. It is about rising above the average and continually polishing personal potentialities. Confucius's concept of xiū-xīn yǎng-xìng ("修心养性") literally translates to "rectifying one's mind and nurturing one's character [with a particular art or philosophy]".[215]

On the opposite hemisphere to the aforementioned philosophers, people from the beautiful continent of Africa have also long produced many stunning proverbs and quotes that embraced a similar ethos. There's this proverb from Rwanda, "If you are building a house and a nail breaks, do you stop building or do you change the nail?"[216] or "you can outdistance that which is running after you, but not what is running inside you." Nigerians may teach you, "We are what our thinking makes of us." While in South Africa, anti-apartheid activist and the voice of Black liberation in the country, Steve Biko (1946-1977), once said, "The most potent weapon of the oppressor is the mind of the oppressed."[217]

Each of these philosophers, from those whose names we still cherish to the unnamed poets forgotten by history, are in accord that nothing can cage and suffocate human beings more severely than the narratives in our minds. Our thoughts are indeed powerful beyond measure.

Your words shape your thoughts

Our words influence our thoughts. We say this knowing full well that there also the mutually re-enforcing relationships between our thoughts and our words to consider. That said, it has been widely agreed that what shapes our thoughts are our interpersonal dialogues which, from a strictly theoretical perspective, encompass the range of methods we use to communicate with ourselves on a daily basis, from self-talk to private speeches or monologues, acts of imagination and visualization, and even recall and memory.[218] In this book, we are using the terms intrapersonal communication and self-talk interchangeably.

Leading researchers tell us that "self-talk is a ubiquitous human phenomenon" and that "we all have an internal monologue that we engage in from time to time".[219] If we are honest about it, we all 'talk' to ourselves, sometimes overtly, and sometimes silently. We likely started this self-talk as children, as part of a natural process of our developmental stage. As children – particularly around the ages of two to about seven – this self-talk may often have been on public display. There is nothing out of the ordinary when we see young children chatting out loud to themselves as they go about their day[220] during these early years, although usually the behaviour starts to diminish around the age of five.[221] Engaging in this type of intrapersonal communication might even be good for children, according to a 2008 study, which found that five-year-olds who talk out loud to themselves might perform motor tasks better than when they are quiet. This sort of vocalised self-talk could even help to improve their communication skills with the outside word.[222]

The words we use when we talk to ourselves also have a weighty impact on our behaviours, as research by Professor Lera Boroditsky has found. Boraoditsky is a highly respected cognitive scientist and professor in the fields of language and cognition who holds accolades such as the National Science Foundation Career Award. She has also been named as an American Psychological Association Distinguished Scientist. Over the years, Boroditsky has been a major contributor to the theory of linguistic relativity – which holds that the way a language is structured ultimately influences how those who speak that language conceptualize the world. Consider, for instance, how gendered languages such as German, Spanish or Portuguese frame gender as a binary construct and how this might impact how speakers of these language perceived the world. Linguistic relativity is also known as the 'Sapir-Whorf hypothesis', after the linguists Edward Sapir and Benjamin Whorf.[223]

Boroditsky's research findings have repeatedly shown that language enables us to shape abstract concepts.[224] In her fascinating and perceptive TED Talk, 'How language shapes the way we think',[225] Boroditsky pointed out how Spanish, Japanese, and Russian speakers interpret certain aspects of their lives through a slightly different lens than individuals who speak other languages. With around 7 000 languages around the world, this raises interesting questions about how language colours our experiences.

In the same talk, Boroditsky mentioned how a five-year-old child from an Aboriginal community in Australia, a society that uses cardinal directions (west to east, for example) instead of left and right, could quickly determine the direction south east – something most of us would have a pretty hard time getting out heads around at a split second.

Why is this the case? Because the words routinely used by the remote Pormpuraaw people[226] help them to sense the world around them in a very particular way. This tells us that the words you repeatedly use help you to be mindful about certain things in a way that guides you to solve certain problems using a specific logic and focus.

"The beauty of linguistic diversity is that it reveals to us just how ingenious and how flexible the human mind is," Boroditsky said, as she wrapped up her discussion. "Human minds have invented not one cognitive universe, but 7 000."

This tells us something rather splendid; that even individuals who do not believe they are creative have creativity within them if only they can make use of the right type of inner dialogue to communicate with themselves in order to unlock this potential. For Boroditsky, the power of behavioural linguistics and psycholinguistics are evidential.

Other thought leaders, such as Tim David, author of Magic Words: The Science and Secrets Behind Seven Words That Motivate, Engage, and Influence,[227] describe the influence which words have on our minds and perceptions as a kind of magic. In Magic Words, David provides a host of practical examples related to just seven words that will motivate people into action. The impact of these seven words highlights how linguistics is indeed a powerful catalyst for cognitive-behavioural shift.

Not convinced? Let's say you are in a transition phase and you are unsure of your next step, or even how to determine what that is. What if you offered up one of the following four options to yourself:

Option A: "I have a big dilemma and I really don't think I can solve this crisis."
Option B: "I am at a crossroads and I am a bit confused about my next step."
Option C: "There is a matter I need to ponder."
Option D: "This is just a pause-point that is inviting me to sit down and rethink my next series of moves."

Option A appears to emphasise the severity of the situation and helplessness thereof. Say this to yourself and you'll already believe that fate has dealt you a bad set of cards. You'll inevitably remain fairly adamant that this crisis cannot be resolved.

In Option B you acknowledged that you are facing a time of significant change, and that's not a bad thing. But the follow up statement draws attention to your confusion. While it's not a bad idea to acknowledge that confusion exists, you may want to add another sentence – a call for action - that might assist you in moving into action to help you move forward.

If you use a more neutral tone like the one suggested in Option C, you may reduce anxiety. Seeing that you already knew this was going to be a big step, calming yourself down could be seen as the first step towards solving your problems effectively. Don't hang up on Option C and its repercussions just yet, we'll discuss this more in the final section.

Option D is an attempt, a courageous offer to self to view this confusing time as just another business-as-usual situation. This option underlines that this confusing time is just one more in a series of pause-points you've experienced before. The statement urges you to believe that all you need is a bit of recentring and time to formulate (or even better, 'to deliver') the right tactics. In other words, this option contains an instruction and a motivation towards taking the right action. We'll delve more into this later when we elaborate on the different types of self-talk.

As we mentioned in Chapter 3, Dr Brené Brown has shared numerous explanations with the world on why it is important to exercise vulnerability in life and in our interactions – especially with ourselves. But it is equally important to recognise that after successfully exposing our soft underbellies, the real magic comes from the subsequent step when we combine that openness and vulnerability with appropriate action. In truth, the power comes from a combination of vulnerability and appropriate action (watch this space, we'll elaborate on this more in the final chapter). If we don't manage to find the right combination, our progress will inevitably stop at vulnerability, leaving us hanging on the cusp of profound change with our best-selves just within our grasp. So read on.

Your multiple identities shape your words

We can agree then that your thoughts can help you accomplish many amazing feats. It all depends on how you approach self-talk, and how you clarify, align and manage the tensions when you speak to your various 'selves'. What does this statement really mean? Let us take you through our assertion incrementally.

Scholars have long been positing assumptions such as the Dialogical Self Theory[228] and Narrative Identity Theory to support the rationales behind the importance of self-talk. The psychological concept known as Dialogical Self Theory explores how the human mind can imagine the different positions of participants in an internal dialogue – just think about how you might hear your father's voice in your head when making a decision or debating a problem. Dialogical Self Theory works on the assumption that the self is not isolated from the rest of the world, it is part of what Dutch psychologist Hubert Hermans calls a 'society of minds', which ensures a close connection between our self-talk and inputs from external dialogues and people.[229] Narrative Identity Theory, meanwhile, postulates that each of us has an internalised life story which evolves as we move through the past and present, into the future. This identity is formed by drawing on our unique life experiences, which are merged together to create a sense of who we are, our purpose in life and our projected path through life.[230] It's a personal anchor of sorts which provides a keen sense of self and a sense of unity.

Some scholars distinguish strictly between these two theories, however we prefer to concentrate on how best to combine these concepts for practical application, rather than getting bogged down in the academic nuances.

If we adopt this approach, then what these two theories tell us is that each individual's inner communication consists of a polyphonic self – a word adopted from the world of music, which describes the layers of a melody which can include more than one voice at the same time. Within this polyphonic self, a multiplicity of inner voices exist. This variety of voices is the result of multiple self-narrated and self-affirmed identities which can be activated consciously in different sequences to shift our thinking and create valuable solutions. However, at times some identities might surface in our subconscious mind and gradually take over our intrapersonal communication advisory board without us even being aware that a hostile takeover is underway.

Internal dialogues and narrative types infer that an exchange of thoughts or ideas between some identities is constantly taking place. Each identity shapes the style in which each inner voice communicates with other identities within us. But typically, the identity with the most airtime dominates the conversation among the assembly of identities. Some of these identities surface naturally without us being conscious about their influences. We might be more conscious of the more prominent identities, but we might not know how to channel them in the right context or utilise them successfully when facing challenges, including life phases where we are required to transition ourselves. Some identities which are essential for making significant personal advancements may still need to be harnessed and enforced.

Yes, you contain multitudes.

These 'multiple selves' become more evident to us - and often to those close to us - when we are faced with different situations and circumstances in our lives. Stop for a moment to think about your responses as a parent, an employee, a friend, a son or daughter, or as a spouse. Are your interactions different? Most likely the dominance of different identities during different interactions or circumstances will influence how you act. David Lester, the creator of multiple-self theory, is an exponent of the idea that our minds comprise multiple selves. Rather than the negative connotations associated with this viewpoint, perpetuated by Hollywood movies such as Sybil (1976), The Three Faces of Eve (1957) and Fight Club (1996), Lester stresses that this is a normal, healthy psychological phenomenon. In fact, he believes a "multiple-self theory of the mind" is necessary for understanding human behaviour.[231]

Award-winning science writer Rita Carter agrees with this view and has contributed to this debate. Her 2008 book, 'Multiplicity: The New Science of Personality, Identity, and the Self', expands Lester's concept and enables Carter to postulate a new view about the 'multiplicity' aspects within all of us. Carter asserts that we all consist of multiple characters, not just a single personality.[232] Each one of these personalities has its own viewpoints, emotions and ambitions. The dad who takes his kids to school, for example, will exercise different modes of thinking from the man who is about to take part in a serious business meeting an hour later, or from the guy who will be with his partner that night. Yet all three identities share the same body, and none are any less or more 'authentic' than another. These identities can largely live in harmony with one another, but when the priorities of one identity come into conflict with those of another then the tension will mount.

Carter's book went on to introduce the idea that within our multiple selves we have major and minor selves, as well as some fragmentary micro selves. The major identities are fully developed characters with distinct thoughts and desires, intentions, emotions, ambitions and beliefs. Minor identities are less complex and prominent, but they emerge during particular situations. What is important to note is that these identities are not independent of one another, but the hierarchy and status of the relationship between these identities within each individual's personal construct system will impact decision making and a person's ability to take action.

To understand this further we need to spend a little more time unpacking the idea of a personal construct system.

Personal constructivist psychology

The theory of personality known as personal construct psychology was devised by George Alexander Kelly (1905-1967). Kelly is an American psychologist, educator and engineer whose personal and professional story was impacted by the economic and human devastation of the 1929 great depression in the United States. Kelly's work focused on the ways in which human beings construct and reconstruct their world views, their thoughts and emotions and ambitions which he collectively termed personal constructs.[233] Such is the depth of Kelly's work that his personal construct concept and methods are applied to a wide range of psychological understanding from cognitive complexity and psychological disturbance, to how we develop (and sometimes destroy) close relationships and how we make decisions.

The foundation of construct psychology theory is, however, rooted in a philosophy which Kelly termed constructive alternativism; the idea that despite only one true reality existing, we always experience this reality from a specific perspective or alternative construction.[234] In other words, our reading and experience of the world around us is not passive in nature, but is coloured by our own interpretations and the knowledge we bring to any given situation. We devise theories, we hypothesise about the past and the future and we seek to explain events using input from our physical environments, our wishes and desires, as well as from our childhood experiences.[235]

Personal construct theory stresses the importance of an individual taking time to make a concerted effort to enter his or her inner world in order to understand the various meanings we assign to the world as a result of this 'inside out' influence. A coach or therapist can use this same approach when working with a client in order to guard against injecting his or her 'rational' or 'objective truth' way of thinking into the session. Instead the coach or therapist will help a client to recognise the coherence within their own ways of construing experience; thereby assisting them to identify the means to modify these personal constructs when necessary. A popular tool during these therapy sessions is the use of psychodrama, where clients use role playing or various types of dramatization of the key thoughts roaming in their heads in order to gain better insights into their lives.

When applying the philosophy of personal construct psychology, it is appropriate to assume that there are some dominant identities that are more deeply rooted inside a person's mind and which influence behaviour and decision making more frequently than less forceful identities. At times, these identities may attempt to supersede one another in a person's subconsciousness. This dynamic means that if a person fails to assign these different identities into an appropriate hierarchy, or is unable to make peace with the hierarchy of identities in place, then the inevitable incongruence will cause stress and may give rise to negative emotions. In other situations, a person may be oblivious to the identities which take the driver's seat during the problem-solving and decision-making process. This lack of awareness can result in a situation where the outcome of a decision does not end up serving the person in question. If this is the case, unless the person can reframe his or her thinking it is likely that this negative outcome will happen again in the future.

The identities developed over the years within all of us can either be loyal enablers or fierce enemies, depending on how we commend them to talk to and influence the multitude of other identities within us.

In some ways, Kelly's highly practical theory is not an earth-shattering concept. Individuals who follow the Christianity doctrine or embrace Islamic faith, for instance, might find themselves asking questions such as 'what would Jesus do' or 'what would the Prophet Muhammad do' as a way of guiding their actions. By appreciating how Jesus or the Prophet Muhmmad might think and act in certain circumstances, individuals can model their cognitive behaviours accordingly when they encounter similar situations.

Meet Mike and his identities

Let's talk about Michael Olivier, an ambitious guy in his early 30s who, at the time of writing, was a manager at a large mining company in South Africa.

In 2019, Mike decided that it was time to disrupt himself. So he issued a courageous invitation to challenge himself with the intention of expanding his vision to catapult his career trajectory. Subsequently Mike was accepted to an MBA degree at a leading global business school, the University of Pretoria's Gordon Institute of Business Science, better known as GIBS. GIBS is a tier-one business school which has been consistently ranked among the world's best by institutions such as the Financial Times and Quacquarelli Symonds World University Rankings. This acceptance itself is an achievement considering that the application acceptance rate is typically below 25%.

As a typical MBA student Mike had to make trade-offs when it came to the allocation of his time. Due to the overwhelming magnitude of assignments and readings, together with ongoing professional commitments, Mike found himself with less time for his family, his friends and above-all, himself. As an aside, and despite being just over 176cm in height, Mike resembled a more handsome version of Jean-Claude Van Damme, so not being able to dedicate time to training really bothered him since he took pride in his bodybuilder identity. To overcome this tension and inner conflict, Mike opted to see himself as a resilient person and decided to ignite his stoic identity (his inner 'Captain Perseverance') to help him persevere. Mike mentioned that he would often encourage himself by saying, "This MBA degree will help me to open doors to other possibilities. In order to pass this degree, I need to make some sacrifices."

But instead of activating his 'stoicism' identity – a philosophy which, when misconstrued, has the tendency to guide people to endure suffering rather than maximising positive emotions – what if Mike decided to narrate the situation from the perspective of an 'investor' identity, something like an internal Warren Buffett, the famed chairman and CEO of Berkshire Hathaway. By so doing, Mike begins to remind himself, "This MBA degree will help me to open doors to other possibilities. To pass this degree, I just have to invest my time wisely by focusing on quality rather than quantity. The dividend in the near future will be amazing."

That is exactly what Mike did.

With this subtle switch of identity (or, to be precise, calling upon another identity instead of suppressing the less helpful one), Mike was able to make peace with his current situation. Activating 'Mr Buffett' helped him to him better invest his time and reduced his tendency to procrastinate. 'Mr Buffett' also prompt Mike to realise that one of the reasons he had signed up for two-year of hard times was to expand his network. However, during Covid-19 when the majority of lectures were carried out in cyberspace, Mike came to realise that he had not been deliberately allocating time to network with his classmates. When his 'Mr Buffett' identity was activated, Mike became more intentional about how he should be spending time, and where it was wise for him to allocate time to important activities such as networking. This also generated within him a greater sense of hope for the future he was currently writing for him and his family.

While we are not disputing that some aspect of stoicism is very much required when faced with such a difficult goal, what should also be explored is the fact that it may not be that helpful for Mike to constantly remind himself of how challenging he expects the MBA journey to be. That said, grit, determination and stoicism certainly do help in the accomplishment of goals. As American psychologist Angela Lee Duckworth, science author Rosa Lee and psychology professor Egbert Chang have demonstrated, grit certainly helps you accomplish goals. When combined with passion and resilience, grit really is one of the cardinal secrets to success.[236] We will chat about this a little more in Chapter 7.

However, it doesn't have to take the lead among the identities that will best serve Mike during his journey. Just the simple reframing of his mind to act more like an investor will yield more positivity and productive outcomes.

Again this has everything to do with the words we use in our self-talk. When Mike uses the word 'sacrifice', his thinking is rooted in trying to reduce his loss over the short term. His thinking and sentiments will be anchored in a deficit-centred mindset. All of us have an aversion for loss. It's a cognitive bias identified by Amos Tversky and Daniel Kahneman in 1979, which subsequently led Kahneman to win the 2002 Nobel Memorial Prize in Economics. The thought of losing something always gives us a greater level of pain, even when we know that we may have the chance to gain something of similar magnitude if we continue our pursuit. So putting his focus on loss and sacrifice might not be the best long-term approach to take.

Conversely, when Mike tells himself that he is actually 'investing' time, then his thinking shifts towards the generation of more value in the long run. The resultant mindset becomes one of abundance, not loss.

Unfortunately, when Mike first reduced his 'stoic' identity – 'Captain Perseverance' – he felt very much out of place. He had to be quite intentional to call upon other identities to outshine Captain Perseverance, who has a tendency to jump in whenever times are tough, when life is handing out a beating or when an individual is feeling like they are on the brink of chaos. The Captain may even encourage the adoption of a motivational personal mantra such as, "When the going gets tough, the tough get going." However, because the Captain always takes over, other identities typically don't get a chance to show their mettle, meaning that when times get tough, they can never elbow themselves to the front as your identity of choice.

We are certainly NOT saying that perseverance is unhelpful. Captain Perseverance has an important role to play, but this is not the only identity in play. We are arguing that instead of automatically activating the Captain, perhaps you should first activate another identity – in the case of our MBA example, 'Mr Buffett' was a better fit to help Mike to prioritise and better invest his time by asking, "If time is a commodity, what would Mr Buffett do?" Would he strategically analyse the associated return on investment? Probably! Would he channel more time to investing in behaviours that create more value and reduce the time spent on less helpful outcomes? Very likely so. Even if you are planning to take time off, Mr Buffett may even help you to spend your downtime in a productive manner and filter out other annoying identities that are nagging you to taking a well-deserved break. Funnily enough, if you activate Mr Buffett first than call upon Captain Perseverance afterwards, you may be surprised with the outcome.

When we use these analogies with ourselves, we will start to realise that our mindset when it comes to approaching problems could be markedly improved. Even though many of our mindsets push a rhetoric of "work smarter but not harder", the foundations of our problem-solving behaviours are still firmly anchored on doing things the hard way because we are proud of our true grit.

Another common trend Mike observed was that the overreliance on Captain Perseverance meant that in situations where identities such as Mr Buffett may have been a better choice, these identities remained forgotten and unused. To guard against this, the best play is to develop another identity to assist Mr Buffett in his quest to outshine Captain Perseverance. The question is how.

In Mike's case, he was highly analytical. So his best bet was to start by leveraging his natural virtues and strengths instead of working hard to supress his flaws or perceived inadequacies.

Mike has the tendency to be quite calm. This was his default for the majority of the time. So he worked to formalise an identity to facilitate a calm internal discussion – let's call this one the 'Calm Facilitator'. Since calmness was actually one of Mike's character strengths (we'll elaborate on these character strengths in Chapter 7), it was almost effortless for him to remember to activate the 'Calm Facilitator' when faced with challenges, particularly when he became aware of the power of this identity.

In so doing he was able to kickstart a round of helpful inner dialogue to probe more deeply into a situation before reacting.

Mike discovered that he was blessed with a tendency to deal with challenges with a sense of urgency, but not just the sort of rushed response that comes with blindly and rashly coming up with solutions. He was able to evaluate the potential value that may arise from a particular choice or response. Mike decided, therefore, to empower this identity and call it 'Urgent Evaluator'. Mike realised he could rely on this newly forged identity to draw all other identities into a deliberation of the preferred approach to solve the problem based on the best avenue for extracting value. By first understanding the value that each identity may bring, the 'Urgent Evaluator' can determine the most helpful option for the particular context.

And there was one more. Mike also appreciated his sense of drive. Having come from a very poor background, one of his biggest goals was to create wealth. This desire was encapsulated in one of his favourite mantras, "Where there's a will, there's a way." So, when things got tough, Mike was able to activate his 'Mantra Enforcer' and get a lift. It may sound cheesy, but having a few mantras up your sleeve may serve you well – motivators like Les Brown's 'stay hungry' or 'act the way you want to be and soon you'll be the way you act'. These aren't just nice-to-haves, their efficacy has been proven by neuroscience.[237]

To synthesise this fascinating and complex area of study into a relatively short sentences, the fact is that the default neurocircuits of the brain are responsible for synthesising thoughts when you encounter an event. Many of these neurological regions are wired together habitually owing to other identities inside your head that have been working collaboratively over the years. For example, one of Mike's hidden personalities predisposed him to change into an 'Angry Hulk' identity and made him erupt like a violent volcano when he was continuously disrespected or when a member of his MBA syndicate team continued to underperform. The 'Angry Hulk' would suddenly surface, wanting to smash everything when things didn't go his way. Mike's 'Angry Hulk' didn't always surface, and it didn't often allow extreme rage to take over, but this feisty identity had stopped others from taking Mike's words on occasion. Additionally, to reduce the tendency of 'Angry Hulk' taking over, Mike also realised that another identity – the 'Poor Neighbourhood Kid' - often put up an arrogant facade that offended others. The 'Poor Neighbourhood Kid' suffered from some degrees of insecurity and an inability to let go the feeling of being disrespected by other kids because of his family's lowly economic status. When the 'Poor Neighbourhood Kid' identity felt Mike had been disrespected, then this identify usually called 'Angry Hulk' in for assistance.

In most situations, confronting the 'Angry Hulk' and the 'Poor Neighbourhood Kid' together was not a pretty sight. Furthermore, when Mike's 'Captain Perseverance' took too much of a beating, for instance by letting that shameful syndicate member get away with slacking off too many times, the combination of the Captain, 'Angry Hulk' and the 'Poor Neighbourhood Kid' resulted in a massive eruption.

Bearing all this interplay in mind, it is easy to see why it might be more useful for Mike to work on amplifying the commanding position of the 'Mantra Enforcer' in his everyday life, particularly when stress is at a minimum. When challenging times arise the 'Mantra Enforcer' identity can reap the benefits of this continual conditioning of the other less-desirable identities to request they step down for the common good, or at least think before they act.

If a 'Mantra Enforcer' identity can forge effective partnerships with other inner advisors, such as Mike's 'Calm Facilitator', 'Urgent Evaluator' and 'Mr Buffett', then together these identities can have a profound impact. By inviting these identities to join his internal dialogue in the right sequence, Mike was able to activate and enhance a much more powerful 'best self' response.

As Mike's MBA journey progressed, his 'Mr Buffett' and 'Mantra Enforcer' began to collaborate. While he was still going to create wealth, the partnership between these two identities led Mike to recognise that other forms of wealth were also important in his life, such as being loved and loving in return, adding value to others, and achieving autonomy and spirituality.

Mike's sense of self-efficacy and self-love began to grow constructively as a result of this shift in his inner dialogue. Funny enough, the 'Poor Neighbourhood Kid' began to fade. His 'Angry Hulk' morphed into 'Astute Hulk' and this identity toned down the level of anger and the need to resort to fury. With the help of 'Urgent Evaluator', 'Mr Buffett' and 'Mantra Enforcer', Mike was also able to establish a fine balance between this newly improved 'Astute Hulk' and 'Calm Facilitator'. Figure 5.1 illustrates how Mike rearranged the hierarchy of his identities to enhance his personal growth. This is, of course, an ongoing journey. While Mike is already a fine husband, a wonderful father and dedicated leader, we have no doubt that he will continue to transition his identities, grow exponentially, make significant progress in life and contribute meaningfully to those around him.

Turning our focus away from Mike, and towards you, we certainly advocate holding tightly to a few phrases that resonate with you and which help you – and your multiple identities – to navigate difficult and confusing times. Nevertheless, using multiple identity theory, it is possible to create narratives which can harness more identities and, in the process, spark self-talk, inner dialogues and narratives that can lead to better outcomes. Furthermore, we would like to suggest you don't spend too much effort suppressing your problematic identities. Instead, we suggest you take these three steps:

1. try to break the strong tie(s) between two or more problematic identities

2. use the characteristics of problematic identities to work for you instead of working against you

3. try to nurture new identities and magnify existing (but less dominant) identities that are helpful to the circumstances you find yourself in.

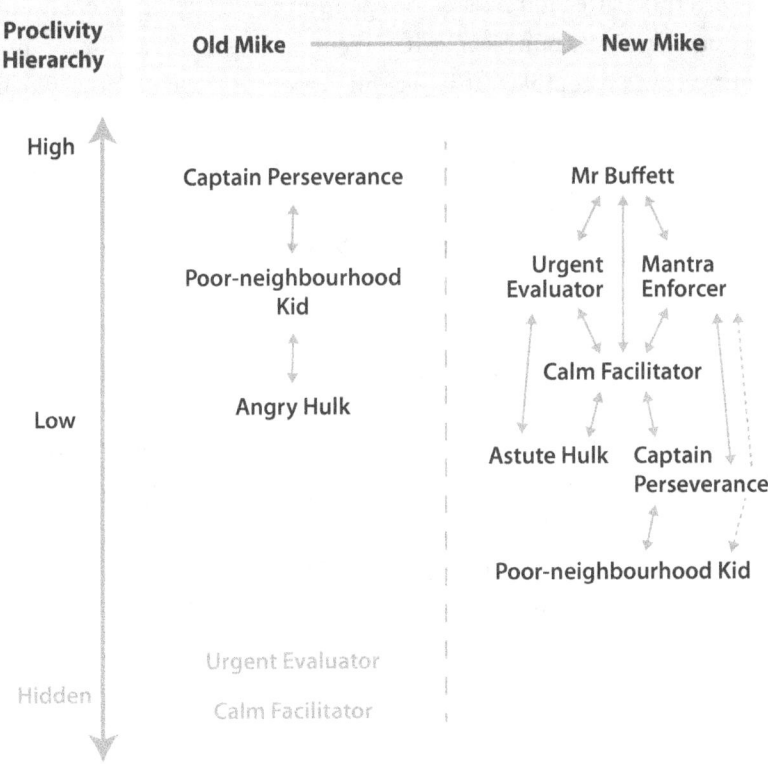

Figure 5.1: Fostering, rearranging, associating, and dissociating Mike's identities.

When completing his Master of Philosophy Degree in Management and Executive Coaching at the University of Stellenbosch Business School, Chen was overjoyed to attend a module and a masterclass delivered by Professor Dusan Stojnov from the University of Belgrade. Stojnov, who is widely regarded as a true master in personal construct coaching and psychology, was insightful and captivating. The three-steps technique above evolved for Chen out of the insights shared by Stojnov.

While the technique is simple it is also extremely powerful as it requires an individual to dig down into their inner constructs (a psychological term that encompasses conscientiousness, intelligence, attitude, emotions, feelings, mindsets, self-esteem and ego). Oftentimes, inner identities can be complex. It is for this reason that the glorious pursuit of personal discovery can be a lengthy and intricate process, and one that may require seeking help from a professional coach. Therefore, in the next section of this chapter, we would like to offer another simple but equally powerful technique that is based on the theories of thought self-leadership and self-talk.

WATCH OUT FOR SABOTEURS

In his New York Times and Wall Street Journal bestseller 'Positive Intelligence', Shirzad Chamine discusses at length the nine common types of identities that sabotage our success. Identified based on neuroscience evidence, these saboteurs can, argues Chamine, become invisible masters that control our lives. To counter this, it's critical to catch these saboteurs red-handed in order to take corrective measures to weaken and rectify them.[238] Conversely, Chamine also suggested there are five identities - which he referred to as sages - that can help you to thrive.

Even though Chamine's book and presentations are both entertaining and insightful, in reality, there are more variations and nuances deserving of the saboteur or sage labels. But that doesn't detract from our sincere recommendation to watch his entertaining TED Talk on the subject, entitled Know your inner saboteurs.[239]

Talk to yourself. It's healthy

While controlling the hierarchy of the multiple identities operating in your own brain is first prize, sometimes this may not be immediately practical or achievable. In these instances, the next best step is to try and modify the content of your self-talk or inner dialogues in order to support your personal growth.

Retracing your way back to the childlike behaviour of talking out loud to yourself may be socially frowned on in some quarters, but it does provide several benefits. If we encourage ourselves to speak out overtly we force our thoughts to slow down and, in the process, give the multiple regions of our brain a chance to make themselves heard.[240] By encouraging this slower, more deliberate approach, different circuits of neurons can be wired to fire up together leading to different cognitive-behavioural patterns.

Talking to yourself has multiple benefits, some of which can be a bit surprising. Research published in 2012, for example, revealed that when hunting high and low for a missing item, just saying the name out loud can help you locate the item more easily than just obsessing about it silently.[241] A more common example is that using motivating language when talking to yourself can transpire into an increase in job performance, job satisfaction and an intent to remain at a current employer.[242] This use of motivational self-talk has even been linked by researches to more resilience in the face of stressful situations,[243] increased self-efficacy,[244] better concentration and improved performance.[245] These benefits are particularly notable in the field of sports science.

Apart from overt and covert styles of self-talk, there are many other variations into which researchers continue to delve. For the purposes of helping you through your personal transition phase, we are going to draw your attention to three of the most common styles of self-talk, paying careful attention to how you can use these different styles to help you navigate this journey. These styles are: first person and third person, positive and negative, as well as instructional and motivational self-talk.

Bearing in mind the multiple identities inside you, we advocate holding permanent seats on your intrapersonal communication advisory board for six distinct identities. Each of these chosen inner advisors should not function in isolation. Rather they should work collaboratively with others on the board.

First-, second- and third-person self-talk

First person self-talk encompasses all the statements or thoughts that use first person singular pronouns, such as 'I,' 'me', 'my', 'mine' and 'myself'. Second- and third-person self-talk utilises pronouns such as 'you', and 'your', as well as 'he', 'him', 'his', 'himself', 'she', 'her', 'hers' and 'herself'. Decades of research affirms that engaging in 'distanced self-talk', or mentally talking to yourself using a third person form, can help foster psychological distance which leads to better emotional regulation, self-control, rational thinking and stress management.[246] This was backed up more recently by research carried in the journal *Clinical Psychological Science* which noted that people who use words for themselves that are usually reserved for others are better able to deal with negative or intense emotions.[247] If this rings a bell about the exercise we asked you to complete when you wrote your short autobiography and eulogy using illeism, then you'd be right. After all, science tells us that referring to yourself in the third person does help you to think more objectively.

In recent years, various empirical investigations have shown that there are multiple advantages to using illeism when attempting to reflect upon certain situations or interpret the meaning of an event. For example, a notable neuroscience study published in 2017 in the Scientific Report section of *Nature*, the highest cited scientific journal, suggests that using the third person self-talk format increases psychological distancing which consequently empowers one to strengthen self-control.[248]

How did the authors arrive at this conclusion? They performed three neuroscience studies using event-related potential (ERP) together with functional magnetic resonance imaging (fMRI). ERP is a technique that evaluates brain responses associated with the stimulation of a specific sensory, cognitive, or motor trigger, while fMRI ascertains the brain activity by determining the changes of blood flow in different regions of the brain when a person is responding to a particular stimulus. The findings suggested that it was possible to leverage third-person self-talk to reduce self-referential emotional reactivity. In other words, when exercising third person self-talk, your brain activities lead to actions that are less influenced by your emotions. As the result of this cognitive shift, it is possible to retain objectivity with less effort.

One of the most intriguing aspects of employing distanced self-talk as a strategy for emotional regulation, is that it seems to take much less cognitive effort to achieve this self-regulation – an important aspect to remember when formulating courageous invitations. As psychologist and Michigan State University associate professor Jason Moser and colleagues wrote in their 2017 paper published in *Nature's* Scientific Reports section, "Third-person self-talk may constitute a relatively effortless form of self-control."

At this stage, you may argue that some egotistical individuals and gaslighters (those who deploy psychological abuse and manipulation) have the tendency to speak to others in the third person. Yes, you are not wrong. But for majority of us, distance self-talk offers us the opportunity to exercise objectivity and reflexivity, especially when it comes to challenges and decisions that require our impartiality. Particularly if the self-talk used is designed to help the six permeant members on your intrapersonal communication board to deliberate freely in order to amicably agree actions which are ultimately to your benefit.

Positive and negative self-talk

What we can't ignore in a discussion about self-talk is the positive-negative continuum. The tendency to use positive and negative self-talk varies from person to person based on considerations such as upbringing and personality. But when it comes to being upbeat and positive versus negative and pessimistic, make no mistake that we human beings innately favour the negative. In 2001 psychologists Paul Rozin and Edward Royzman termed this the 'negativity bias'. It's a cautious approach which served humankind well 120 000 years ago when there were real, physical threats to contend with, but in our modern world it's just become a reflex which sticks to negativity like glue while finding any possible way to mistrust positivity.[249] Yet, harnessing optimism really does unlock some positive outcomes.

Researchers also tell us that it helps us better achieve goals and manage stress. A 2009 study published in the *Journal of Applied Social Psychology* actually found that optimistic college students were less likely to drop out than pessimists, simply because they were more motivated and less overwhelmed by the situation.[250] So there's a lot to be said for trying to shift negative self-talk onto a positive territory.

One way you can do this is by actively working to create and uphold identities that possess a slightly higher affinity towards optimism and positivity. Then under the right circumstances, activate these identities to help you to narrate your thinking and give meaning to your experiences. Activate these identities in ways that can help you to generate happiness and wellbeing, instead of merely visualising how you are enduring pain and hardship while taking a beating from life.[251] But don't do it too much or all the time, because researchers warn us that keeping up a positive dialogue with yourself all the time isn't always good for you.[252] Nor does positive self-talk always leads to fruitful outcomes.[253] In fact, misusing positivity can even lead to harmful or disastrous outcomes, particularly when forced positivity does not resonate with the challenges and threats on the horizon.[254]

Journalist Barbara Ehrenreich certainly didn't shy away from the controversy attached to an anti-positivity stance in her book *Bright-Sided: How Positive Thinking Is Undermining America*,[255] in which she explored the tenets of positive psychology and argued that this sort of wild optimism errs on the side of mass societal delusion. Ehrenreich came to this conclusion after her cancer diagnosis was met by unjustified positivity and exaggerated cheerfulness, leaving no space for pragmatism. While Ehrenreich's book was not a treatise for negativity, it certainly was a slap in the face to boundless optimism.

That's not to say that negativity doesn't have a bright side either. Interestingly, high-performing athletes can sometimes use negative self-talk to boost their performance – after all some negative emotions (such as increased blood flow to the brain or elevated breathing rates) can be regarded as healthy if they are viewed rationally and logically,[256] or if they speak to cultural or personal interpretations and motivators.[257] Another study posits that some athletes might even interpret negative self-talk as a form of self-encouragement.[258] That said, switching things up between negative and positive self-talk might actually hold the key. For instance, rather than negatively telling yourself "my legs are tired" when you are half-way into a marathon, why not add a challenging statement such as "but I can push through" to add a touch of positive encouragement.[259]

While optimal levels of negative self-talk can spur on motivation and help to activate your best self, constant negativity can have a demoralising effect which has the opposite effect. Similarly, giving yourself a boost of positivity and affirmation can be very beneficial, but you should always guard against misusing positive self-talk as it may morph into warm and fuzzy platitudes.

Perhaps the secret lies in remaining keenly observant of your mood when inner dialogue is taking place. Psychologist and neuroscientist Lisa Feldman Barrett refers to this as understanding the power of mood, because how you are feeling is impacted by everything you see, hear, smell, taste and touch. In other words, you are constantly impacted by something academics refer to as 'affect'. Affect – or your mood - colours how you experience daily events. It can also be harnessed as a source of wisdom which enables you to make better and wiser choices.[260] If you are aware of affect it can be used to your advantage, for instance by using affect as a cue to step back from deeply held beliefs in order to connect with people different to you.

As we discussed in Chapter 3, in the application of rational thinking to master new behaviours, the rationality of your intrapersonal communication is what really counts, not the positive or negative nature thereof. As Ehrenreich would attest, blind optimism for the sake of it can sometimes be more damaging than a logical assessment of the situation which could result in activating another inner identity capable of rising to the challenge at hand. Or, as Barret might tell us, it's about pushing the pause button, opening your mind and challenging the logic of your existing views.

Putting a practical spin on all of this, it's clear that not all positive sentiments and self-talk are good. Similarity, not all negative sentiment and self-talk is bad. What matters is the context. Therefore, we recommend that you take this positive-negative dichotomy into account when appointing identities to serve as permanent board members on your intrapersonal communication committee: A 'Negative Policeman' and a 'Positivity Nudger'.

The 'Negativity Police': When there are red flags that your brain is producing neurocircuits that lead to negative self-talk and thoughts, the 'Negativity Police' can step in to bring awareness to you and whatever identity or identities are causing this pessimistic trend to your inner communication. The 'Negativity Police' analyse whether or not the harmful statements in your mind are constructive given the current context. This identity aims to catch you when you slip into self-doubt, rumination, anxiety, irrational fear or if your mind starts spinning out of control. Instead of confronting the identity or identities that are causing this unconstructive negativity, like a veritable lone ranger, the 'Negativity Police' immediately request back-up and call on the 'Positivity Nudger' to swing into action (we'll get to know the 'Positivity Nudger' next). However, when the 'Negativity Police' finds your negative inner dialogue is constructive or the statements are warranted for the situation, the identity will attempt to collaborate with another persona, for instance 'Agent MacGyver' (we'll elaborate about this identity shortly), in order to link the negative self-talk with value creating and innovative self-talk. Of course, other identities such as the 'Positivity Nudger', the 'Sensible Energiser' and the like can be invited into your boardroom to support 'Agent MacGyver'. We circle back to these identities in a subsequent section, but first it is necessary to understand the polar opposite of the 'Negativity Police', the 'Positivity Nudger'.

The 'Positivity Nudger': While we often know better, many times we make choices that simply aren't good for us. Sometimes we regret these decisions at a later date and feel guilty about giving in to temptation. What researchers tell us, however, is that we can strengthen our self-control by making simple changes to our environment. This is a process which behavioural science experts Ralph Hertwig and Samuli Reijula call 'self-nudging'. In an article published in Behavioural Public Policy[261] the concept is explained as an empowered approach to structuring our own environment. For instance, you might turn off your smartphone while working to avoid distraction; thereby helping yourself to make the right choice to focus on the job at hand rather than following a juicy thread on Twitter.

External nudges have been shown to work well, so it follows that the nudges which come from within will be even more powerful. Just ask Dr Tara Swart, a psychiatrist, neuroscientist, senior lecturer at MIT and author of 'The Source: The Secrets of the Universe, the Science of the Brain'. After dedicated years to studying self-nudging, she agrees that it is indeed a powerful way to help overcome challenges and a lack of willpower.[262]

The 'Positivity Nudger' is an identity that works to align your thinking and action with your courageous invitations. It also galvanises all other identities to carry out their conversations in a slightly more positive way. The 'Positivity Nudger' constantly modifies words to increase positivity authentically, without stepping into the dark-side of positive psychology. Hence, it nudges, it prompts and it cajoles you to see the brighter side of life. For instance, when the 'Negativity Police' call upon the 'Positivity Nudger' to deal with strong blanket statements such as "I cannot do it" or "I am not going to find the solution", this identity will help you to nudge the inner conversation to "I am not sure how to do it yet" or "the ah-ha moment is yet to come". 'Yet' is a powerful three-letter word that gives hope that, with the right amount of time and effort, you will see the light.

Instructional and motivational self-talk

Both positive and negative self-talk can be motivating, even though positive self-talk does lead to better self- encouragement. The power of motivational self-talk does yield several benefits. However, it does not mean that there is no merit for individuals to exercise instructional self-talk. In fact, it is puzzling that the majority of popular articles and vblogs focus on motivational self-talk instead of paying an equal amount of attention to instructional self-talk as well.

In an unpublished research study, Chen, with his collaborator, Dr Vivienne Spooner, managed to assist their MBA student Estelle Craig to gather 58 participants to join Part I of the research. All participants were either junior manager, entrant level employees, or interns of large corporates. Additionally, the researchers ensured that none of these participants had any prior entrepreneurship experience and all have obtained a business degree. In Part II, the 30 participants included senior and middle managers as well as entrepreneurs.

For both sections of the research, these participants were then divided into three groups (One control group and two experimental groups). Each group had to completed two rounds of challenges, with each round consisting of two tasks. In round one, each participant from both groups were given an A4 paper that consisted of a rudimentary shape marked in the centre of the paper. They were then tasked to exercise creativity to create an artwork by incorporating this shape as part of their creative piece. In the second task, both groups of participants were instructed to formulate an innovative business strategy for launching an ice-cream store in a large, fancy indoor shopping mall located in a vibrant, affluent, and popular urban area. Participants were given 10 minutes to complete each of the two tasks.

The second round of the challenge consisted of two tasks that were similar to the ones given in the previous round. However, before a participant was permitted to start a task in this round, unless assigned to the control group, he or she was required to read a cue card written in a manner as if he or she was exercising self-talk. They were also requested to make a concerted effort to assimilate the messages of these cue cards, embracing the fake-it-till-you-make-it attitude.

In this round, the participants from the control group received no self-talk instruction and continued to respond to tasks similar to the ones they had just completed. Whereas two different types of cue cards were handed to the participants according to the particular experimental group to which they were assigned.

Participants from the MST (Motivational self-talk) Experimental Group were all given motivational self-talk type of cue cards before each task. Their cue cards for the first task would state, "I am brilliant! I am creative enough to do this task well!". When it was time to work on the second task – to formulate a business strategy for launching a toy store in a rural area – each of the MST Group participants was given a card that read, "I shall believe that I can do this task well! I know I can think innovatively!"

Conversely, participants in the IST (Instructional self-talk) Experimental Group were given the same tasks as participants of MST Group, except they were given instructional self-talk type of cue cards. For example, before embarking on Task 1, their cue cards would instruct them to "let me spend 5 minutes to construct as many different artwork options as possible on another piece of paper before I work on the task sheet. I will then use the last 5 minutes to pick the best option to develop it further on the original task sheet". Following this, the cue card for Task 2 would state, "Spend the first 2 minutes to list all the elements that will wow your customers, the parents, and your customers' customers, the kids. Then spend another 2 minutes to list down all business components, such as marketing, operations, and the like that can channel your attention to come up with something innovative. Then spend the last 6 minutes to complete the task."

All inputs from all participants were evaluated by 5 different judges. This was to ensure that there are enough judges to minimise the possibility of individual judge's biases skewing the grading process.

Do you know which group of participants performed the best? Interestingly, not the control group nor the MST Experimental Group.

During the subsequent qualitative interview sessions, some of the participants from the MST Experimental Group cited that even though they felt motivated in the first few minutes of each task, they did not know what to do. Some suggested that they had their "blinkers on" as they neglected some critical components of the business or did not consider other possible options. Others stated that by the end of each task, they were doubting themselves again as they felt that they struggled to come up with great ideas. Whereas for the participants in IST Experimental Group, even though they were a bit nervous in the beginning, they were guided to create options for their artwork and to use a helpful strategy formulation framework to confront the business strategy task.

This suggests that despite the fact that motivational self-talk can have a positive impact in one's life, the ability to come up with the right formulae to solve challenges still underpins the overall success. Spending some time discerning the challenge that lies ahead, before just rushing into solution mode, will help you to make better decisions and resolve problems more effectively.

Previously, we discussed how adding a 'what-to-do-next' type of instruction – even in the face of negative self-talk - could lead to helpful outcomes. Remember those athletes we discussed? This doesn't just apply to the world of sports, it also has merit for creative and innovative tasks where having a set of highly helpful instructions can help to reduce blindspots, prevent linear thinking and guard against unhelpful cognitive-behaviours, such as various types of biases and preconceived notions which arise due to environmental considerations or inner emotions.

This simply serves to underline that because we do not live in a binary world, we cannot rely exclusively on binary ways of thinking. Instead, we should be exploring ways to develop quality motivational and instructional self-talks, instead of focusing on only positive interventions. We should focus on the context and follow up with the right instructions in a motivating way, since motivation without the knowledge could lead to unproductive and even dangerous outcomes if the disconnect between reality and self-talk results in significant cognitive friction, as we noted when we discussed the science behind over-positive pushes and how this too can prove negative.

To help counter a binary, one-size-fits all approach to fostering self-talk, we suggest you try to appoint inner advisors similar to the 'Sensible Energiser' and 'Agent MacGyver', both of which work well with Mantra Enforcer. As promised, let's get to know these two identities a little better.

'Sensible Energiser': How vividly can you conjure up images of your future? Writing your eulogy will have given you a pretty good idea of how easy, or hard this process was for you. This ability is important because it plays a key role in how you energise yourself at the opportune time.

In academic terminology, we call it self-prospection or consideration of future consequences. Yes, that's quite a mouthful, so let's break it down more practically. If you can imagine both your near and distance future-selves to be more desirable and if you can visualise ways to connect this vision back to your current self, then it is likely that you will feel more energy when you are in pursuit of these objectives.[263]

Of course, our energy is also being influenced by both progress and setbacks – not just vision and intention. Sometimes, 'Sensible Energiser' just has to show up to celebrate small successes that keep us motivated and which help to sustain our mental energy. This is according to Brian Jeffrey Fogg, director of the Persuasive Tech Lab at Stanford University who postulates that you don't need to wait for big wins to get out the champagne, frequent small successes actually matter more than the big wins. He is an advocate of finding ways to celebrate yourself daily, remembering that your brain doesn't perceive progress or perceives progress differently; so you'll stay energised and keep your brain motivated.[264]

This inner advisor may even gently remind you to use power posture as a way to energize yourself. As Harvard business professor Amy Cuddy reminded us in her well-received TED Talk, body language can profoundly shape who we think we are.[265]

When an identity is evaluating or judging itself or an event more harshly than it should, this may well be caused by getting angry over silly mistakes or beating yourself up because of unexpected setbacks. Living under the influence of any critical mind will not enable you to live a satisfied life. Although you may deceive yourself into thinking it will make you a higher achiever, this constant self-criticism is actually sapping your brain of precious mental energy. Once the 'Negativity Police' detect this behaviour and call in other re-enforcements, the 'Sensible Energiser' will monitor the mental energy level and attempt to lift your spirits as others inner advisors help you to deal with minor missteps as they occur.

'Agent MacGyver': Not many popular TV shows became so successful that the name of the main character becomes a verb and finds a spot

for itself in the Oxford English Dictionary. MacGyver, the action-packed show that ran from 1985–1992, is one of the rare examples.[266] According to the official definition, to MacGyver is to make or repair something "in an improvised or inventive way, making use of whatever items are at hand", which is exactly what the fictional character, Angus 'Mac' MacGyver did. Played in the original series by American actor Richard Dean Anderson and his famous mullet, and Lucas Till in the 2016 remake of the series, MacGyver was able to use anything from a paperclip to a rubber band to get himself out of seemingly impossible situations week in and week out. Armed with his trusty Swiss Army knife and duct tape, his name became synonymous with quick, ingenious thinking and innovative methods.

MacGyver came to be associated with utilising resourcefulness. The cognitive ability of resourcefulness means to find quick and clever ways to overcome difficulties using the resources at hand. Instead of wishing for more assets or better circumstances, individuals who exercise resourcefulness will dig deeper to reach their goals, which is why resourcefulness is regarded as one of the important cognitive traits for leaders in this disruptive era.[267] This MacGyver-like ingenuity can be displayed by almost everyone.

Lee Zlotoff, the creator of the TV character MacGyver, coined the term, 'inner MacGyver'. During an interview in 2019 Zlotoff put it this way, "It turns out we have extraordinary resources inside of us which we are generally not aware of." Tapping into this innate ability, he explains in 'The MacGyver Secret: Connect to Your Inner MacGyver & Solve Anything',[268] comes down to three steps. In Zlotoff's words, "It's really simple. You write down whatever question or problem you have in long hand, it's better than typing, the neuroscientists can tell you why. But you write down the problem. And then rather than standing there and racking your brain you just say to yourself 'you're going to work on that problem inner MacGyver subconscious, I'm going to go do something else, when I come back you're going to have an answer for me'. Then you can go do one of hundreds of activities available to you. Whatever you do choose something that is physical as it keeps that conscious mind occupied so it can't get in the way. Then when you come back after an hour, four hours, a day, look at that question again and say to that inner self, 'OK, what's the answer'. Then you just start writing. It does not matter what you write… within 30 to 45 seconds the answers will simply flow out of you."[269]

We believe there is another way, which involves issuing deliberate self-talk instructions that can take you back to the starting point of a situation or problem, allowing you to analyse the context and ask pertinent questions that ultimately lead you to insights regarding the resources at your disposal.

In 'The Sleeper and the Spindle', Neil Gaiman paraphrased a fellow English writer, GK Chesterton, when he wrote, "Fairy tales are more than true - not because they tell us that dragons exist, but because they tell us that dragons can be beaten." How you utilise and develop the right type of identities can help you construe meaning and generate value-yielding 'dragon slaying' self-talk that has the power to create magic in your life. Strictly speaking, you will be better equipped to lead yourself well and reframe your perceptions if you are able to pin down and understand your own combination of major identities. As you clarify the hierarchy and relationships between these identities, and isolate the kind of self-talk each of these important identities shapes in your mind, you become more adept and more skilled at utilising these inner advisors to advance your goal of 'being more'.

The process of developing this deep understanding starts with questions, observing your responses and how your self-talk changes depending on different situations. For instance, ask yourself if you exaggerated a setback you had recently. Then dig deeper. Which identity or identities led you to overstate this setback? How do you think this identity or identities were formed within your mind? Can you identify ways in which these identities are working to sabotage your success?

It is crucial to play around with combinations of different inner identities and identify the value they might unlock for you if harnessed correctly in different circumstances. To design your inner advisors' narratives and dialogues, it is important to first filter, then select and then appoint the right inner identities as your advisors. Thereafter, help these identities to make a concerted effort to craft and refine the words, narratives and dialogues that they exchange inside your mind. Give them names, just like we've done here, to help you better understand their personalities, characteristics, strengths, and the situations in which they shine.

Once your behavioural linguistics have been appropriately adjusted, these four self-talk-oriented identities can form a fruitful partnership to create value for you. To illustrate the power of these four simple identities, we would like to give you a quick summary of Terashni Pillay's personal disruption journey. Of course, you do not have to term these four identities exactly how we have named them – in this case: the 'Positivity Nudger', the 'Negativity Police', the 'Sensible Energiser' and 'Agent MacGyver'. What is important is that you have effectively scoped out an appropriate identity per each of these four self-talk styles, both positive and negative as well as instructional and motivational. To help get the best out of each of these identities, it's often helpful to creatively come up with different terms that resonate with you and your story.

Shine brighter: An inspiring journey

Growing up in Durban, Terashni Pillay had always been a competitive individual. Since her late teens she had begun to develop an ambition to advance in her career. Although at this point her determination might not have been a full-fledged purpose, she did set some high-level strategic goals for herself.

In 2005, Pillay enrolled at the University of the Witwatersrand in South Africa for a Bachelor's degree in science majoring in environmental science. She progressed to honours level and graduated in 2008. However, Pillay was dissatisfied by her future career prospects and unsure about her direction, so she decided to sign up for a Bachelor's engineering degree in chemical engineering at the same university. She completed that qualification in 2012.

Pillay worked briefly as a chemical engineer, before taking up a position as risk engineer for global insurer American International Group South Africa in 2013. She was promoted to the rank of senior risk engineer in 2015. In 2018, the 30-year-old Pillay was headhunted to head up the risks engineering unit at Discovery Limited, a highly innovative and successful South Africa-based listed financial services group.

Pillay's portfolio up until this point in her career had usually involved highly technical risk engineering work. She had never really led a team, let alone been tasked with managing a group of head-strong employees. Furthermore, being the newly appointed head of a newly created unit, Pillay would be responsible for the design, implementation and execution of strategy for that unit. She would have to take charge of all aspects of the new unit, from setting up operational and financial plans to formulating technological and human resource tactics. It was a big leap, and almost akin to launching and running a start-up within the Discovery group.

As her first big task, Pillay was invited to present her strategy to Adrian Gore, the founder and CEO of Discovery, and a room full of executives. Gore remains one of the most successful leaders and entrepreneurs in the world, and his corporate creation is renowned for shaking up the finance industry through business-model innovation and the roll out of highly ingenious strategies. Since Pillay had never really formulated a strategy for an entire unit before, she was understandably extremely anxious. We don't think anyone could blame her. It was at this moment in time that Chen happened to sit next to Pillay in an airport lounge. They started talking and Pillay decided to try the coaching route.

To Pillay's detriment (disclaimer: the former version of herself) she had a tendency to spiral into negative self-talk and overemphasize what she did not have. But that was not the real problem. Oftentimes during their coaching sessions, it was clear that Pillay was sabotaging herself and diminishing her brilliance. Despite having a wealth of amazing attributes, Pillay failed to recognise these abilities and took refuge in devouring one self-help book after another. After a few coaching sessions, Chen asked Pillay to pack away all her self-help books and hand them to her personal assistant. She needed to start relying on herself to 'do' self-help as oppose to 'reading' self-help. (Yes, the authors can see the irony of this as we push on with writing our own self-mastery book.)

Chen then asked Pillay to activate her "Negativity Police" identity she needed to observe when she started sabotaging or downplaying herself. Chen also encouraged her to reflect on the specific conditions and situations that would lead her to sabotage and downplay herself. She was asked to identify these triggers so the 'Negative Police' could catch these culprits.

Pillay and Chen discussed the possible strategic intent which could form part of the new Discovery business unit and worked through some aspects of the strategy. Even though the strategy was still incomplete, it began to take shape and Pillay's anxiousness at presenting to Gore and the top executives began to wane. Chen asked Pillay to call upon her "Positivity Nudger" and went through a few different statements aimed at nudging Pillay to see this as a growth opportunity. At one point, her "Positivity Nudger" pointed out that Gore and his team were prolific business leaders who probably only hired individuals capable of helping them to create more successes. It is unlikely, therefore, that they had hired Pillay only to see her fail. This realisation completely changed the game. Pillay was happy to buy into this argument and place her trust in the senior executives.

As her anxiousness subsided slightly, her "Agent MacGyver" was then activated to find solutions. Within less than a few minutes of coaching conversation, "Agent MacGyver" suggested that Pillay did not have to know everything, she just had to be highly skilled at relying on and extracting valuable information and wisdom from key stakeholders and experts. What aided Pillay in this mission was her natural charm, approachable demeanour and a sunshine personality filled with humility and sincerity.

Based on the self-talk conversations undertaken by these different identities, Pillay became more enthusiastic and excited about the prospect of knocking this big task out of the park. Her "Sensible Energiser" was actuated, and then accentuated. She found herself re-enforcing her own belief system and caught herself saying that Discovery hired her because she knew the field so well. Pillay agreed to continue to energise herself, rehearsing her positive self-talk. She also opened up to discussing the gaps she might want to work on.

The "Sensible Energiser" and "Agent MacGyver" identities also prompted her to realise that she did not have to follow the same script as others when presenting a business strategy. She started believing that she could bring something different to the table. She also began to sense that she was meant to shine. She was able to walk into the boardroom with her own spin. What was the outcome? Well, not only did her first big meeting go down well, but Pillay received a high five from Gore and a number of the senior executives.

Two years after joining Discovery, Pillay was invited to take up a post at Marsh & McLennan Companies Africa as a strategic manager dedicated to assisting one of the managing directors. It didn't take long before the company gave her the opportunity to head up its property risk consulting and strategic projects portfolios. Part of her task was to turn a business unit around.

Being 32 at the time, Pillay had to lead people who were older and had that been working for the company for a long time. Within the first week of assuming the job, the whole team decided to call a Zoom meeting and declared that they did not want to work under Pillay's leadership. Pillay had to rely on her 'Positive Nudger' to hide her anger. This identity allowed Pillay to talk to herself and remind herself that this could be just a small bump along the way to greater things. This unpleasant event was just a small test of her leadership. Her 'Negative Police' identity went into overdrive, just so she could allow her team to speak with minimal interruptions. She was very careful not to use words that would reflect her true emotion or further strain the fragile relationship between the team and its new leader.

The combination of her "Sensible Energiser" and "Agent MacGyver" helped to minimise the tension. "Agent MacGyver" prompted her to question why her team felt this way. Why was this unit making a loss? Could that be linked to the negative sentiments being raised? Could providing hope to these staff members and empowering them to do more, help the situation? Her "Agent MacGyver" also instructed Pillay not to neglect anyone's input, so she allowed everyone to fully express their views. She also followed her instincts by asking genuine questions. As the result of such a forthcoming, transparent and courageous dialogue, many of her subordinates started to drop their guard.

While the tone of the team began to soften, the handful of individuals who had instigated the meeting continued to express their dismay. The "Sensible Energiser" cheered on Pillay's small accomplishments, encouraging her to see her true worth, and assisting her to back herself. With her self-efficacy energised, Pillay decided to inform her subordinates that she would be very willing to accept all resignation letters. She quickly added that it would be regrettable for anyone to quit now before they had a chance to work together to turn around the business unit.

Fast-forward a few months and Pillay's subordinates have made a remarkable transformation and the unit had gone from in the red to bringing in the lion's share of profitability for Marsh & McLennan Companies Africa. That initial confrontation quickly became water under the bridge, and Pillay began to adopt an empowering leadership style to engage with her team – a completely different approach to the previous leader of the business unit. Pillay's belief in her team's ability to shine was rewarded and she, in turn, worked hard to share information with them and inspire and upskill each individual.

Pillay continues to disrupt herself, along the way creating new successes and attracting opportunities to her.

These paragraphs do not do justice to Pillay's transformation and have skipped over many of her smaller wins and accomplishments. However, it is important to note that Pillay was able to tick a milestone in her career progression checklist as we were writing this book. On 31 August 2021, Swiss Re Corporate Solutions formally announced that Pillay would officially take over as its South African CEO from 1 November 2021. In this role, Pillay would be responsible for managing the strategy development and performance of the company in South Africa and across Sub-Saharan Africa. She was just 34 years old.

Bringing in her age is more than cosmetic, it's an important part of this story because Pillay always felt that her age imposed a glass ceiling. Fortunately her inner identities provided her with the right kind of self-talk that encouraged her to keep moving forward. This progression is illustrated at a high level in Figure 5.2. This snapshot highlights how Pillay's identities helped her to overcome hurdles or created successes in opportune moments, which she was able to accumulate into invaluable experiences to help her make her next big leap. Pillay's self-talk-oriented identities will continue to evolve as she develops her own executive gravitas and continues to emerge as a strategic yet human-centric leader.

Have a close look at Figure 5.2. Perhaps you would like to do a similar mapping exercise for yourself?

Why not try to create and list the self-talk-oriented identities that you wish to develop? Then map out how you wish to leverage them for your short-term journey of personal disruption by clarifying the values that each specific identity can help you to create. Thereafter, and based on activating the different identity or combination of identities, you can formulate self-talk to help you respond to different situations.

It's a simple but powerful technique.

As we bring Chapter 5 to a close, we would like to note that the process of appointing inner advisors is individual and unique. You can choose to uncover all your identities, rearrange their proclivity hierarchy, and shape new complementary identities so they can help you to develop better sense-making dialogues when you encounter a challenging situation. This way you can foster quality strategic narratives in how you arrive at solutions. You can also try to design a few different identities that enable you to shape and utilise your positive, negative, instructional and motivation self-talk approaches more effectively. Alternatively, you can push the boundary a little bit and try to adopt a style that combines these approaches.

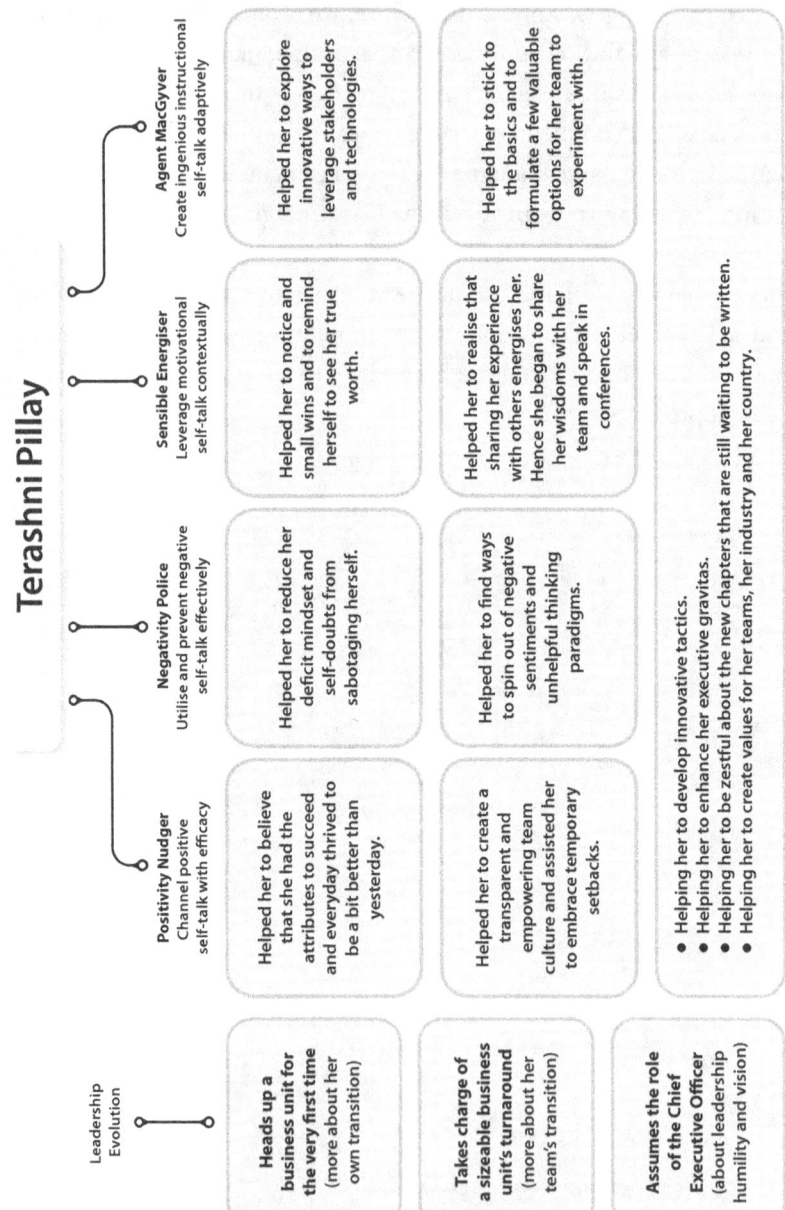

Figure 5.2: A transformation journey through self-disruption

After all, a multifaceted range of values can be generated when you know how to fragment and recombine different elements. Just ask Davlin Richardson. This was the main topic of his MBA research and an investigation that continued informally after he had submitted his thesis. Chen and Richardson interviewed close to 80 highly innovative leaders and entrepreneurs to uncover some of the factors that enabled them to disrupt themselves and come up with disruptive business ideas. The majority showed they were capable of fragmenting a business concept and a relevant situation into different parts, then they used systems thinking to pick the adequate parts they deemed valuable for the context, and recombined them along with some other elements to increase the product-market fit of their offerings.

There is a whole lot of combining going on in that approach, which is why the next chapter delves into a concept we call 'ampersand thinking'. Within this concept lies the magic to enrich your life. All you have to do is adopt it contextually.

Self-enrichment Exercises

Looking back at your own reflections so far (as you have read through the chapters of this book) it is time to focus on your own inner advisers and how you can use them to support your courageous invitations, your personal growth to a better self and ultimately your goals. To assist your growth, we have summarised the areas of focus into the following questions, and we encourage you to work through before you move on to chapter 6. Revisit figures 5.1 and 5.2 if you need a reference point.

List two or three distinct cognitive-affective behaviours that you will need to ensure you can progress towards your goal(s) more meaningfully and rapidly. Now assign the name of the identity to each cognitive-affective behaviour. These are your enabling identities.

List two or three distinct cognitive-affective behaviours that may be hampering your progress. Now assign the name of the identity that matched each cognitive-affective behaviour. These are your derailing identities.

List one or two distinct cognitive-affective behaviours that help you create, sustain, and enhance your enabling identities. Now assign the name of the identity that matched each cognitive-affective behaviour.

_____

_____

List one or two distinct cognitive-affective behaviours that help you calm, reduce, and/or eradicate your derailing identities. Now assign the name of the identity that matched each cognitive-affective behaviour.

_____

_____

_____

_____

_____

Take a moment to think about how these identities can interact with each other, and how you will arrange their hierarchy so that you can maximize your growth and strengthen your best self. If you have some spare post-it notes, try to make use of them. Write down each of your identities on a post-it note.

Based on the above responses, rearrange the post-it notes in the hierarchy to maximise your growth and strength as your best self. What does your hierarchy of identities look like? We encourage you to look back at figure 5.1 if you need some guidance, noting that we are focused here on their interaction with one another. Before moving to the next question, consider where there is self-talk between the identifies and connect them with a line.

Now assign a number to each of the self-talk interaction lines between your identities. Write down the self-talk phrase that you would like these identities to use when they interact with each other. Consider how you could use this self-talk to benefit your growth and activate your best self.

_____

_____

_____

_____

_____

_____

Are there any areas of self-talk that may be limiting your personal growth that you need to be aware of? How can you refocus / reframe this self-talk to be beneficial for growth / goals achievement?

_____

_____

_____

_____

_____

_____

_____

_____

What further incremental changes may occur to your identities and their interaction in the future as you seek to transition your identities for personal growth?

_____

_____

_____

_____

_____

_____

It is now up to you to revisit your hierarchy of identities often. These identities will be your inner advisor and provide you with the right kind of self-talk you need in this journey of self-disruption.

Having regard to the above, what updates do you need to make to your Best Self Goal Setting canvas? Make your updates.

Chapter 6
The Magic Of Ampersand Thinking

The simple and unassuming word 'and' might not, on first acquaintance, seem like it warrants shortening. It's just three letters, after all. And yet this well-worn conjunction has just that, its own shortcut: the ampersand. History tells us that the highly recognisable '&' symbol has a rather interesting backstory; one which starts as far back as the first century BC. During this time Roman slave Marcus Tullius Tiro served as private secretary to famed Roman lawyer and orator Marcus Tullius Cicero. After Cicero's death Tiro was freed and went on to become a respected writer in his own right, who leaned on his unique and firsthand insights to pen an extensive four-volume biography of Cicero.[270]

The symbol we know today – the one which high-end fashion labels, well-known chocolate brands and telecommunications firms such as Dolce&Gabbana, M&M's and AT&T have all taken to with aplomb – is what is known as a ligature. It's a combination of the letters 'e' and 't' (the Latin word 'et' which means 'and'). Its purpose, however, is far more than stylistic.

Anyone who has ever tried to take verbatim notes when someone else is speaking will know how hard it is to keep up with the flow. Therefore, in order to speed up his writing process, Tiro devised a form of Latin shorthand – which became known as Tironian Notes and included a glyph known as the 'Tironian et', which looked something like a reversed digit seven or '7'. Yes, it doesn't look much like the symbol we use today. While Tiro's name remains inextricably linked to the roots of the ampersand, it wasn't until centuries later that the symbol actually evolved into the shortcut we know today, and found its unusual name.[271]

The name ampersand is in itself a quirky tale which was born out of schoolchildren in the early 1800s learning the symbol as the 27th letter of the alphabet, so X, Y, Z, &. The problem was that the symbol, at that point in time, remained unnamed, so these youngsters concluded saying their ABCs with the words "… and, per se, and' (with the final and standing for &). Over time the kids, as they do, garbled the words into a single word, which is what we use today.[272]

Why all of this background about a handy, but let's not kid ourselves, a relatively innocuous symbol? Well, the ampersand has a remarkable ability to link, to blend and to co-create seemingly disconnected ideas and themes. It is this ability to cement connections which gives the ampersand its power, not in the power of the symbol itself. Similarly, in life, if you choose to open yourself up to ampersand thinking in your quest to develop your 'best self' then you can tap into a remarkable ability to link a convoy of seemingly unconnected and disparate train carriages, thereby enabling them to work together as they head towards a single destination.

Sometimes, in your quest to create a masterpiece, you may already have gathered all the skills and mindset shifts required, but all you need are the connections to slot everything together. Together we are going to walk through a few examples of ampersand thinking, and how you can apply this approach in your day-to-day life.

The second-largest orchestra vs super-spicy chilli

Unless you are an opera lover, the name Claudio Monteverdi (1567–1643) might not resonate strongly with you, but the impact this Milan-born, Renaissance-era composer and visionary had on the world of music is incalculable. A font of creativity at a time when self-expression was at its peak, Monteverdi challenged traditional ideas about harmonic progressions and became known for his progressive techniques and modernist ways.[273] Today, more than 450 years after his birth, historians regard Monteverdi as one of the world's most influential composers and credit him for developing a new genre of classical music, the opera. His first opera, *L'Orfeo* (or *La favola d'Orfeo*), was composed in 1607 and is still performed today.

In 2015, when *L'Orfeo* was included as part of the BBC's classical music festival, Proms, at the Royal Albert Hall, conductor John Eliot Gardiner wrote: "It may be that the radicalism of Monteverdi has yet to be fully grasped... In *L'Orfeo* we can follow him [Monteverdi] veering away from the old modal systems and inching towards what we now recognise as tonal harmony - one of the developments that defines the very essence and bounds of Western music (including, of course, opera) right up until the 20th century."[274]

In this musical masterpiece, Monteverdi decided to combine more than 41 instruments in a way that had never been achieved before. Trombones, trumpets, harpsichords, chamber organs, strings, woodwind instruments and brass were drawn together to create, what Gardiner described as, "a vibrant, living work". While Monteverdi gave a healthy dose of latitude to future conductors in terms of how this large ensemble would play his work, he did carefully specify which instruments should be used for certain sections.

Today, this ensemble approach is regarded by some scholars as the antecedent of the modern symphony orchestra.[275] While orchestras come in different shapes and sizes, from smaller chamber orchestras of less than 50 members to philharmonic orchestras of 50 to 100 musicians, the composition of a full-size orchestra typically consists of string, woodwind, brass, and percussion instruments. From time to time, other instruments, including vocals, may be introduced depending on the work being performed.

Over the years, famed composers such as Bach, Beethoven, Mozart, Schubert, Debussy, Stravinsky and Tchaikovsky crafted clever arrangements of different patterns of musical notes, using expert timing and the right sequences to guide this combination of musical instruments towards musical perfection. When these masterpieces are performed by an orchestra in harmony with itself, it still sends shivers down the spine.

Consider, for instance, how Beethoven used the seventh chords and syncopation in first movement of his ground-breaking Symphony No.3, 'Eroica'. It was unprecedented. On other occasions, such as the fourth movement of Beethoven's Symphony No 6 'Pastoral', the crescendo from the strings stirs emotions to their fullest, before they fade away as the brass and percussion instruments come into their own, evoking our imaginations and creating the sensation of being immersed in a thunderstorm.

The wonderful thing about music is that, in the hands of an expert orchestra, the same emotions can be stirred up within us centuries after these compositions were created. There is a wonderful story which highlights the power of music to transcend time and space. It was 9 July 2016 and amateur and professional musicians from the Netherlands, Germany and Austria gathered in Frankfurt's Commerzbank Arena with the sole purpose of breaking the Guinness World Record for the largest orchestra. A staggering 7 548 musicians united to create a mega-orchestra that went on to perform excerpts from symphonies by Dvorak and Beethoven, as well as performing some popular pieces. The event trumped the previous record of 7 224 musicians, who had gathered in Brisbane, Australia in 2013.[276]

While the German record was subsequently broken in 2019, when 8 097 musicians gathered in Saint Petersburg, Russia, on 1 September

2019 to play the Russian National Anthem,[277] the 2016 event holds a special meaning due to the deeper intention behind the record-breaking effort. As organiser Jens Illemann, a trumpet player from the Germany city of Hamburg, said at the time: "We wanted to show how music can connect people, and how important it is for Germany."[278]

For many people in our digital, social-media dominated modern world connection is less likely to be achieved through live classical music events and more likely to be facilitated through content carried on online platforms. YouTube, for instance, has 2.29 billion active users each month and, at the start of 2021, was ranked as the second most popular social media platform in the world, just behind Facebook with 2.74 active users a month.

In the case of Germany's 2016 record-breaking orchestral event, the videoclip with the highest YouTube view was posted on 12 July 2016 by India's *Hindustan Times*.[279] The total number of views was just over eight thousand views when we checked the statistics on 4 March 2022. Not bad, but certainly a long way from achieving Illemann's goal of using the power of music to connect as many people as possible. While it took home a Guinness World Record, the German event fell short of connecting to many of the four million *Hindustan Times* subscribers. (It is worth noting that the Germany record was eventually broken by Venezuela's National System of Youth and Children's Orchestras which gathered 8,573 musicians to successfully play 'La Marche Slave' by Pyotr Illyich Tchaikovsky on 13 November 2021).[280]

This comparison may seem slightly disrespectful to die-hard classical music lovers, but there is a point to be made in this example about the best way in which to connect on a grand scale. And, to take this further, we'll need to bring in another example; this time the good-humoured stylings of Danish musician and chili connoisseur Claus Pilgaard, also known as Chili Klaus or Klaus Wunderhits. After developing a keen interest in chillies of all shapes, sizes and potencies, Chili Klaus came to appreciate that he could spread his knowledge about these varieties, while simultaneously entertaining others by getting celebrities, musicians, and other interesting individuals to try his hot chillies.

What does this have to do with an orchestra? Perhaps you have guessed it? If not, press on.

In 2014, Chili Klaus acted as conductor and trickster to the Danish National Chamber Orchestra when he compelled the musicians to eat – on cue – eye-wateringly hot chillies before continuing with their rousing rendition of Tango Jalousie, a gypsy tango written by Danish composer Jacob Gade in 1925. To the untrained ear the professionals executed their mandate flawlessly, despite the grimacing, tears, glowing red faces and obvious discomfort. Only when the very last note was played did the musicians carefully place their prized instruments on the floor and rush off stage.[281]

The YouTube video that captured this amusing event was posted on 31 October 2014 by Chili Klaus.[282] By 4 March 2022, same date as we checked the video of the German mega-orchestra event, this funny video has gained 5.5 million views – approximately 735 times more views than the massive gathering of musicians. What is particularly interesting to note is that while Chili Klaus only had 161 thousand subscribers at the time, his video managed to overshadow the *Hindustan Times*' 2.89-million subscribers by a ratio of around one to 19.

What does a comparison between these two stories tell us? That how you choose to combine different elements matters.

From Baby Shark to viral videos

To put these two orchestra videos into some YouTube context, consider that a children's music video called Baby Shark Dance, made by Pinkfong Kids Songs & Stories, had garnered 10,2 billion views between 18 June 2016 when it was originally posted until 4 March 2022.[283] When you consider this in the context of the two orchestra videos, their combined tally seems like a drop in the ocean. However, if you were able to combine Illemann's mission of connecting people by creating a megaorchestra with a fiery chilli gimmick, then you might just find that social media content quickly goes viral and connections tick up at a faster rate.

According to marketing expert Johan Berger, an international best-selling author and marketing professor at the Wharton School of the University of Pennsylvania, the virality of social media content is the result of combining six factors, which he abbreviated as STEPPS. STEPPS stands for social currency (people talk about things that make them look good), triggers (we talk about things which are top of mind), ease of emotion (if we connect, we tend to share), public (we often imitate what others do), practical value (we share information that can help others) and stories (we lean towards sharing great stories or narratives). In his book *Contagious: Why Things Catch On*, Berger advocates for making sure these boxes are ticked when developing marketing content.[284]

Keeping STEPPS in mind when crafting social media content is just part of the battle one, the next step is to make sure that the combination is just right. At least, this is the view of James Currier, a venture capitalist and one of Silicon Valley's leading growth and network effects experts.[285] The founder of Tickle Inc. (formerly known as Emode.com), a media company that produces quizzes and tests that offer everything from IQ to personality insights, Currier successfully directed operations from 1999 to 2008. The tickle.com offering relied heavily on people sharing their psychology tests and quizzes, so a significant amount of time and effort was poured into understanding why people share some content and not others. For Currier, the secret sauce came down to eight psychological buttons: status, identity, being helpful, fear, order, novelty, validation and voyeurism.

Most of these buttons speak for themselves, but let's run through them quickly.

Status is an important element since many people want to be seen as cool or influential or authoritative in their online interactions. Another big reason people share things is to project their own identity; they will share more when in doing so they express, advocate, or defend their identities or the identify of their tribe. In addition, if you can convince other people that your content will be of use to them, then it is more likely that people will share this valuable or novel information.

Fear too is a powerful emotion – after all we all know that bad news often travels faster than good news. But, according to Currier, many people do not like chaos, or things that are not aligned to their perception of the world order. They will share anything that gives them the perception that they are making this world a bit more orderly and systematic. Currier further suggested that content which provides a glimpse of novelty, in order to help people differentiate themselves from the crowd, is more likely to be shared. Sadly, however, content that falls on the nasty spectrum of social media, such as voyeurism, also resonances with some people, who freely share things that enable them to live vicariously through another.

In short, there is a proven recipe for achieving success in the fickle and fascinating world of social media. You just need to know which buttons to press and how to create effective linkages.

Create your own cocktail of fusions, remixes, mashups, cross-overs and blends

It is not only viral videos on social media that benefit from combining the right ingredients in the best order. If you pause quickly to take stock of how you navigate your way through life, you will soon recognise that most things which might be regarded as spectacular are so because of the unique combinations they possess. Consider a stunning Italian supercar that incorporates finely tuned electrical and mechanical devices, or a beautiful sunrise moment in the mountains that is made all the more beautiful because the rising sun plays off the winter morning dew and brings the landscape to life. While we see the whole, it is often the sum of the parts that provides the magic.

Music, yet again, offers up the most wonderful examples of how sometimes unexpected combinations can generate the 'wow' factor.

In 1978, during the era of disco and hi-NRG (pronounced 'high energy') upbeat electronic dance music, an American DJ and composer Patrick Cowley created a remix of disco queen Donna Summer's 'I Feel Love'. When the over 15-minute-long track was officially released in 1982 it went on to become the first remix to make the charts, hitting 21 on the UK singles chart. With overdubbed effects and the use of synthesisers, the new version was a far cry from Summer's 1977 original, but no less foot tapping or effective. Today's Cowley's mega-mix is still a cult classic.

Similarly, if you think that combination will never mesh, consider the blend of classical music and heavy metal. That is exactly what a two-man band called Mozart Heroes pulled off when they blended Mozart's Symphony No. 40 with Metallica's iconic heavy metal offering 'Enter Sandman'. Since its release in 26 April 2015 on YouTube, this unique – and surprisingly uplifting - combination has been viewed more than 58 million times.

While the likes of Heriot-Watt University's Professor Adrian North have determined that classical music and heavy metal fans have a lot more in common that you might think – including a flare for the dramatic – the surprising marriage of seemingly contradictory styles into a successful blend often stirs something within us simply by virtue of thinking outside of the prescribed lines.[286]

The same goes for the culinary world, which has long dabbled in the art of fusion cooking, which combines diverse elements and traditions from a variety of cultures and geographies into a single cosmopolitan dish.

Many renowned chefs, Michelin-starred restaurants and simple eateries around the world are faced with a similar problem: how to standout from others. After all it's no long sufficient to serve up an Italian-inspired pasta, an all-American burger or a simple Mexican taco when everyone in the city is selling the same. Instead you might try a chicken wonton taco, which adds a dash of Asian flare. Or a Mexican ravioli complete with chorizo. Or perhaps a tandoori chicken burger, for a touch of India exoticism.[287]

The cross-over of cultural recipes and culinary arts are often well-received by consumers, and give top master chefs the opportunity to play with new and unique combinations of ingredients, recipes and cooking styles while leaning on their in-depth knowledge of ingredients and methods likely to enhance a dish. British celebrity chef-cum-science pundit Heston Blumenthal even adds a dash of biochemistry and physics knowledge into his process, when creating impressive gastronomical artworks. Consider, for instance, his savoury bacon and egg ice-cream or a mousse palate cleanser poached in liquid nitrogen.

Blumenthal is an outstanding illustration of how shaking up the establishment and being prepared to stretch the line requires more than just combining different ingredients. To create memorable – if crazy – outcomes you also need know-how, a keen eye for timing and an overarching view of the end result. During his illustrious career, Blumenthal has opened several acclaimed restaurants in the UK and Australia, all of which necessitated more than just his reputation and culinary flare to succeed. From produce to ambiance and services to marketing, everything had to be combined in the effective way in order to achieve the desired experience for customers.

Einstein's combinatory play

In early 1900s, a respected French mathematician called Jacques Hadamard conducted a survey of 100 leading mathematicians of the day – including a chap called Albert Einstein – to try and untangle their mental processes. Hadamard went on to publish his findings in *An Essay on the Psychology of Invention in the Mathematical Field*.[288]

In responding to Hadamard's questionnaire, Einstein described his own thinking process by coining the term 'combinatory play'. In a letter to Hadamard, which was later incorporated into a book entitled *Ideas and Opinions*,[289] Einstein described this creative process as "act of opening up one mental channel by dabbling in another" and added that: "combinatory play seems to be the essential feature in productive thought". The process hinged on bringing unrelated ideas, disciplines and topics together and allowing them to feed off one another with the hope that creativity is sparked. For Einstein, whose interests ranged from sailing to writing travel journals to playing the violin (he was self-taught) and the piano, this blending of science and art was his magic elixir.

This form of ampersand thinking takes seemingly unrelated facts and ideas and moulds them into creative, innovative and novel forms. The process, which is at the same time both conscious and subconscious, can – with some deliberateness – become a value-creating way to solve challenging issues by putting a different slant on them.

This approach is not exclusive to Einstein, it was harnessed to powerful effect by iconic technopreneur Steve Jobs who once told *Wired* magazine: "Creativity is just connecting things. When you ask creative people how they did something, they feel a little guilty because they didn't really do it, they just saw something. It seemed obvious to them after a while."[290]

Similarly Jørgen Vig Knudstorp, who we met previously in these pages, joined the Lego Group in 2004 at a time when the Danish toymaker was in all sorts of trouble with depressed sales and saddled with around US$800 million in debt.[291] The future did not look rosy. So how did Knudstorp turn Lego around, from the brink of bankruptcy to a highly profitable business before he stepped down as CEO on 1 January 2017? In part, Knudstorp ascribes his success to a leadership philosophy of knowing how to build the right combinations. In an interview with Meet the Boss, Knudstorp noted that his job was to gain clarity around all the important strategic levers at his disposal and then come up with creative ways to help the company fine-tune this combination to create added performance.[292]

A similar ethos has also been applied as part of the discipline of combinatorial chemistry. This chemical synthesis method relies on preparing and testing a large number of chemical compounds rapidly on a small scale, using small reaction cells in high-throughput parallel approaches. The process is generally aided by computer software and chemical libraries so researchers can effectively pre-screen the potential chemical features required to form part of the drug molecule in order to produce the desired effects. Combinatorial chemistry prepares a large number of different compounds at the same time, instead of synthesising compounds in the traditional manner. This saves time and increases output. As a result, this combinatory approach has been used for both drug lead discovery and optimisation.[293]

The same combinatory play mentality, when used to combine human, technology and new business models, can provide certain companies with differentiating factors that can be used to outcompete their rivals and disrupt the industries in which they operate. Certainly, the ability to arrive at creative solutions using a variety of inter-related and even unconnected ideas can – and does - spark innovation. But the key seems to rest in how best these inputs are combined, in other words how they are linked together by that common, every day 'and'. By combining possibilities and concepts with an 'and' it is possible to not only clarify the desired outcome which is being targeted, but also to better filter through all options on the table and recognise others which may have been out in the cold but are deserving of attention and inclusion.

In other words: It is not sufficient to only identify and embrace divergent concepts and approaches but also to create linkages which interconnect and network ideas, thereby harnessing the tensions and potentialities rather than clinging to an either/or approach. And this is where ampersand thinking comes into its own, expanding on Einstein's combinatory play concept and inviting us to greedily look for more and deeper connections and linkages which when fused together can create truly dynamic combinations.

Sometimes by combining 30% of solution A with 45% of solution B, while infusing both with 25% of solution C in the right ratio and under the right sequence, it is possible to deliver something quite impressive.

That weird-looking ampersand symbol - the Latin shortcut for 'and' - can really help to expand your thinking. You just need to learn how to harness it.

Ampersand thinking

The solutions we seek to enrich our journey through life do not commonly limit themselves to binary forms alone. Oftentimes they are not a case of 'either/or'. Instead, they are waiting for you to discover them when you apply a mindset of 'and/plus'.

While many of us think we have a grasp on this approach, more times than we care to elaborate on we come into contact with people who are looking to enhance and fire up their lives and for whom the theory behind ampersand thinking makes sense. However, they struggle when it comes to applying this mindset to their day-to-day lives. To help guide you through the process, we're sending you back to class – to business school actually. During some innovation and creative thinking modules, Chen likes to ask his MBA students this simple but deliberate question, "Tell me right now, do you prefer this lecture to be, A) very practical or B) theoretical? If you wish to pick option A), then put your hand up now."

Let's pick up the action with the participants under intense pressure to make a quick decision.

Without pausing for long, Chen presses again. "If you pick option B), then put your hand up now."

Frequently, the majority of participants attending the lecture will pick option A, with normally about less than 25% picking option B.

Chen then asks the class, "Are options A and B, mutually exclusive? If not, why do you pick only one? Wouldn't it be nice to know that the approaches you learn in my class and the suggestions you have been provided with are practical because they are, in fact, anchored on sound theoretical underpinnings?"

Often, after Chen's follow-up questions, participants turn around and protest that it was due to the wording of Chen's question, and his pressing for an answer, that caused them to respond in the way they did. Chen asked for an either/or response, they'd argue. This closed question approach led them to pick one of the two options on the table.

In truth, this sort of binary mentality is deeply rooted in our thinking processes. From an early age our teachers, parents and elderly family members have generally provided us with limited options to pick from coupled with threats of dire consequences if we do not choose wisely. For example, these authority figures may propose a question similar to this one: "You can listen to me now or there will be consequences".

This binary approach has carried over into our spheres of learning too, even at tertiary level, where you may receive a complicated equation to solve, or an intricate case to study, which asks you to consider option A versus option B in very clear terms.

As the result of this pre-programming, we tend to reduce the options in our heads down to either/or decisions or processes. Does this sound familiar, "Should I quit my job to pursue my entrepreneurial idea? Or should I stay in corporate and let go of the entrepreneurship?" Instead, why not ask: "What is my 'reasonable utopia' in this case?" In other words, while it is not physically possible to have your cake and eat it at the same time, how can you formulate ideas and approaches that help you to get the best from both of these words? If you push the binary question aside for a moment, maybe this thinking could see you formulating a question like: "How can I enhance my happiness and personal growth while remaining in corporate and developing a side hustle?"

When ampersand thinking such as this comes into play, the results can often be quite astounding, as was the case with Antoinette van der Merwe, who we briefly mentioned in Chapter 3.

Antoinette started her professional career as a cleaner, sweeping floors and polishing toilets. Perseverance and hard work paid off and eventually she become an executive in a large South Africa-based cleaning company. Despite her successes, and the fact that she was now at a point in her life when she was reaping the benefits of her hard work, Antoinette was not entirely fulfilled. Nor was she confident in the future that lay ahead.

In a coaching session with Chen, she asked: "I am at a crossroad. Should I quit my job to start micro-farming?"

Chen smiled and asked, "Do you like your job?"

Antoinette responded with enthusiasm in her eyes, "The majority of the time, it's a resounding yes."

"Do you like micro-farming enough to quit this job?" probed Chen.

Antoinette hesitated before she responded. "I am doing micro-farming now. But I am not sure I can answer you."

"Well," said Chen, "since you are already doing micro-farming but you are not sure, can I assume that your corporate career still holds some attraction?"

"Yes", a concise answer, but one that fully represented Antoinette's personality. She was, after all, a person who thrived on efficiency.

"So what aspects of your job do you love and what aspects make you want to leave?" asked Chen.

Antoinette shared that she enjoyed the pressure, the challenges, the complexity, as well as the comradery she shared with her colleagues. She even mentioned that the negatives people often mentioned when talking about corporate life, such as organisational politics, did not bother her. She also admired her line-manager, she said.

With a bit more probing, the pair were able to establish why

Antoinette labelled this point in her life as a 'crossroad', and it had less to do with any indecision on her part about choosing between micro-farming or her corporate job and more about her need for certainty. Antoinette has climbed the corporate ladder to the very top, but where was her next challenge? She had a deep resistance to being stagnant and now, ensconced in the executive, she felt unclear about her future. Her desire to re-establish herself as a micro-farmer was, therefore, born out of a need to retake control of her life.

To diffuse the intensity of the conversation, Chen asked, "What does your girlfriend say?"

"Even though she does worry about me for constantly investing so much time and energy to my corporate job, she made it clear that the lifestyle of a micro-farmer will be too passive for me in the long run."

A solid observation, to which Chen responded, "So am I correct in assuming that in an 'reasonable utopia' state, which means a place of ideal perfection within sensible conditions, you would love to continue doing interesting and challenging tasks at your company, while also doing something - or even many things – on the side that challenge you and give you the sense of growth?"

Antoinette began to smile. "Yes," she responded.

"So why can't you be slightly greedy and find ways to combine things so that you can achieve your reasonable utopia?" Chen nudged.

Subsequent to this conversation, Antoinette reframed and realigned the internal dialogues between her inner advisors. She had a frank discussion with her line manager and the outcomes were very promising. At the same time, Antoinette hired some family members to take on the tedious errands and chores required to run the micro-farming operations while she took care of the fun part of the business. Furthermore, and in line with her need for constant growth and development, Antoinette began learning how to assemble LED lights and bought another house as a renovation project, again so she could keep learning new things.

While the conversation with Chen was pivotal, if truth be told,

Antoinette was already a leader who applied an ampersand mentality to her life and her career. She often asked her subordinates what other businesses they could pursue and what more could they offer to their clients, even if the ideas were just low-risk, quick-win diversification options. This approach, coupled with the fact that Antoinette trusted her subordinates and their views, meant that they were able to effectively collaborate to create interesting and gratifying successes. The problem, it seemed, was that she had temporarily forgotten to let the Chief MacGyver-type of inner advisor take charge of her life.

Ampersand thinking nudges us to consider the options available and then to explore ways in which these can be uniquely combined to extract value. For instance, when you ask, 'and what else?' or 'and who else?', you are actually trying to exercise lateral thinking to create other viewpoints and unlock additional options for addressing problems or creating solutions. Most importantly, this approach allows you to explore these options without getting bogged down in either/or thinking and without rushing into mental fixedness.

It is for this reasons that we refer to ampersand thinking as a person's sensible insatiability to generate plausible options which are so necessary when building a best self and a better life. Oftentimes, solutions to our problems are in plain sight but we just don't seem to be able to access them. Ampersand thinking allows us to connect certain dots, thereby bringing options and ideas together. That's where the magic happens.

We are not saying that at times the old binary mentality might resurface, or that unhelpful behavioural patterns and cognitive biases might creep up on us, but rather than trying to force yourself to eradicate old patterns that no longer serve you it is often a lot easier to invest your effort into formulating the right combination of plausible tactics that can better carry you forward. Funnily enough, being mindful about thinking and acting in more collaborative and creative ways often helps to diminish the mental reliance on unhelpful thoughts and behaviours.

Self-innovation for personal growth

Your own double S curve, which we discussed in Chapter 2, is another form of ampersand thinking. After all, the double S curve is an illustration of your current place and future potential in this world and should focus you on ways in which to phase in your new S curve while introducing other, smaller changes to phase out the old S curve. As you make this transition it's necessary to ask yourself what you need to take forward and what skills might need to be developed. For instance, some old traits might still serve you in the future if they are combined with the new traits that you are currently developing.

A great way to apply ampersand thinking as part of your self-innovation and personal growth journey is to use a popular business innovation model known as the Ten Types of Innovation.

In 1981 two of the foremost experts in industrial design, systems thinking and innovation methods, Jay Doblin (1920-1989) and Larry Keeley cofounded a strategic design planning consultancy which they named Doblin. Unlike other firms offering advisory services in innovation and design, Doblin embraced an ethos of design and innovation based on human-centricity and multi-disciplinarity thinking. This successful company was eventually acquired by Deloitte in 2013.

One of the most well-recognised tools developed by Doblin came about as a result of more than four decades of studies and research into corporate innovation, incorporating insights from more than 2 000 successful companies including Amazon, IBM, Cirque du Soleil and Ford. Keeley invested considerable effort in identifying patterns evident in companies that have successfully innovated in the past, as well as the reasons why innovation endeavours failed. By around 1997 Doblin's methodical research had led them to uncover the drivers of how organisations can spur on innovation by seamlessly orchestrating 10 organisational dimensions. In 2013, Keeley codified this framework with the aid of Helen Walters,

Ryan Pikkel and Brian Quinn and published the acclaimed book, *The Ten Types of Innovation and the Discipline of Building Breakthroughs*.[294]

To ensure the robustness of the framework, Keeley and his co-authors beefed up the analysis by exploring more than 1 200 game-changing innovations created in the past 200 years. Their research not only affirmed that the Ten Types of Innovation was a viable framework to help executives craft a sound innovation strategy, but it also led them to the startling realisation that innovations which really count always use five or more types of innovation. By combining distinctive types of innovation, even if the cocktail was arrived at accidentally or unintentionally, the innovation that ensues was almost guaranteed to have the power to change industries - or even the world. That's quite a recipe, if you know how to use it.

Let's take one step back before we push on with the Ten Types of Innovation framework by touching on how this approach applies to individuals. Ask yourself if it is logical for you to consider yourself, as an individual, to be a Proprietary Limited (Pty Ltd) company. If you are an entrepreneur, you are essentially behaving like a company. Whereas if you are employed by a large company, irrespective of your ranking, you are in principle a micro-enterprise within a large enterprise. If this comparison seems sensible to you, then the Ten Types of Innovation framework becomes a useful tool when examining how you can increase your personal innovativeness in order to enhance your professional capacity. We encourage you to undertake this exercise.

Keeley and his co-authors split the Ten Types of Innovation into three categories. At the centre they placed the 'offering', which contains the core product elements as well as how the product is organised and integrated. To the left they put 'configuration' or how the company is organised to make a profit. And to the right 'experience', or how the company interacts with its customers. The accompanying graphic illustrates the three categories and their subcomponents. As we delve into each of these elements in more detail, we ask that you keep that Pty Ltd example in mind, remembering that you can apply this framework to the enrichment of your own life.

Offering	Configuration	Experience
• Product Performance • Product System	• Profit model • Network • Structure • Process	• Service • Channel • Brand • Customer Engagement

Figure 6.1: Adapted from The Ten Types of Innovation and the Discipline of Building Breakthroughs

Offering

The first Ten Types of Innovation category – 'offering' – includes two types of innovation: product performance and product systems.

Innovation Type One: Product Performance

Product performance innovations look at how a company provides value from its core offerings. This type of innovation involves incrementally refining and updating some of the existing offerings to ensure the company remains competitive and is able to explore new offerings in order to deliver the next wave of competitive advantage. Product performance is not just about how many innovations a company can deliver, but also the timeliness and the level of product-market fit of the innovation.

In the context of personal innovation, product performance can be regarded as the skills for which you were initially hired. For example, if you are scientist, it is important to advance your knowledge in the scientific domain should you wish to maintain your reputation. As technology evolves and new techniques are invented, the ways in which a scientist continues to upskill will be a key determining factor of success.

Similarly, it is important for you to be clear about your core offerings and how you can continue to fine-tune these. Unfortunately, core skills or product performance are often the easiest areas in which others can compete with you; after all in the information era it's not hard to develop similar skillsets.

Innovation Type Two: Product System

Moving on to product systems which, in the context of a company, refers to how complementary offerings are adopted, connected, bundled and integrated together to form a more robust and valuable offering for customers. From an individual perspective, let's look at this using the example of an accountant. Simply acquiring corporate finance knowledge or understanding the financial projection of your company may not enable you to accelerate your professional trajectory substantially. Other important skills such as leadership, influence, listening, grit, strategic thinking, lateral thinking, navigating organisational politics and the likes will play an increasingly critical role as you climb the corporate ladder. The higher your rank within a corporate, or the more impressive your own business, the more you need to revisit the suitability of your product systems and explore the practical ways you can expand your offering or, on a personal note, innovate within yourself.

The components highlighted under the 'offering' category can also be applied to your private life. Think about the key stakeholders in your life. Each of your children have different needs. Showing your partner that he or she is valued also requires a unique approach. Then each of your friends and family members probably needs your support, closeness, or connection in different ways. Have you ever thought of how you might fine-tune what you are offering them so they feel more appreciated, loved and supported? Have you considered how this might allow them to enhance their own lives and journeys?

Configuration

Within the 'configuration' category of the Ten Types of Innovation framework, four key types of innovation are outlined: profit model, network, structure, and process.

Innovation Type Three: Profit Model

How an organisation manages to ethically maximise its profitability is one of its main concerns. Leaders seek to create innovative profit models to transform a firm's offerings into flattering valuable returns. However, when applying the 'profit model' for the context of personal radical shifts, one should not limit this to thinking only of monetary renumeration or bonuses. Instead, could you ask your line manager or company executives to provide you with mentors instead? Or could you push yourself to work on a project that isn't part of your job description, but which may bring about new opportunities for you or, at the very least, boost your CV? Perhaps ask to partake in training courses? Or to be considered in the business's succession planning to take on a line manager role? Maybe at this point in your life you crave autonomy, so how should you go about achieving that? Do not be short-sighted to merely focus on your salary and bonus. There are so many aspects in your life you can negotiate for a better deal. Our recommendation is to spend time exercising a healthy dose of strategic selfishness and negotiating more rewards for your good work.

It is very important to understand what possible 'profits' you stand to gain when you enter into a predicament or an engagement with people. This allows you to push towards more win-win outcomes or nudge or negotiate your way close to your initial desire. Therefore, understanding how many types of profits you are after will enable you to negotiate with your key stakeholders more effectively. Keep on questioning how you can gain maximum profitability using innovative ways to unlock opportunities that accelerate your growth.

Innovation Type Four: Network

Moving onto the 'network' component, this aspect relates to partnerships, connections and relationships. In the business arena this speaks to the power that lies in creating, nurturing and seeking out potential collaborators with which to form business relationships in today's hyper-connected world. Similarly, for individuals, the secret here is to realise that you cannot rely on yourself alone to accelerate your progression.

When applied correctly, you can build social capital and generate enormous value from interacting with others in your network, by tapping into new resources and unlocking useful information to capture opportunities and exchange mutually-beneficial 'favours'. When you pause to consider the value of your network, perhaps start by asking if the depth and the breadth of your network can help you reposition yourself for a career change. How many people within your network would be happy to make a referral or provide other kind of assistance? When you wish to get something done, how quickly can you call upon a few people to provide a helping hand?

If you can couple this network component with some of the strategic selfishness topics we discussed in Chapter 4, then you may be able to uncover a number of new opportunities and resources that previously seemed out of reach.

Innovation Type Five: Structure

Similarly, the structure around you and the structure of an organisation is key to ensuring competitiveness. Structure within the context of an organisation encapsulates the rules, roles and responsibilities which create a framework in which activities are directed towards the pursuit of goals. When an organisational structure is properly designed and well-executed, it is easier to coordinate the assets and talents of the business to create competitive advantage. Without a good structure, no leader can deliver on the strategic imperatives required.

This applies to personal shifts too. Being able to establish a good support structure will certainly facilitate vast and gratifying returns. As you unpack this layer of innovation, start by asking yourself the following questions: What does a solid structure look like during this transition phase of your life? How can you leverage this structure to do more and be more? First and foremost, you need to know which family members, friends and other acquaintances have valuable resources which can help you on this journey. Who do you go to in order to refuel your motivation when you feel down? Who helps you to look after your kids when you are busy pursuing your goals? Sometimes, your pets can make great supporting structures too – so don't forget those furry cheerleaders either.

Another example to consider is the role of appointed advisors as part of this support group - something akin to the board of advisors which a company might have in place to support leaders. On a personal note, do you have a board of advisors (beside the ones inside you which we discussed previously) which you can call on to guide your thinking and critique ideas? What is the composition of this board? Are these advisors diverse enough? Do you only ask people who think the same as you for advice? Are some advisors actually much younger than you and see the world in a more curious way? Do you know if your support structure would be effective in the face of a radical shift? These are some of the questions you should take the time to ponder.

One of Les Brown's tips is to surround himself with 'OQP' – only quality people. People in your network and structure have the potential to offer you access to important resources, in the form of tactical knowledge, innovative ideas, financial support, favours, audacious ambition or just plain old positivity. You just need to be courageous enough to ask (and then to take) what is on offer and to give back in order to create a mutual gratifying experience.[295]

Innovation Type Six: Process

Process, the final innovation type in this category, is probably one of the most under-appreciated components when it comes to innovating. Oftentimes we talk about developing new mindsets as a way of unlocking great results, and this is not wrong, but an equally important and often neglected facet is the new process required to make it happen. Unless you have changed your process – your patterns of behaviour - nothing will ever change, and you will never enjoy those shiny new results.

How a company goes about producing products and delivering services as part of its core operations can be a major distinguishing factor. Without establishing a highly efficient process and continually adapting that process to suit an ever-changing context, the competitiveness of any organisation will suffer as ideas fall short of delivering tangible value. Similarly, at a personal level, refining your daily and weekly processes or the routine you follow when executing tasks can help you to become more efficient and accomplish more with less time. Here we point you to the following questions that might help you fine-tune your processes and optimise your effectiveness: How do you nourish your body and mind? How do you deliberately introduce randomness into your professional life to expose yourself to new thinking?

In *Own the Day, Own Your Life: Optimized Practices for Waking, Working, Learning, Eating, Training, Playing, Sleeping, and Sex*, Aubrey Marcus, a human performance expert and self-styled 'modern philosopher', shares a number of practical tips which we can all include in our processes to help us live better and stronger lives.[296] As Marcus shared on his YouTube channel: "We are talking about ... all of the natural elements you can use to really upregulate your life. We are talking about air, water, cold, hot, exercise, sex and of course the different foods you can eat and the different practises you can do throughout the day, including just social companionship."[297]

Just like organisations, personal process can also be bureaucratic, which goes against the ebb and flow which an author like Marcus recommends. Consider, perhaps, if you impose unnecessary rules on yourself. What does that do to your psyche? Have you ever said: "It's 10:22 now, let me start working at 10:30." Well, why not 10:23? Why do we have to wait for the time to reach the increment of 10 or 15 for us to act? Or, because you don't like change, do you prefer to keep going just a little bit longer using the old way of doing things, instead of thinking how you can be more agile and re-engineer your processes to accomplish different tasks more efficiently?

To extract real value, in both an organisation and at an individual level, it is important to optimise the processes that direct the important aspects of our lives. If you don't, you'll always be a step or two away from extracting enormous value.

Experience

'Experience' is the last category on the Ten Types of Innovation framework, and it comprises service, channel, brand and customer engagement. Before you exclaim that these corporate-sounding words will surely have little relevance to your personal situation, trust us: they do. Just read on.

Innovation Type Seven: Service

To get the ball rolling, we are going to draw on the words of Italian poet and author Cesare Pavese, who once wrote: "We do not remember days, we remember moments." In line with Pavese's thinking, the moments of our lives during which we are most enamoured by someone, or something automatically creates memories that last for decades. Similarly, moments in which you can make another human being feel that he or she has your complete and undivided attention, empathy and understanding, will stay with that person for life. The power of the moment, of the experience, cannot be overstated.

In the world of business something called service innovation underpins how a company strives to delight its customers by creating thorough and attentive services. But, of course, human needs are forever changing. Therefore, it is important to constantly re-examine your ability to anticipate the needs of your key stakeholders in order to help them to achieve their goals. Why? Because ultimately you and your company stand to benefit from delivering what customers want.

Innovation Type Eight: Channel

In business, channel encompasses all the ways and approaches a company uses to connect with customers. It is probably hard for anyone to take you seriously if they cannot reach you to access your services or you fail to connect to your key stakeholders owing to an inadequate or distant communication style. Therefore, paying attention to how your key stakeholders and customers access your services, as well as ensuring you don't overcommit your services, is vitally important. As is taking the time to determine the optimal level of service which different people, or groups, require. Additionally, do not narrowly regard that channel is directly between these individuals and you. You can leverage other people to act as the channel. Sometimes, when you want to convey certain message to an individual, it may be better to partner with another person who this individual and you mutually have established a good relationship and trust with. If you can get these actions right, then you inevitably increase your 'customer engagement innovation'.

How you represent yourself is also important. And this is where branding comes into play.

Innovation Type Nine: Brand

Branding is a key innovation for most companies. Even successful organisations like Apple have had to go through brand renewals and brand extension strategies to propel growth and remain in step with customer needs. Brand innovations help to ensure that key stakeholders recognise and remember your organisation favourably. Your brand either attracts stakeholders to work with you or causes them to be repelled by your offering. While corporates spend incredible amounts on rebranding efforts, developing a personal brand often happens irrespective of whether you nurture your brand or not. Therefore, even if you are not inclined to do so, it is in your best interests to manage and clarify your personal brand from to time. Otherwise, other people may brand you in ways that are not conducive to your personal growth. Consider how you might be received when you turn up at a new place of work, where nobody knows you or what you are capable of. Why not dial up the elements you wish to enhance and manage others' perceptions of you before they arrive at conclusions of their own which don't fit your personal narrative?

Innovation Type Ten: Customer Engagement

Lastly, we have customer engagement innovation. This concerns the ways in which successful companies build a deep understanding of customer aspirations. From the personal innovation perspective, we will swap out the word 'customers' with 'stakeholders'. Your ability to exercise empathy, and your capacity to profile your stakeholders' idiosyncrasies and preferences, will help you blend a winning formula that enables you to engage with your key stakeholders. It allows you to design different types of engagement tactics to gain rapport rapidly and wow different stakeholders depending on a range of circumstances. For some stakeholders, compliments might do the trick and help them to drop their guard. For others, your knowledge will really instil confidence.

Across each of these three main categories – 'configuration', 'offering' and 'experience' – and their various types of innovation there exists a wealth of ways in which you can re-examine your personal or business attributes and embark on a process of renewal. While this is infinitely important at a corporate level, it is vital when you find yourself at a personal impasse. Maybe you are in between jobs or waiting for a new opportunity? Perhaps you are at a personal crossroads? How you use the Ten Types of Innovation to position yourself during an interview, a moment of reflection or in your quest to uncover your best self will set the stage for the future. So answer the questions we've suggested honestly, openly and with a focus on the past, the present and the future.

Your unique '&' combinations

Many of us have contributed towards the formulation of strategy for our company, division or business unit. Some of us even helped our respective organisations to design tactics to empower the entity to become more innovative. Yet, many of us do not take time regularly to think about our own 'PTY Ltd' strategy. Nor do we frequently revisit this personal strategy or refer to this strategy when making decisions about our future.

Maybe at this very moment, you realise that you would like to introduce one or two more components to the Ten Types of Innovation framework, components which best suit your unique context. If so, please ignite your ampersand thinking and add these to this framework. Remember the power of adding an 'and' and do so at every opportunity.

As a way of illustrating the uniqueness of our personal combinations, we'll leave you with the story of Dan Thurmon. In his childhood, this motivator and author was absolutely captivated by juggling. He was so intrigued by this skill that he spent hours watching the same street juggler performing, until the juggler noticed him and decided to teach him how to juggle. While he might be skilled at juggling, Thurmon is also highly practical about the notion of juggling in our personal lives. In fact, his ability to practice the ampersand thinking philosophy enabled him to combine his strengths as a motivational speaker with his unique juggling skills and deliver a knock-out and thought-provoking TED Talk entitled Off Balance On Purpose. He has also written a book with the same title.[298]

In this talk, Thurmon advocates for freeing yourself from the torment of pursuing a 'balanced life'. He argues that you waste valuable energy by trying to achieve balance during difficult times. You only serve to heighten your levels of anxiety, but still find yourself back in the same spot.[299]

Instead, Thurmon motivates us all to adopt a new approach to creating a happy, fulfilling life by purposefully leaning into the unknown. He believes the only most effective way to initiate positive change in our lives is for us to embrace reality, lean forward with concerted effort and find new cognitive-behavioural patterns to solve the challenges we are experiencing. He encourages us to recognise that there are many spheres in our lives, from work and relationships, to health, spirituality and other interests. These spheres are constantly changing and evolving. The interrelated pattens between the spheres are constantly changing and evolving, therefore, we need to explore ways to transcended by being deliberate in living off balance so we can find the combinations of pattens that best serve us.

It's a great TED Talk, which is well worth watching.

Once you've watched Thurmon in action and seen how he moulds the ideas encased in the Ten Types of Innovation framework to suit his own agenda, you'll have a blueprint for ways in which to accelerate your own growth, be it in career development or other spheres of your life.

A word to remember

What sets most of us apart from the great masterminds of history and modern innovation is our ability to combine seeming unrelated elements and ideas together. Why on earth would you combine peanuts and popcorn when creating an ice-cream blend? Well Ben & Jerry's did just that. They merged caramel ice-cream with white fudge-covered caramel popcorn and toffee-coated peanuts, with a caramel swirl to finish it off, and made a limited-edition ice-cream. Did this seem like a natural fusion? Maybe not, but it has gone down in the history books as one of the weirdest flavours the company has ever made.[300] It worked because, in that moment, that unique combination worked.

Imagine you are a limited-edition ice-cream. What combinations can you blend together to ensure that you stand-out from the crowd? And how can you create a personal recipe of success that enables you to embrace your self-innovation journey and generate gratifying returns?

Self-enrichment Exercises

It's time to pull out your pencil and jot down some ideas. Let's work our way through these questions.

What are the simple ingredients you can leverage in combination so that you can maximise the success of your goal attainment?

_____

_____

_____

_____

_____

Are there any other options / combinations that may be worth considering?

_____

_____

_____

_____

_____

What are the simple ingredients you can leverage in combination so that you can maximise the success of when you attempt to activate your best self?

_____

_____

_____

_____

_____

_____

_____

Are there any other options / combinations that may be worth considering?

_____

_____

What are some of the inner identities and different forms of self-talks you need to create or enhance?

Now armed with ampersand thinking, explore how you will apply the Ten Types of Innovation to develop your personal innovation strategy (refer to Figure 6.1 if you need some assistance). The following questions will take you through the Ten Types of Innovations:

OFFERING

Innovation Type	Key Questions	My Responses
Product Performance	What are my core offerings? What are the core offerings I need to expand on to achieve my aspirations while being competitive?	
Product System	What are the other complementary skills that I need to acquire or master in order to boost my offerings?	

CONFIGURATION

Innovation Type	Key Questions	My Responses
Profit Model	What can I do to maximise my personal profit (monetary and non-monetary)? What rewards should I secure for my growth and zest?	
Network	How can I build social capital by leveraging my network? Who (and which tribes) can I tap into? What opportunities may be created?	
Structure	What structure (friends, family, and peers) do I need around me to achieve my goals? What value could I tap into from these individuals?	
Process	What routines and mindsets do I need? What are the courageous invitations I need to issue and fulfil to create values for me?	

EXPERIENCE

Innovation Type	Key Questions	My Responses
Service	Who are my key stakeholders? How do I anticipate their needs? What and how does each of them like me to help them with?	
Channel	How many ways can I leverage to connect with each my key stakeholders? How does each of them like to be connected?	
Brand	What do I think my personal brand is? How do my key stakeholders see me? How do I manage key stakeholders' perception of me?	
Customer Engagement	How do I get an understanding of what your stakeholders' aspirations? How do I build deep and meaningful relationship with them?	

Table 6.1: Creating your personal innovation and building breakthroughs using The Ten Types of Innovation framework

Is there anything that I need to change in my goals framework in response to what I have discovered about myself and how I approach things?

Now before we circle back to your Best Self Goal Setting Canvas, let's just pause and consider your pre-programs, constraints etc that are holding you back from achieving your goals. Remember, we have already considered your fears back in Chapter 3 (Courageous invitations).

_____

_____

_____

_____

Reflect back on our comments about 'binary mentality'.

How can you address these to ensure that they do not prevent you from achieving your goals?

_____

_____

_____

_____

Before we bring this chapter to a close, reflect on whether there are any other components that would be worthy of consideration in your innovation framework for your own life context.

_____

_____

_____

How will these contribute to the achievement of your goals (much in the same way as you considered above for the Ten Types of Innovation categories).

_____

_____

_____

Now that you have explored these concepts, are there any changes required to your goals framework that we have been reflecting on since the beginning of the book? Update your Best Self Goal Setting Canvas accordingly.

Chapter 7
It's Not About Fate, It's About Navigation And The Journey

It's hard to get to where you are going if you don't have a clear direction. Fifty years ago, would have been talking about using a topographic map, with all its contour lines and references to scale and distance, as the best tool for the job. Today everything we need to navigate our way around is available through our smartphones, which tap into the 31 operating global positioning system (GPS) satellites orbiting the Earth (June 2021 figures).[301]

To fully appreciate the impact of these space-age objects, and the importance they hold in our day-to-day lives, we are going to transport you back in time. Back to a period of fear and uncertainty, divided loyalties and a clash of ideologies: the Cold War.

The Cold War was a period of geopolitical tension. The protagonists were largely the United States and the Soviet Union, with their respective allies also coming into the equation. Generally the Cold War is regarded as beginning in the wake of the Second World War, from the onset of the Truman Doctrine on 12 March 1947 (when the United States pledged to help nations resist communism to halt the spread of the ideology) to the Dissolution of the Soviet Union on 26 December 1991.[302]

About a decade into the tension, the Cold War took a new turn when, on 4 October 1957, the Soviet Union sent a metal sphere into orbit – the beeps of the Sputnik satellite were heard around the world for 21 days before it went silent, but the impact of this moment lives on today. The space race had begun.

The United States countered by pushing its Navy Navigation Satellite System into overdrive in 1958. The country launched a protype satellite towards the end of 1959, which failed to reach orbit. They eventually achieved success with their second satellite in April 1960. By 1964 a constellation of five satellites was up and running as part of the so-called Transit system.[303]

At the time, the United States' primary objective behind this satellite programme was to support its Polaris ballistic missile submarine fleet, but relying on just five polar orbiting satellites meant that accuracy could be a LOWand, for the most part, was only achievable by most military users within 200 metres. Signal strength was also a frustration. Of course, over the years these accuracy challenges were addressed and, as the tension of the Cold War eased, the once highly classified Transit system began to be adopted for purposes such as commercial shipping. By 1974 the United States' first NAVSTAR Global Positioning System satellite had been launched and a fully-fledged system was up and running by the 1980s, expanding to 24 satellites by 1994. Over the years, as constellations from the likes of Russia, the European Union, China, India and Japan joined forces with NAVSTAR to create the Global Navigation Satellite Systems (GNSS), the number of satellites swelled with the aim of achieving more than 120 in orbit between 2021 and 2023.[304] Add to that the various other satellites orbiting the Earth, both active (3 372 according to the United Nations Office for Outer Space Affairs in April 2021) and inactive (3 170), and it is clear that our dependence and acceptance of this technology has grown in leaps and bounds since 1956, when scientific papers that advocated the use of satellites for geodetic purposes began to emerge.[305]

Using the Doppler effect, or wave frequencies, listeners could determine if satellites were moving towards or away from them based on the change in frequency of the waves in relation to the observer. Using this natural physics phenomenon, scientists could pinpoint a satellite's exact location by observing it in a single pass. They soon came to realise that an observer on Earth's location could also be determined using the known orbit of a single satellite. It was this realisation that really gave birth to the GPS system we know today,[306] which enables us to determine – within something like a 7.8 metre accuracy – where we are at any given time on the surface of the Earth by locking in the signal emitted by seven or more of the satellites spinning above our heads.

Your GPS satellites

That's all very interesting, we hear you say, but what does that mean for my own enriched navigation journey?

Let's circle back to the main premise of this book (established in Chapter 1) and our focus on how best to navigate your way effectively through life, irrespective of whether you have found your purpose or not. To make our point we'll take you into the classroom.

Each year, Chen lectures more than 1 200 delegates and students. For the past three years, he has been asking them the following question: "What are the 'GPS satellites' you use to find your position as you navigate through this period of your life's journey? In other words, what do you pinpoint your progress against?"

This is a question which the authors use to gain a wider perspective, both personally and professionally. When Chen uses this informal qualitative surveying technique he always emphasises to the participant that he is not aiming to uncover the process through which the participants benchmark their progress – such as talking to a spouse, having a chat with line managers, or engaging with mentors or coaches. Instead, he is trying to find out how participants determine or measure their progress through life.

The responses vary, but can be broadly categorised into the following themes:

- The attainment of career advancement goals
- Meeting financial ambitions
- Achieving a greater feeling of general wellbeing
- Drawing and giving comfort and happiness to family and friends
- Making a contribution to others and the world in general
- Finding alignment with personal core values
- Using an external objective as a benchmark and measuring progress based on that marker.

Generally, when these themes arise in a session or presentation, the co-authors rarely challenge the validity of responses received. After all, the above-stated criteria can serve as a very helpful GPS for validating a person's 'position' in life. However, on the occasions when we have elected to probe a bit deeper, we've noticed that many participants fail to identify their GPS satellites or fail to convince us that all of these important GPS satellites are being utilised frequently. Participants' responses are often inconsistent with their actions. For example, general wellbeing may have more to do with living out religious beliefs and sustaining mental and affective states – but physical wellbeing is something many participants fail to mention.

The co-authors also found that even though some people suggested that their happiness and the happiness of their family and friends were both important, there was often a level of cognitive dissonance among those highly ambitious individuals and the workaholics in the crowd. Many of these participants, therefore, tend to navigate their lives based on the signal received from just the first and second 'satellites' in this list, rather than looking for input from the full range of options available to them.

Given that a GPS position requires at least seven satellites to help determine your location on Earth, how can you hope to determine your position in life using just two interconnected satellites?

When Chen facilitates strategy formulation workshops to c-suite executives and senior directors, he always ask his clients to question themselves, outline which leaders they benchmark their style against, and interrogate whether these benchmarks are still relevant in the current context. He has often been surprised to learn that in the early stages of their careers, many clients often identified their performance and thinking against some iconic leaders and personal mentors. But as these clients rose up the corporate ladder, they forget to find new benchmarks, or even undertake any benchmarking at all. The most frequent excuse for this oversight was: "I just don't have the time." When faced with this response, Chen politely helps them to translate this statement into its real meaning: "I just don't set this as a priority and, therefore, I don't allocate time to it."

The big question is, how can an executive expect his or her organisation to grow by setting ambitious strategies and new directions when their own growth agenda does not match the ambitions they have for their own organisations?

You are not lost

What are the GPS satellites you pinpoint yourself against when you are feeling a bit lost in your life's journey? What do you lock into to help find your audacious purpose? How do you focus your intention needed to issue courageous invitations or practice strategic selfishness if your internal GPS is still battling to pick up a signal?

Ask yourself if these GPS satellites are enough to get you where you want to go? Do you need a new approach for engaging with your surroundings? What else can you do to complement your existing GPS satellites? What other options are out there? Do you need to take a moment to ponder some of the plausible answers and evaluate the quality of your answers?

If you find yourself protesting this question rather than honing in on an answer, or arguing the point of even having a GPS, if you are feeling lost and confused, then we ask you to circle back to Chapter 1. After all, how can you hope to crystalise and clarify the GPS satellites needed to guide your life's journey is you have yet to find a purpose. And don't be disillusioned about retracing your steps, remember this is a journey and purposes change over the course of a voyage.

Yes, it's lovely if you can find your purpose. But purpose changes. Additionally, it is erroneous to think that you are lost if you don't have a purpose. After all your position never changes, so you can NEVER be lost.

Don't get frustrated if you think we are just playing with semantics. There are plenty of significant reasons why we would like to suggest that you should reframe from thinking you are lost. First and foremost, your inner advisors will tell you not to adopt this defeatist mindset when conversing with yourself. By insisting you are lost, you only serve to mentally magnify the problem – possibly blowing up the problem beyond proportion or making a problem where none really exists at all.

But the most fitting explanation of our rationale is as follows: If you have the courage to examine your situation, then you always know where you are. When you've taken the time to arrange your inner advisors effectively, then the voices in your mind will always come up with useful recommendations. Let's look at a few examples of how this might play out in reality:

If your loved one passed away suddenly and you have developed a sense of guilt, you know where you are in life. You are just temporarily unsure of your next step.

If your partner cheated on you or you got thrown under the bus at work by a manipulating colleague and subsequently got fired, you know where you are in life. You are just temporarily unsure about how to channel your emotions and face the unknown.

If you routinely choose to party the whole weekend and surround yourself with fair-weather friends who endorse bad habits then, deep down in your mind, you know where you are in life. You are just temporarily in denial and may be refusing to recognise that what you are doing actually does not serve you.

There are many plausible reasons which might contribute to a feeling of being lost, not just these reasons. However, these or any other similar series of challenges and life changes have the potential to trick your mind into declaring that you are lost, directionless, rudderless.

The primary reason why this feeling of being adrift arises is that many people just don't want to spend time objectively analysing the intrinsic and extrinsic factors that led to this situation. They feel uneasy with this depth of interrogation, so they steer away from it. Since that majority of us suffer from negative bias – defined as our tendency not only to register negative stimuli more readily but also to dwell on these events – it is simpler and more natural to focus on the negative and became increasingly uneasy. A failure to put your current stage under the microscope and clarify your own mental interpretation of this situation only leads to vagueness, which in turn builds that feeling of being lost.

There is also another reason to consider: Counterfactual thinking. This psychological term speaks to the human tendency to create possible alternatives to life events that have already occurred; creating an alternative that is contrary to what actually happened. Downward factual thinking also comes into play in such situations and is a thought process that can drag your thinking to places that are not useful to you since you cannot change the past.[307] Psychologists have long said that humans have a tendency not to accept the bad things that happened to them. Instead, some of us keep on imagining what our lives could have been if certain undesirable events or misfortunes did not happen to us. The associated 'would have' and 'could have' responses associated with this lack of acceptance ultimately make us feel more 'lost' than we should, and more than we actually are.

The third reason at play, and perhaps the most common, lies in the unknown and our tendency to attribute the sentiment of feeling lost to the fears sparked by uncertainty. We may claim that we are lost simply because at that particular moment in time we cannot confidently predict what the long-term future may hold for us. Or at times, we may simply believe that we are lost because certain factors have placed us in an unfavourable position, causing our initial plans to crumble before our eyes. The secret in these instances is to remember that we are still very much in possession of those plans.

Faith Magidigidi, an executive in the contract services industry, used to suffer as a result of these exact three issues. Despite being a go-getter with enviable intellect and ambition – which were clearly evident in the successful track records she'd achieved in her career - when it came to making big decisions in her personal life she struggled to apply an evidence-based approach to help pinpoint her position. Instead, she frequently made decisions based on overemphasising that she was lost. However, with some guidance she came to acknowledge how these three reasons were contributing towards her problem-solving approach. Faith ultimately reached a level of eudaimonic happiness,[308] which speaks to the ability to extract happiness and contentment in life through self-actualisation and the determination of one's purpose.

During our journey through life, we are bound to encounter unpleasant situations. Some we will stumble across when we make a careless mistake. Some will be imposed on us through circumstances beyond our control. Irrespective of what these unpleasant situations bring about, be it big heartache or small miseries, we are seldom fully lost even when we are in the midst of them. We hasten to add that it may well be challenging to overcome some of these situations; and that struggle should never be downplayed. Our view is that if you have taken time to set up your personal GPS satellites and if you check in with them consistently, then you will not be lost. You will always know where you are. You may be in the midst of a vast ocean, there may be harsh waves and deep currents, and sometimes the storm will rage for longer than you would like, but your thinking and your actions will help you to move closer and closer to the shore, leaving the troubled waters behind until you find yourself back on *terra firma*.

Anyone who has ever sailed, or swum in the sea will know that the power and force of the world's oceans are tremendous. However, they are not impossible to traverse successfully if you have the right tools and the right attitude. Certainly, having defined GPS satellites is an important step but all of us need to do more than just define one big GPS satellite in our life which we use to check our position periodically. When it comes to finding our way across the ocean of life, we must pay close attention to the nuances we sense and feel in any given moment. Inspired by the book *The Power of Moments*[309], by Chip and Dean Heath, we call these 'micro-moments', and they can be highly effective in guiding us out onto the water and into the journey of our lives.

From Polynesia to Scandinavia

Eye-popping blue waters, impossibly radiant turquoise lagoons, palm trees, powdery beaches and perfect sunny days probably spring to mind when you dream of the fabled paradise of islands known as Polynesia. Incorporating about 1 000 islands including Samoa, the Cook Islands and French Polynesia, the region covers a 160 million square kilometre triangular area of the east-central Pacific Ocean renowned for its luminous aqua lagoons, fish-rich coral reefs and dazzling beaches with silky-soft sands. The Hawaiian Islands form the apex of the triangle in the north, with New Zealand (Aotearoa) in the west and Easter Island (Rapa Nui) in the east.[310]

Yes, the region is staggeringly beautiful, but its waters are not always tranquil and inviting. Three of the five deadliest waves on the planet can also be found in Polynesia. For instance, Teahupo'o (pronounced 'tear-hoo-poh-oh' or 'cho-poo', which means 'hot head')[311] is a village on the southwestern coast of the island of Tahiti which is renowned for its surf break and heavy, glassy waves which can reach up to two or three metres and, on occasion, as high as seven metres. Making these powerful waves all the more dangerous is the fact that they break over a shallow sharp coral reef which is home to shivers of sharks.

Just imaging that you decided to jump into a small canoe and set sail from Hawaii with the aim of reaching a small island thousands of kilometres away in the middle of this geographic triangle. It would certainly be a daunting task. Yet, linguistic evidence and recent DNA studies suggest that western Polynesia was first settled some 500 to 2 500 years ago by the Melanesian people.[312] A more recent genetic study suggests that Polynesians also made an epic voyage to South America 800 years ago.[313]

Obviously ancient Polynesians didn't have sophisticated GPS technology at their fingertips, and it's equally unlikely that any of those early adventurers had a map to help them navigate these challenging waters. That luxury only came about when Tupaia, an arioi priest, chiefly advisor and master navigator from the Leeward Islands, collaborated with members of the crew on board Captain James Cook's HMS Endeavour to chart the region and create what we know today as Tupaia's Map. Tupaia's feat, created during his time on board the Endeavour between August 1769 and February 1770, is a clear indication of the mastery of Polynesian seafarers at the time.[314]

For thousands of years, Polynesians achieved non-instrumental oceanic navigation without the help of modern navigational aids. These ancient navigators settled the Pacific Islands through the sacred art of wayfinding, which is rooted in a sacred connection to the Earth and deep knowledge of the planet's movements and patterns. Using the constellations as navigational guardrails and seabirds as clues to what lies ahead, these ancient wayfinders were successfully able to navigate the oceans.[315]

Wayfinding is hardwired into us humans, and it is evident in animals too. You only need to consider pets that return home after escaping their yard, birds that migrate long distances, or aquatic animals capable of finding their way to a particular beach, bay, or stream during mating season. The term touches on any and all processes that help humans and animals to orient themselves and travel with confidence into the unknown.

That said, the early Polynesian voyagers were some of the best wayfinders in history. They could find their way across vast reaches of the Pacific Ocean navigating by the sun, stars, seabirds, clouds and other natural cues, like the impact on wave patterns and oceans swells when an island was blocking their course. A seasoned navigator was able to see and feel the refraction of the waves and how this could warn of low-lying islands which were invisible to the human eye.

On the opposite end of the globe, the fierce Vikings aroused as much fear and respect as the ancient Polynesians.

During Scandinavia's Viking Age (starting in the late eighth century to around the mid-11th century) Norsemen and Norsewomen navigated icy lands, islands and fjords using agile ships which took them from northern Europe to Russia, the Mediterranean Sea and Newfoundland. Famously, the Vikings conquered the British Isles and areas of mainland Europe, where they mixed and married with the local populations.[316]

Like the Polynesians, the Vikings relied on nature - birds, whales and celestial bodies – as well as deeper connections to the sea and the land to navigate their way to new shores. The behaviour of fish or marine mammals held clues to the presence of land, as did birds. Some experienced sailors could even smell the difference in the air when land was close. Their formidable navigational skills saw the Vikings establish the first European settlement in the New World in Newfoundland, Canada some 500 years before Christopher Columbus even set sail on his voyage. Joining skipper Leif Erikson, 90 men and women travelled from Iceland to establish what we know today as the L'Anse Aux Meadows National Historic Site.[317]

Remembering these ancient adventurers and how they tapped into all available resources to make their way across the perilous oceans, let's return to our GPS satellites. If you hope to pinpoint your position in life, what elements should you be using to help you assume the role of wayfinder? You, after all, are your own wayfinder. To do so you need all the options at your disposal to unlock the path ahead.

Unlocking the strengths and virtues of your character

To help you find your inner wayfinder we are going to move on from the beauty of Polynesia and the rugged ice-scape of Scandinavia and shift our attention to post-war Hungary and into the life story of Mihaly Csíkszentmihályi, considered one of the early pioneers of positive psychology.

Born in Hungary in 1934, the impact of the Second World War had a marked impact on Csíkszentmihályi's life and work. He observed that many people were unable to live contented lives after suffering the loss of their homes, jobs and security during the war. So his response was to throw himself into learning about art, philosophy and religion as a way of determining what makes a life worth living.[318]

In a 1995 interview with author Dava Sobel, Csíkszentmihályi explained how he first came to learn about psychology at a ski resort in Switzerland when he attended a lecture by Swiss psychologist Carl Jung, who spoke of the traumatized psyches of the European people after the Second World War. He told how he was detained in an Italian prison as a child where, amidst tremendous loss and fear, he began to first formulate his ideas about flow and optimal experience. In the interview, he explained: "I discovered chess was a miraculous way of entering into a different world where all those things didn't matter. For hours I'd just focus within a reality that had clear rules and goals."

As one of the pioneers of positive psychology, Csíkszentmihályi held that when a person was in a mental state of flow they are fully immersed and completely enjoying the activity and the process. The ability to tap into such a state helps people to feel greater joy and energy. Describing this state in an interview with Wired magazine, Csíkszentmihályi said: "The ego falls away. Time flies. Every action, movement, and thought follows inevitably from the previous one, like playing jazz. Your whole being is involved, and you're using your skills to the utmost."[319]

We experience flow when the task at hand is either well within our capabilities or slightly out of our competency zone, allowing us to enjoy the natural state and positivity that comes with doing something we have the ability to tackle with confidence – this creates a mutually re-enforcing relationship between the individual and the state of flow. As Csíkszentmihályi puts it: "Flow also happens when a person's skills are fully involved in overcoming a challenge that is just about manageable, so it acts as a magnet for learning new skills and increasing challenges."[320]

In addition to making activities more enjoyable, flow also has a number of other advantages. It contributes to:

- *Better emotional regulation*: With increased flow, people also experience more growth toward emotional complexity. This can help people develop skills that allow them to regulate their emotions more effectively.

- *Greater enjoyment and fulfilment*: People in a flow state enjoy what they are doing more. Since the task is enjoyable, undertaking it is also more likely to be rewarding and fulfilling.[321]

- *Increased happiness*: Research also suggests that flow states may be linked to increased levels of happiness, satisfaction and self-actualization.[322]

- *Higher intrinsic motivation*: Flow is a positive mental state. As such, it can help increase enjoyment and motivation. Intrinsic motivation involves doing things for internal rewards.

- *Increased engagement*: People in a flow state feel fully involved in the task at hand.

- *Improved performance*: Researchers have found that flow can enhance performance in a wide variety of areas including teaching, learning, athletics[323] and artistic creativity.

- *Learning and skill development*: The act of achieving flow indicates a substantial mastery of a certain skill, therefore people have to keep seeking new challenges and information to maintain this desired state.

- *Heightened creativity*: Flow states often take place during creative tasks, which can help inspire greater creative and artistic pursuits.[324]

Over the past decade, Silicon Valley executives such as Eric Schmidt and Elon Musk, Special Operators like the Navy SEALs and the Green Berets, and maverick scientists like Sasha Shulgin and Amy Cuddy have turned everything we thought we knew about high performance upside down. Instead of grit, better habits, or 10 000 hours, these trailblazers have found a surprising short cut. They're harnessing rare and controversial states of consciousness to solve critical challenges and outperform the competition.

New York Times bestselling author Steven Kotler and high-performance expert Jamie Wheal spent four years investigating the leading edges of this revolution—from the home of SEAL Team Six to the Googleplex, the Burning Man festival, Richard Branson's Necker Island,

Red Bull's training centre, Nike's innovation team, and the headquarters of the United Nations. What they learned was stunning: In their own ways, with differing languages, techniques and applications, every one of these groups has been quietly seeking the same thing: to boost the level of flow states.[325]

This is not a wild fad or an intriguing idea. The theory of flow has been supported by neuroscience research. Firstly, researchers have found that there are changes in brain activity during flow states.[326] Secondly, other studies suggest there is also an increase in activity of dopamine (a brain chemical involved in pleasure and motivation) when people are experiencing flow.[327]

Another stunning discovery is that one tends to find and sustain one's flow state if one utilise one's innate strengths.[328]

Strength-based practice is a social work practice theory that emphasises a person's self-determination and strengths. It is a philosophy and a way of viewing clients as resourceful and resilient in the face of adversity. This type of approach builds on an individual's strengths, specifically seeing them as resourceful and resilient when they are experiencing adverse conditions. Nevertheless, studies have shown that individuals who can utilise their strengths frequently possess higher levels of subjective well-being.[329]

In some quarters the strength-based approach is not held in high regard[330] however an analysis by American analytics and advisory company Gallup reveals that people who use their strengths every day are three times more likely to report having an excellent quality of life, six times more likely to be engaged at work, 8% more productive and 15% less likely to quit their jobs.[331] You can also find a wealth of literature, from the likes of Marcus Buckingham, Steven Kotler, Jamie Wheal and Tony Robbins, outlining why utilising your strengths is the right approach to engaging with your world.

Studies have also found that when managers adopt a strengths-based appraisal approach, it has a positive effect on perceived supervisor support and employee motivation to improve.[332] Additionally, researchers have also found that when coaching interventions are grounded in a strengths-based approach and focused on setting a specific goal for personal and professional growth for non-executive workers, the psychological capital of these coachees, and their goal-related self-efficacy improved.[333]

In short: Flow and strength utilisation are critically linked.

Since the introduction of positive psychology,[334] the study of character strengths (CS) has been at the forefront of research on human well-being and optimal functioning. One of the most well-known scales is probably the one popularised by Gallup, a pioneer in the strengths movement which conducts research into workplace outcomes, individual well-being and employee performance and engagement based on 34 talent themes sorted into four domains.

In 2003, the American Psychological Association honoured Dr Don Clifton, who formulated the CliftonStrengths assessment distributed by Gallup, with a presidential commendation as the Father of Strengths-Based Psychology. Clifton co-authored the 2001 book *Now, Discover Your Strengths* with consultant and motivational speaker Marcus Buckingham, offering advice on how to determine the strengths of your employees and how to put these qualities to work to ensure success. It's a fantastic book, which is well worth reading and since Buckingham's work has had a profound impact on the careers of successful executives such as Lori Goler, the Vice President of Human Resources and Recruiting at Facebook.[335] In fact, the strength-based recruiting approach remains a critical element of Facebook's international recruiting approach to this day.[336]

But back to Clifton and the CliftonStrengths classification he first developed as a foundation upon which to research the character strengths and virtues that enable and promote good character and a good life.[337] Today, Clifton's classification is regarded as one of the main building blocks of positive psychology, but it started life based on the work of a group of 55 scientists undertaking a systematic review of existing psychological, philosophical and theological literature to identify, classify and measure universally valued positive traits. CliftonStrengths defines 34 talent themes, which are grouped according to strategic thinking, execution, influencing and relationship building.

But CliftonStrengths is not the only game in town. If you are interested in knowing more about character strengths and virtues then the handbook of the same name by Christopher Peterson and Martin Seligman[338] comes highly recommended. It's a chunky tome, which breaks down character strengths into the 24 character strengths which we all possess to some degree. These 24 strengths are regarded as the 'psychological ingredients' which can then be used to explain positive virtues. A variety of assessments are now used to measure character strengths, but the most popular is the VIA Inventory of Strengths (VIA-IS), which has been applied to more than 13 million people around the world, each time telling us a little bit more about the makeup and structure of character strengths.[339]

According to Peterson and Seligman, the 24 character strengths are generally grouped into six broad categories. Here's how they fit together:

- **Wisdom and Knowledge**: Creativity, Curiosity, Open-mindedness, Love of Learning, Perspective, Innovation
- **Courage**: Bravery, Persistence, Integrity, Vitality, Zest
- **Humanity**: Love, Kindness, Social Intelligence
- **Justice**: Citizenship, Fairness, Leadership
- **Temperance**: Forgiveness and Mercy, Humility, Prudence, Self-control
- **Transcendence**: Appreciation of Beauty, Gratitude, Hope, Humour, Spirituality

It is worth noting that while Gallup's CliftonStrengths is highly regarded for helping to define talents and skills, little by way of academic interrogation and research has been undertaken around the classification – much like the lack of scholarly criticism of a popular online personality test like the Myers-Briggs Type Indicator has not been interrogated at scale by the academic community. Peterson and Seligman's Character Strengths and Virtue scale, meanwhile, is the result of interrogating hundreds of peer-reviewed empirical studies and distilling these findings into the basic building blocks of positive personality and the ingredients needed to live a full, fulfilled, satisfied and prosperous life.[340]

A recent study in the United States rolled out the VIA-IS assessment to test the relationship between character strengths and various measures of well-being among college students at the University of Colorado at Boulder. The study scored students according to a diversity of factors from physical health and academic scores to alcohol consumption and undertaking risky behaviour. It showed that character strengths were most strongly related to positive measures of well-being, such as a zest for life and enthusiasm.[341]

That word – zest - is an important one and it's a character strength we are going to dive into in more depth. Yes, we may be slightly biased by focusing on this particular strength above the other 23, but we believe the rationale for our choice is sound and support for this rationale can be found in several scientific studies. So our next step focused on the strength element known simply as zest.

SHIFT towards a quest for zest

What is zest? The Cambridge English Dictionary tells us it is an enthusiasm, eagerness and interest. An energy. According to the VIA Institute, zest speaks to throwing yourself into a situation or activity with gusto, giving all you have and being enthused and excited about the process. They also highlight zest as being a robust contribution to physical and psychological wellness.

Zest, however, is not the same thing to all people. Not all of us display our enthusiasm by jumping on couches or exclaiming at the top of our lungs. Some, the introverts among us, can be equally excited about life without displaying the outward signs we have come to expect from the likes of a Tony Robbins, Oprah Winfrey or Dwayne Johnson. Rather the common denominator is that zestful people approach tasks with full commitment and tenacity. They encapsulate the beauty of zest, which French fashion designer Christian Dior once declared was the 'secret to all beauty', and the benefit from the powerful attraction of positivity which Norman Vincent Peale noted in his best-selling book *The Power of Positive Thinking* when he said: "If you have zest and enthusiasm, you attract zest and enthusiasm. Life does give back in kind."

The core idea of zest is to feel alive, excited and motivated by any activity or task or life direction you embark on. It is the exact opposite of a feeling of 'blah' which emerges when we are just existing rather than living, which is why zest is such a key ingredient in building positivity and radiating it to those around you and it is so essential to performing at your best and being committed and happy in your work.[342] Zest can, because of the positivity it generates, serve as the fuel for rapid learning and self-transformation. Furthermore, when applied properly zest generates grit. It helps you to enter the state of flow[343] and drives you to constantly seek out ways to utilize your skills and abilities to the fullest.

In 2009, a study of 228 schoolteachers in Hong Kong showed that the character strength zest was often associated with positive emotions and increased levels of life satisfaction in teachers. It was suggested that by cultivating zest in teachers it might be possible to counter burnout in the profession.[344] A similar study in Turkey, which sampled 600 teachers from 27 primary schools in Ankara, also showed that a zest for work contributed positivity to the perceived success of the teachers involved in the research.[345]

And it's not just the teaching profession that yielded such findings. A survey involving 9 803 adults, all of who were employed at the time of the study, found zest to be highly correlated with undertaking work associated with being a calling, and with general work and life satisfaction.[346]

Of all the character strengths, zest is associated closely with positive behaviours like creativity and leadership and ambition; which tells us that if you can build zest within an organisation that you can create more satisfied workplaces[347] and also counteract the impact of burnout and the associated doldrums that causes to productivity and enthusiasm.[348] Indeed, in high-stress professions such as teaching and nursing, where patience and kindness is so essential, studies also show that having a zestful attitude ensures better productivity and can help individuals to better accomplish their daily tasks with energy and humour.[349]

A similar study in 2007, conducted with the involvement of more than 10 000 American and Swiss adults, showed that people derive happiness in life through three channels: seeking pleasure, engagement and meaning. Zest is strongly associated with each of these methods of extracting happiness, showing that no matter how we tap into our job in life, there is always a component of zest at play. The study also revealed that zestful people were less neurotic and had better coping mechanisms than those who lacked zest.[350]

Youngsters also benefit from a feeling of zestfulness in their lives, seemingly across the age spectrum and a range of schooling levels. In 2006, when parents were asked to write about 200 words describing their three to nine year old children as part of a study, phrases such as 'full of life', 'energetic' and 'enthusiastic' were linked to levels of zest. In line with adult studies, those children with higher levels of zest also tended to be happier.[351] What was also revealed by another 2006 study, this time of middle schoolers in the United States, was that zest was more common in youth. Like the previous study, the presence of zestfulness was associated with all sorts of positives, such as fewer instances of depression and social withdrawal, less neurotic personality traits and a better stress response.[352] In addition, empirical studies have also shown that higher levels of zest foster resilience[353] and it can also lead to a reduction in suicidal tendencies among the youth.[354]

As if you needed more convincing, there is yet more to chew on when you consider the impact of zest on your life's journey. A recent study published in The Journal of Positive Psychology concluded that strength-based interventions have a role to play in alleviating chronic pain and increase confidence that, despite pain, the individual can still perform various tasks. This research surveyed 491 participants and found pain self-efficacy was most strongly associated with zest, as defined by the VIA-IS character strength classification.[355]

From our perspective, as we seek to find ways in which to boost your navigation through life, zest can certainly help to empower your inner advisors to guide on the right path and nudge you to steer away from troubled waters. This invaluable internal resource also helps you to align your values and re-enforce your belief systems in line with your actions. Above all, zest has the ability to heighten all other strengths. If you are zesty about bravery and self-control, it is likely you will prevail in the face of challenges. If you are zesty about curiosity, open-mindedness and learning, it is likely that you will become more innovative. Zest almost seems to have an ability to ramp up these other characteristics to be their best-selves.

This means that you don't have to hold on to the mantra "fake it till you make it". Instead, try "face it till you make it by injecting zest".

The challenge with zest, however, is how we measure or quantify it. How do we know how much energy one person has versus another? How do we gauge how much enthusiasm they feel at a given moment? Like many different constructs of positive psychology, accurately estimating the amount of zest in a person has proved challenging for researchers in the field. But the truth is, this only matters to the scholars and researchers, because deep down in you, you know if you are harnessing and utilising zest or not.

So, putting the textbooks and journals aside for a while, let's turn our attention to ways in which you can shift yourself to generate and magnify zest in your life.

We suggest that you try the SHIFT mindset approach.

Getting to grips with the SHIFT mindset approach

SHIFT stands for Sincerely, Heuristics, Intentionality, Fortitude and Transfers. We believe each of these mindset components has a mutually re-enforcing relation with the character strength zest. To help you on your way, we are going to take you through each aspect of the SHIFT approach.

Sincerity

The word sincerity, according to the Oxford English Dictionary, is derived from the Latin *sincerus* meaning clean, pure and sound. *Sincerus* may once have meant 'one growth', making it a possibly the purest form of self-growth. It is also a word linked closely to the notion of honesty, which is often associated with being fair and telling the truth. Sincerity forms the basis of honesty by encapsulating the ability to speak and act in accordance with and about your own feelings and beliefs. This is a powerful moral force which involves naming and owning one's truth. As a result, it is beneficial to shine the light of sincerity on ourselves when we go in search of our 'authentic selves'.

If you are sincere about your feelings and actions, it will enable your zest to be rooted on a solid place. When applied sincerely and in a positive sense, individuals are able to hold a truthful mind. They are less affected by eternal influences, because their focus is on being sincere to themselves and others, and this permits them to be creative and to channel their zest without imposing mental constraints.

Sincere zestfulness allows us to be genuine in our caring, authentic in our curiosity, engaged in our desire and intentional about being and becoming more. Displaying sincere zestfulness acts like a magnet to others, drawing people in to what we do and who we are. Looking back on the people we've met through these pages, the stories we shared and the challenges that have been overcome, it is clear that the majority either exhibit or channel sincere zestfulness in their own unique way. Were you attracted to their stories? Were you inspired by these individuals? If so, you too were being drawn to their sincere zestfulness.

What is clear, in a world that is changing at a rapid pace, is that we need more people – more leaders – who have the ability to display sincerity in what they say and what they do. Sincerity prompts leaders to empathise, love and care for others. It empowers leaders to be honest, vulnerable and transparent. So it should be advocated for as a mainstream approach to leadership development. The world doesn't need more fakes and phonies, it needs people who embrace sincerity in all they do and leaders who display the purest form of self-growth.

Heuristics

A heuristic is a mental shortcut to problem-solving that employs a quick, less complexed though-processing approach. This approach may not guarantee optimal nor perfect answers because it is associated with tapping into mental habits and recipes for sense-making, but it is sufficient for reaching immediate, short-term goals or approximations. A lot has been written about the strengths and weaknesses of resolving challenges with heuristics, including extensive work from trailblazing psychologists Amos Tversky and Daniel Kahneman. Despite working together to further our understanding of behavioural economics, Kahneman alone won a Nobel Prize in Economics in 2002 since Tversky's death in 1996 made him ineligible for the prize which can only be awarded to a living laureate. However, their 1974 paper[356] was ground breaking. In it they state: "These heuristics are highly economical and usually effective, but they lead to systematic and predictable errors. A better understanding of these heuristics and of the biases to which they lead could improve judgments and decisions in situations of uncertainty."

And that is exactly what we've seen in recent years, a flood of new and exciting information about how our brains work and how our minds handle decision making. One example comes from American neuroscientist, author and science communicator David Eagleman, who argues that it doesn't matter whether consciousness is involved in the decision-making process, since most of the time it is not. In *Incognito: The Secret Lives of the Brain*,[357] Eagleman explores the gap between our conscious and unconscious selves and arrives at the conclusion that our brain's unconscious processes are a lot smarter, more adaptive and complex than we give them credit.

Of course, some heuristics are more useful than others depending on the situation, which is why it is important to pick up when bad heuristics are coming into play as part of your decision-making and problem-solving processes in order to avoid making mistakes. That said, heuristics can also improve decision-making effectiveness by simplifying our ability to make difficult decisions, thereby avoiding 'analysis paralysis'.[358] This is a popular concept in the study of heuristics, as is the term thin-slicing. Even though the term as first used back in 1992 by Nalini Ambady and Robert Rosenthal in a meta-analysis study published in the Psychological Bulletin,[359] the idea really gained traction thanks to Canadian author Malcolm Gladwell. In one of his New York Times bestselling books, *Blink: The Power of Thinking Without Thinking*, Gladwell devoted page after page to discussing the advantages and disadvantages of finding patterns in situations based only on a 'thin slice' of experience.[360] This was contrary to the widely held view that the less we process our decisions the less accurate they are. However, studies increasingly show that when we are in times of certainty, battling a lack of information and being pushed for a quick decision, that heuristics allow for what is known as the "less-is-more effect', in which less information actually leads to greater accuracy.[361]

In short: While heuristics might not always give us perfect answers, it can create significant value in spheres where we can't have perfection or when perfection isn't required – ideal, in other words, for our ambiguous modern world. Furthermore, as we seek to navigate the uncertainties of our own journeys – as well as the challenges of a disrupted and changing world – heuristics are often our first port of call when faced with making a decision, before we switch to a deeper, more effortful and algorithmic style of reasoning.

All of this insight tells us that it is important, and indeed valuable to invest time and effort in continually conditioning our heuristics to be more effective. One way to do that is to infuse our heuristics style with some degree of positivity, when then empowers us to be adaptive and zestful.

By allowing heuristics to be rooted within a mindset of abundance, problem-solving capabilities will be enhanced as will the quality of our brain's output. An abundance mindset refers to the belief that there is a plentiful supply of everything we need in the world from resources to love, relationships, wealth and opportunities. It brings us to a place of knowing there are many more chances to 'be more', even if an opportunity is missed or messed up. There is always room to create more, get more and be more if only our reasoning style is one of plenty, rather than hinged on a scarcity mindset that inevitably leads to a life less fully lived and focused on loss and deficits.

If your heuristic instinct (your default mode) is to bring out enthusiasm that is rooted in abundance, then this mindset will help you to be slightly more (or a lot more) zesty about every step you make on your life journey. Can you imagine the difference in approaching decision-making from a positive place of certainty rather than one of fear and lack? If not, take the time to give it some thought.

Intentionality

Phenomenology is the study of structures of consciousness as experienced from the first-person point of view. When it comes to intentionality, the core doctrine in phenomenology focuses on performing every act we conduct with consciousness, deliberateness and directedness. By doing so, we are able to steer our minds and actions toward something more frequently and repeatedly.

In philosophy, intentionality is the power of minds and mental states to be focused on things, ideas, beliefs or hopes. To do so intentionally links mental representations of the world to the efforts required to pursue a particular set of goals.[362] To illustrate what this means in practice we are going to whiz off to the tip of Africa, to a town called Bronkhorstspruit where the Van der Walt brothers, Dirk and Faan, grew up. The brothers endured years of hardship before they built WeBuyCars, a R4 billion (about US$270 million) used-car reselling company.[363]

Dirk and Faan's zest for cars can be traced back to their father, Koos, who taught them how to fix cars. From an early age they spent a lot of time under the hood tinkering with their old family car, which was unreliable and often let them down. In 1988, after Faan bought, fixed and sold a Yamaha XT500, he first thought this could be the start of something. Both brothers went on to study and pursue their respective career paths, so it was only in 2001 that they founded WeBuyCars.[364]

In the early years, Dirk and Faan handled all aspects of the business themselves. If they got a lead, even if they were almost home after a full day on the road, they'd turn around and go visit the client who had just called. When business was slow and they found themselves with nothing to do, they still rolled up their sleeves and set about polishing tyres and ensuring that all the cars in their small warehouse looked neat and appealing to a potential buyer. Even when they had built WeBuyCars into a behemoth enterprise, this intentionality of always creating more values never disappeared. In fact, the brothers, their fellow executives and staff actively based the best self activation for the business in intentionality. This was no accident, it was a deliberate ambition to build enthusiasm for the company, its customers and its future within the organisation. It started and was perpetuated in the company's boardroom - the place where Faan, Dirk and the company's other executives gave themselves permission to dream big, envisage the future more courageously and invite themselves to engage more zestfully about the possible futures of WeBuyCars.

This relentless display of intentionality is something which the majority of successful people display in life. Turn your mind back to our DJ-motivator-politician Les Brown. Brown's zest for the radio business was undeniable, but it was his intentionality to maintain those high levels of zestfulness that empowered him to constantly explore new opportunities. This zestful intentionality landed him the first big break in this life and he continued to harness the benefits of this mental approach from then on. Similarly, almost without a shadow of a doubt, the other successful people we mentioned in this book accomplished impressive feats due to their intentionality. Maybe you can think of a few examples from your own circle too? People whose enthusiasm and zest, whose dogged determination and intentional focus, set them apart from the crowd. Take note and learn.

Fortitude

Fortitude, by its very definition, refers to an ability to show courage in the face of pain or adversity. It's the sort of bravery we associate with elite athletes, social and political activists or corporate whistleblowers and, yes, members of elite fighting forces such as India's Marine Commandos, the US Navy SEALs or Russia's Alpha Group.

In 2014, when United States Navy Admiral William McRaven addressed students at the University of Texas in Austin,[365] he included some key insights into the intense training SEAL candidates receive, and the courage these specialist forces need to display in life and in the field. He described in detail the day-in-and-day-out mental and physical torture of training, the camaraderie that this forged in trainees and the bravery it took to push aside discomfort and remain focused on the end goal.

Finally, in a galvanising cry to the Class of 2014 McRaven said: "Start each day with a task completed. Find someone to help you through life.

Respect everyone. Know that life is not fair and that you will fail often, but if you take some risks, step up when the times are the toughest, face down the bullies, lift up the downtrodden, and never, ever give up – if you do these things, the next generation and the generations that follow will live in a world far better than the one we live in today. And what started here will indeed have changed the world for the better."

The zest which McRaven so clearly articulates, which (as we've already noted) makes it easier and more bearable to endure chronic pain or discomfort, is a factor which no doubt separates the SEAL candidates who make it through this gruelling process from those who opt out by ringing the bell. The trainees who are able to get comfortable with discomfort, who are able to find the motivation to push on in the most trying of circumstances, those are the ones who win in the end.

Of course, success in life is not only about being comfortable with discomfort and pushing through the pain, it is also about learning from constructive failures. Picking yourself up when you fall and dusting yourself off, taking the lessons and moving forward.

Paul Tough, the Canadian-American writer and broadcaster, once suggested that the secret sauce when it comes to achieving success is actually experiencing a whole lot of failure. In his book, *How Children Succeed*,[366] Tough drew on insights from a variety of educational leaders, including a man called Dominic Randolph.

Randolph was, and at the time of writing still is, the principal of Riverdale Country School, an elite private school in New York City. As an educator, this level of schooling and the largely privileged children it attracted exposed him to a unique problem: the experience of too few setbacks to overcome. Randolph was concerned that his students would know nothing (or very little) about this foundational skill on the ladder to success. As a result, when these students encountered failure it was so far outside their comfort zones that they lacked the skills to adequately deal with it, the persistence to keep pushing through and to try again, and zest to keep their own inner motivation to keep going. In Randolph's own words: "The idea of building grit and building self-control is that you get it through failure. In most highly academic environments in the United States, no one fails anything."[367]

There is a wealth of empirically evaluated evidence when it comes to the relationship between success and fortitude.[368] When you ask Professor Angela Duckworth, the author of *Grit*,[369] success is the outcome of a web of factors including grit (or resolve, courage and bravery), passion and resilience. It's a cocktail of traits similar to the Finnish concept of 'sisu', which can be described as a combination of stoic determination, tenacity of purpose, grit, bravery, resilience, and hardiness.[370]

Sisu is more expansive as a concept that the Danish term Janteloven that we encountered in Section 4, but like the Law of Jante sisu is also well embedded in the Finnish national character. Indeed, the people of Finland pride themselves on their stoic nature and resilience. However, sisu goes much deeper than just perseverance. The concept – which has no single equivalent in English – talks to surpassing one's preconceived limitations by accessing stored-up energy reserves. Adversity unlocks sisu and the energy needed to fuel the mental will and fortitude to keep going. This single word embraces the very essence of human endurance and achievement, by celebrating the fortitude needed to embrace failure, learn from past mistakes and, in the process, build character strengths and enhance capabilities.

Fortunately, as every good Finn knows, the fortitude embedded in sisu is not an innate quality bestowed only on the lucky few. It is very much a learned behaviour that must be practiced until it becomes habitual. By practising fortitude we are better able to engage in our lives with more zest. Having zest for life allows us to exercise fortitude more successfully when we encounter challenging situations. By embedding fortitude into our responses and reactions, we are better able to recharge and sustain high levels of zest.

Fortitude is a crucial component of the SHIFT approach. Without it, our lives may feel just like another four-letter word.

Transfers

In the context of SHIFT, transfers comes from the psychological term transference which describes the phenomenon in which an individual redirects emotions and feelings, often unconsciously, for another person to an entirely different person. It's a concept that was first outlined by psychoanalyst Sigmund Freud in 1895 when he noted that the deep and often unconscious feelings that sometimes developed within the therapeutic relationships he established with patients.[371] Transference is often noted during clinical therapy sessions when a patient attaches anger, hostility, or a host of other possible feelings to a person or a group of people with similar characteristics who resemble an individual or individuals who might have poorly treated the patient in the past. Such transfer is destructive, but this is an extreme case, so let's bring this down a notch with another example.

Let's say you realise that you misread an instruction and forgot to submit an important document to your client. Or you encountered an unexpected traffic jam that made you 15 minutes for a very important meeting. Or you received a passive aggressive comment from your boss on the same day that you and your partner also had a fight before you left the house.

Suddenly every minuscule inconvenience ignites your inner fury. When you get into this state, life plays up by throwing curveballs that push us out of our optimal zone. As a result, our emotions often go down a slippery slope of infuriated huffs and puffs and crankiness. We don't shake off our negative mood easily. We fester in it.

This tendency to stew in a destructive thought-pattern is common in human beings, but just wait a moment and think through this response rationally. Let's say that there are 24 large-denomination bank notes inside your wallet at this very moment and that by accident you take out a note and tear it, or it is blown away by a gust of wind. Do you throw the other 23 bank notes away in anger? No. So why let one hour out of 24 ruin the rest?

The word transfers, which we use in place of the concept transference, talks to the mentality to put a stop to the negative spiral sparked by one bad incident or experience. As such transfers is a constructive approach which channels bad into good. Of course, we aren't advocating that you forget harm and hurt, rather that you stop glorifying your pain and hurt. So many people dwell on the melancholy periods of their lives instead of accepting that these incidences happened and then actively refocus their energy to move on. Using this approach you are able to transfer your thinking away from the negative and the destructive after effects of anger and fear. Without transfer you will inevitably drag yourself down and reduce your ability to activate and sustain your best self. Conversely, by applying transfer, you reclaim your zest.

Always remember that while the discomfort of the moment can be inconvenient, or the pain debilitating, you can always bounce back with a bit of zest. This is something each of your co-authors has experienced first-hand, and which we'd like to share with you now.

During the writing of this section, Chen was placed in a bad position in a project thanks to the mistakes and poor attitude of his colleagues. When he decided to push back, he was set up for failure and fired from the project since his colleague felt he was the cause of poor chemistry in the team and with the client in question. At the time, the injustice of this outcome was highly frustrating to Chen.

Similarly, Duggan was also placed in a difficult position on the executive management team of a large organisation and felt pressured to take decisions that she was uncomfortable with. She left the organisation feeling disenfranchised about her career and corporate culture more generally.

Rather than throwing our hands up, giving up in the face of these challenges and perceived failures, each of the authors were able to summon their inner zest and push through. We each achieved this by putting the insights contained in this book into practice.

We called on our inner advisors to help us find gains amidst these plot twists. We sought out moments to craft our courageous invitations. You can too.

At times, we crafted these invitations in a just-in-time fashion – maybe issuing a quick 30-second invitation to 'be more' before going into a serious meeting – and sometimes we had to recommit ourselves to lifestyle changes or a life-changing choice which had turned complex. We asked questions of ourselves to keep ourselves on the right side of positivity by using transfer, such as: If things do go according to your plan, how will you behave and what will you do? If things do not go according to your plan, how will you carry yourself and will you be able to improvise or modify your plan without the influence of negative emotion?

Each of us held to zest, both for ourselves and those around us. Don't forget, zest can be infectious. Through the phenomena of 'emotional contagion', a term that describes the spontaneous spread of emotions and related behaviours between people, zest can be transferred to those around you. Emotional contagion really is like the gift that keeps on giving, enabling you to inspire others with your zest and then, when their zestfulness returns, enabling you to stoke up your level of zest by feeding off their enthusiasm. What's more, just like emotions can be shared between individuals, so too can you transfer wisdom, experiences and inspirations.

Over the course of the Covid-19 pandemic, during which this book was written, the enormous challenges impacting people around the world opened up novel opportunities to research and better understand constructive transfers and how to create moments that encourage these transfers to occur. As we gain more information on this phenomenon, however, it's important to remember that human beings are not robots, we don't have one default mode, we are governed by cycles, hormones and rhythms, all of which impact how we SHIFT in a given moment.

SHIFT spirals and micro-moments

As human beings we are always oscillating between a virtuous spiral and vicious spiral. In some weeks, we create virtuous spirals one after another and ride these spirals - like a bird soaring - to progress significantly in our lives. On other occasions, we stumble by failing to apply some of the SHIFT five components well. As the result, we experience a state of vicious spiral. Oftentimes, in the course of just one day, we bounce between the two.

According to Nobel Prize-winning scientist Daniel Kahneman, human beings experience some 20 000 distinct moments in any given day and each 'micro-moment' lasts a few seconds.[372] That's a lot of micro-moments, so it's hardly surprising that some of these micro-moments slip by and some we just fail to notice or take advantage of, particularly when we are in the wrong mindset or under stress. Sometimes these micro-moments are hidden from view, awaiting a bit of ingenuity on our part to turn them into great memories and defining milestones. And, in case you doubted it, we actually can.

A team of neuroscientists from MIT recently found that the human brain can process entire images which the eye has seen for as little as 13 milliseconds.[373] This compares to the roughly 100 to 200 milliseconds it takes the brain the process a known word.[374] While this figure may seem impressive, remember that the human brain in not just dealing with one image or one word in any given millisecond, it's processing a wealth of information both consciously and unconsciously. Where it gets interesting is when we start to look at the processing power (to borrow the computer term) of the human brain. It has been suggested that the sensory systems of the human body sends 11 million bits per second to the brain for continual processing, and yet the conscious mind – which certainly wasn't designed to deal with the wealth of data being thrown at it each moment of the day - seems able to only process up to 120 bits per second.[375] How does human perception and comprehension cope with this gap? One ubiquitous solution is chunking, which involves grouping information into a larger whole. However, these sorts of shortcuts mean that inevitably much of the information we receive every second of our lives is either being selectively grouped for compression or underprocessed before brain shelves or discards it.

Also, chunking can sometimes fail to recognise important micro-moments if we are not careful about it. Given the imbalance between information input versus information processing, it is possible that you may not even be aware that you are filtering out and subjectively interpreting everyday experiences through the lens of various biases.

Fortunately, the impact we aim to create for ourselves, and for others, depends on how we apply SHIFT in these micro-moments (Refer to Figure 7.1). When we live with zest, we will be gifted with creating and experiencing micro-moments in the right way and with the right intention when they occur, rather than having a vague after-image of them. The more you practise SHIFT, the more embedded these strengths are into all your responses, and the easier it becomes to take full advantage of your micro-moments.

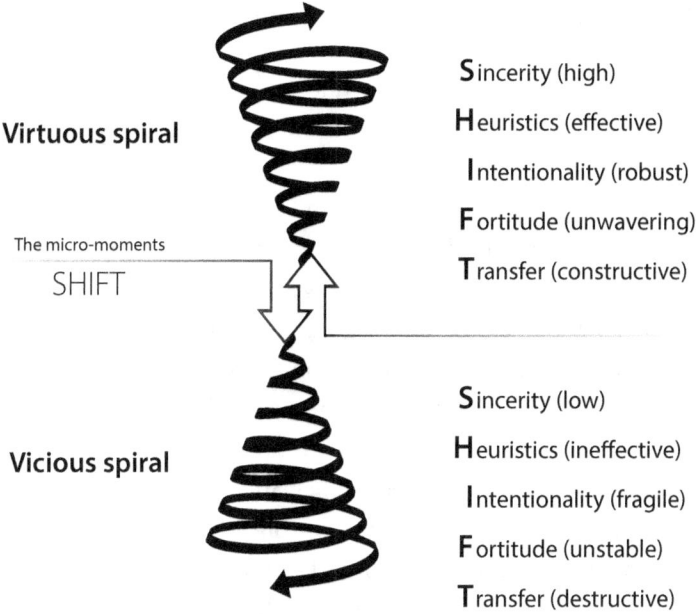

Figure 7.1 The two spirals of your life

If it's not just fate, how will you measure your life?

Richie Norton is the author of leading Amazon download *Résumés Are Dead* and *What to Do About It* as well as the popular blog Start Stuff. Recognised as one of the best and brightest businessmen in the United States under the age of 40 in 2010, Norton once commented that: "Destiny is not fate, it's navigation." We fully agree.

As you head into the final section of this book, we'd like to invite you to ask yourself once final question. Respond as honestly as you can. Here goes: "If an author decides to capture various stories of my life, both the good ones and the bad ones, and turns them into a self-master book, what can people learn from the stories and how many stories will inspire the readers?"

We ask you to ponder that while we pause for a moment to chat a little about Professor Clayton Christensen: one of the greatest thinkers of our time.

Thinkers50 is a well-respected and reliable resource for identifying, ranking and sharing leading management. Every two years, Thinkers50 pays tribute to top business and management ideas by releasing a ranking of management thinkers and singling great minds out for recognition. Christensen, who is a recognised authority on innovation and the architect of the Theory of Disruptive Innovation, featured four times on the Thinkers50 list and twice topped the rankings, in 2011 and 2013. In 2019, he was inducted into the Thinkers50 Hall of Fame.[376]

Before his passing in January 2020, one of Christensen's most revealing comments was that it was high time his own Theory of Disruptive Innovation was disrupted. An open-minded approach to his life's work.

Christensen authored a number of books during his distinguished career, and the one in particular we highly recommend is *How Will You Measure Your Life?* which he co-authored with James Allworth, and Karen Dillon.[377] This book is result of a powerful speech that Christensen delivered to Harvard Business School's graduating class in 2010, during which he drew on his business research to offer a series of guidelines for finding meaning and happiness in life. He incorporated examples from his own experiences to explain how high achievers can all too often fall into traps that lead to unhappiness.

The speech was memorable not only because it was deeply revealing but because it came at a time of intense personal reflection for Christensen, who had just overcome the form of cancer that had taken his father's life. As Christensen struggled with the disease, the question 'how do you measure your life?' became more urgent and poignant, and he began to share his insights more widely with family, friends and students.

In this ground-breaking book, Christensen puts forth a series of questions to help interrogate this question. They are:

1. How can I be sure that I'll find satisfaction in my career?
2. How can I be sure that my personal relationships become enduring sources of happiness?
3. How can I avoid compromising my integrity—and stay out of jail?

Then, using lessons from some of the world's greatest businesses, he provided incredible insights into these challenging questions.

So, in an homage to Christensen, and a nod to you and your new, enhanced journey through life, we'd like to compliment his thinking by offering a few closing thoughts and inquiries of our own which might help you craft your answer to the final question we posed above.

How will you measure your life? What are the GPS satellites and wayfinding techniques you intend to use to navigate your life journey? And how often do you use them? Have you forgotten to find new GPS satellites or have you continually neglected to use your wayfinding techniques as you moved up the career ladder?

Holding tightly to who you are becoming is always more important than focusing on who you were once upon a time. Know that even though having a purpose may help you, your purpose will change as you journey on. Even without a purpose for a while is perfectly all right, as long as you keep striving to activate the best possible versions of yourself.

Capture as many micro-moments that you can at the intersection of where your two stories collide and use these to oscillate upwards using the virtuous SHIFT spiral, which can help you to make exponential progress.

Do issue yourself with clear and firm courageous invitations so you will venture on with conviction and be in the position to turn all micro-moments into multifaceted values.

Restructure, align and gather your inner advisers to help you to recognise and capitalise on micro-moments with ongoing success. Do consider applying strategic selfishness to enlighten yourself and others.

At each micro-moment in your life, strive to navigate your way in order to combine all that you do well and in line with your character strengths. The magic does come from your ampersand thinking – especially if this thinking style is supported by all the key constructs we have mentioned in this book.

To lean on the words of the great French author Marcel Proust, who gifted the world the book *À la recherche du temps perdu* (In Search of Lost Time): "The real voyage of discovery consists, not in seeking new landscapes, but in having new eyes."[378]

We hope that with the lessons, anecdotes, research findings, controversial views, and recommendations for setting specific approach-oriented goals included in this book, you will start looking at your life's journey from a new perspective (i.e a new set of eyes). We urge you to use these windows into your world wisely to take in all the nuances of the transformational journey you are embarking on, and to recognise the massive strides you are making. Know that the path of your success does not hinge on a single phrase or formula, the wisdom locked in a self-mastery book or the advice of a single guru. It lies in your ability to consistently, consciously and carefully craft the life you desire. Your success lies in the zest you bring to this question, how boldly you are prepared to disrupt yourself and those around you, and in your ability to break patterns in search of new and magnificent opportunities.

Just gather your inner advisors around you, point your GPS satellites into the unknown and press 'go'.

Self Enrichment Exercises

As we bring this book to a close, we believe that this is a good opportunity to complete three final exercises. Firstly, lets round out this chapter by considering how you can apply SHIFT in your self-disruption journey and how this may contribute positively to the achievement of your goals. The following questions should assist you in getting your thoughts together:

How can I apply sincerity to increase my zest level when I undergo this self-disruption journey?

_____

_____

_____

_____

_____

How can I enhance the effectiveness of my heuristics so that I can sense and seize those value-creating micro-moments?

_____

_____

_____

_____

_____

How can I be more intentional in issuing and executing effective courageous invitations?

How can I increase my fortitude in this self-disruption journey?

How do I exercise constructive transfers and prevent destructive transfers?

If you are asked to write the bookmark between your autobiography and eulogy now after having completed this book, what would the statement look like? Give it a try.

_____

_____

_____

_____

As a final exercise, we would now like you to revisit all the exercises that you have completed on your journey through this book and take one final look at your Better Self Goal Setting Canvas and make any changes / updates that you think are necessary.

Don't forget to note down your reflections or other thoughts that may be useful to your ongoing journey to the achievement of your goals and your best self.

We encourage you to revisit the concepts in this book and your Best Self Goal Setting Canvas regularly as you continue to grow personally and professionally.

We wish you all the best on your journey and would love to hear from you as to the progress you have made, the challenges and the achievements. We salute you for taking the first big step towards achieving your best self.

IT'S NOT ABOUT FATE, IT'S ABOUT NAVIGATION AND THE JOURNEY

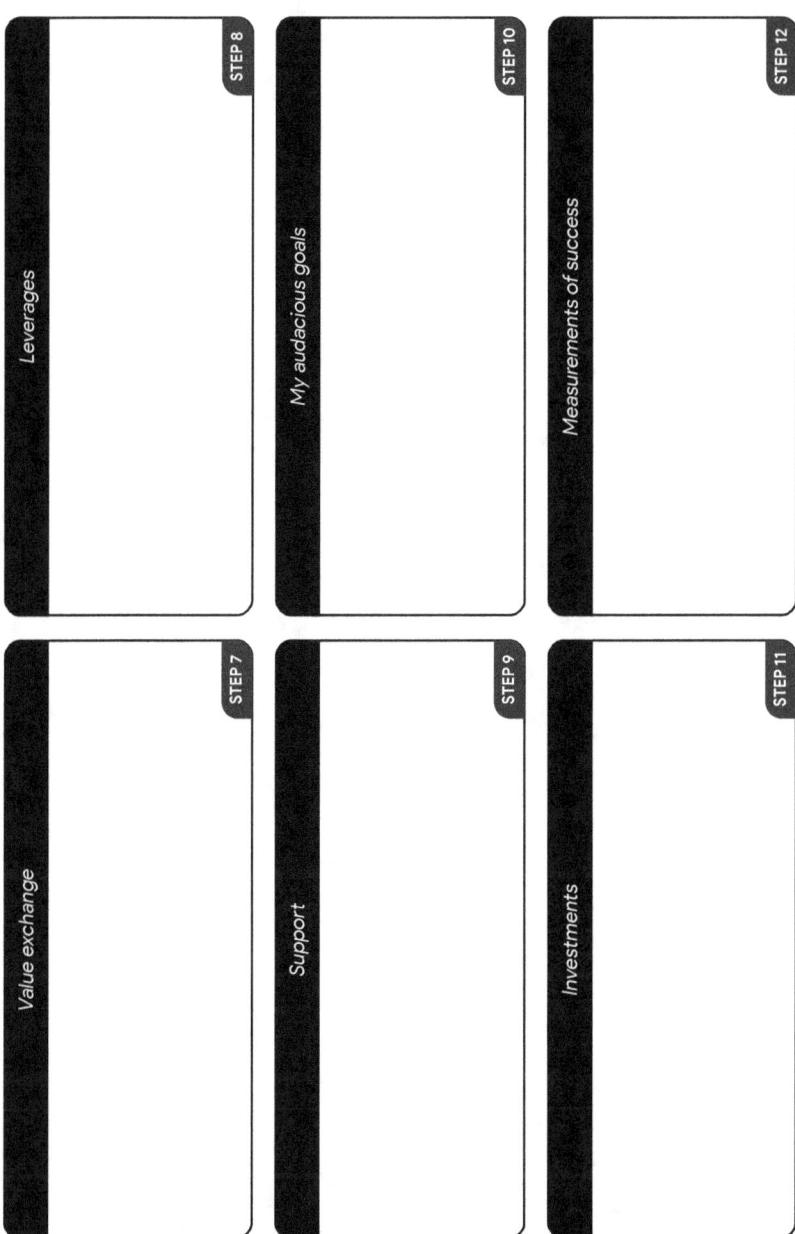

References

1. Lamb-Shapiro, J. (2013, November 29) A Short History of Self-Help, The Word's Bestselling Genre. *Publishing Perspectives*. Retrieved from https://publishingperspectives.com/2013/11/a-short-history-of-self-help-the-worlds-bestselling-genre/

2. Fontaine, C.R. (1981) *A Modern Look at Ancient Wisdom: The Instruction of Ptahhotep Revisited*. The Biblical Archaeologist 44, no. 3: 155-60. Doi:10.2307/3209606.

3. Ptahhotep, Donaldson, F. (1990) *The Maxims of Ptah-hotep: Humankind's Earliest Wisdom Literature*. Vantage Press Inc.

4. Gunn, B. (2019) *The Instruction of Ptah-hotep and The Instruction of Ke'gemni: The Oldest Books in The World*. Amazon Digital Services.

5. Norcross, J.C., Mrykalo, M.S. & Blagys, M.D. (2002). Auld lang syne: Success predictors, change processes, and self-reported outcomes of New Year's resolvers and nonresolvers. *Journal of Clinical Psychology*, 58(4), 397-405.https://onlinelibrary.wiley.com/doi/abs/10.1002/jclp.1151

6. Bauer, J. J. & McAdams, D. P. (2010). Eudaimonic growth: Narrative growth goals predict increases in ego development and subjective well-being 3 years later. *Developmental psychology*, 46(4), 761.

7. Matthews, G. (2007). The Impact of Commitment, Accountability, and Written Goals on Goal Achievement. *Psychology | Faculty Presentations*. https://scholar.dominican.edu/psychology-faculty-conference-presentations/3/?utm_source=scholar.dominican.edu%2Fpsychology-faculty-conference-presentations%2F3&utm_medium=PDF&utm_campaign=PDFCoverPages

8. Novellino, T. (2015, March 26) *Billionaire Spanx founder Sara Blakely has stacks of advice for teens*. The Business Journals

9. Rosten, L. (1991) *The Joys of Yiddish*. New York: Pocket

10. Instagram. (2018, March 30) *@sarablakely*.

11. Blakely, S. (2018, December 4) *Stand-up comedy days...* Facebook. https://www.facebook.com/watch/?v=500250117137143

12 Blakely (2013, April 25) *Spanx's Sara Blakely - Tips for Success*. Primeau TV: YouTube

13 Blakely, S. (2019, March 8) *How to find your higher purpose*. LinkedIn

14 Brown, J. (2021, October 27) Atlanta entrepreneur, Spanx founder surprises her employees. *Alive*. https://www.11alive.com/article/features/spanx-employees-surprise-delta-flight-money/85-28860ea4-2bda-4e38-944c-1208ee8b1d17

15 Saliers, E. (1997) *Everything In Its Own Time*. New York: Sony Music Entertainment

16 Klein, D. (2014) *Travels with Epicurus: A Journey to a Greek Island in Search of a Fulfilled Life*. London: Penguin Publishing Group

17 Van Norden, B.W. (2011) *Introduction to Classical Chinese Philosophy*. Indianapolis: Hackett

18 Eleojo, E.F. (2014) *Africans and African Humanism: What Prospects?* American International Journal of Contemporary Research, Vol 4 No 1.

19 Sinek, S. (2009) Start with why – how great leaders inspire action. TEDxPuget Sound: YouTube.

20 Sinek, S. (2011) *Start with Why: How Great Leaders Inspire Everyone to Take Action*. New York: Portfolio Penguin

21 Schein, M. (2018, June 13). *Author Simon Sinek Is Full Of Hot Air (And Other Reasons You Should Follow His Lead)*. Forbes

22 Hemerling, J., White, B., Swan, J., Kriesman, C.C. & Reed, J.B. (2018, August 16) *For Corporate Purpose to Matter, You've Got to Measure It*. Boston Consulting Group

23 Lee, D. (2016, April 1) *Apple at 40: The forgotten founder who gave it all away*. BBC News

24 Isaacson, W. (2011) *Steve Jobs: The Exclusive Biography*. New York: Simon & Schuster

25 Morgan, C. (2021, February 19) *Steve Jobs left Apple to start a new computer company. His $12 million failure saved Apple*. INSIDER

26 Fell, J. (2011, October 27) *How Steve Jobs Saved Apple*. Entrepreneur South Africa

27 Weinberger, M. (2017, July 31) *This is why Steve Jobs got fired from Apple – and how he came back to save the company*. Insider

28 Carr, A. (2010, May 11) Video: How Steve Jobs's Early Vision For Apple Inspired A Decade Of Innovation. *FastCompany*. https://www.fastcompany.com/1776369/video-how-steve-jobss-early-vision-apple-inspired-decade-innovation

29 Podolny, J. M., & Hansen, M. T. (2020). How Apple Is Organized for Innovation. *Harvard Business Review Nov.-Dec*, 86-95. https://hbr.org/2020/11/how-apple-is-organized-for-innovation

30 Isaacson, W. (2011) *Steve Jobs: The Exclusive Biography*. New York: Simon & Schuster

31 Gladwell, M. (2011, November 6) *The Tweaker: The real genius of Steve Jobs*. The New Yorker

32 Christensen, C.M., Hall, T., Dillon, K. & Duncan, D.S. (2016, September) *Know Your Customers' "Jobs to Be Done"*. Harvard Business Review

33 Pansari, A. & Kumar, V. (2017) Customer engagement: the construct, antecedents, and consequences. *Journal of the Academy of Marketing Science*, 45(3), 294-311.

34 Sinek, S. (2009) Start with why – how great leaders inspire action. TEDxPuget Sound: YouTube.

35 Schlender, B. (2015) *Becoming Steve Jobs: The Evolution of a Reckless Upstart into a Visionary Leader*. New York City: Crown Business

36 Harris, J. (2020, February 21) *'Miracle' revived the memory and glory of the 1980 U.S. hockey team's triumph*. Los Angeles Times

37 Whack, E.H. (2016, November 21) *Rocky: 40 years later, he's still a loveable underdog*. The Associated Press

38 McCullough, D. (2016) *The Wright Brothers*. New York: Simon & Schuster

39 Monash University. (2004) *The Pioneers: Samuel Pierpont Langley (1834-1906)* Retrieved from https://www.ctie.monash.edu/hargrave/langley.html

40 Park, E. (1997, November) *Langley's Feat – and Folly*. Smithsonian Magazine

41 Park, E. (1997, November) *Langley's Feat – and Folly*. Smithsonian Magazine

42 Ferrante, R. (2017, November 28) *Getting Your Due, Samuel Pierpont Langley*. Smithsonian Institution Archives

43 Seto, J.L. (2020, February 20) *How Enzo Ferrari Built Ferrari From the Ground Up*. MotorBiscuit

44 Luxurious Magazine. (2015, February 19) *Ferrari and Pavarotti come together at Modena's Enzo Ferrari Museum.*

45 Kurczewski, N. (2018, November 16) *Lamborghini Supercars Exist Because of a 10-Lira Tractor Clutch.* Car and Driver

46 Salim, Z. (2021, February) *How Hawker Chan Earned The World's Cheapest Michelin-Starred Meal With His S$2 Chicken Rice.* Vulcan Post

47 Alves, G. (2019, December 19) *Hawker Chen, the man behind cheapest Michelin-starred meal, reveals what he likes to eat after a long day.* The Economic Times

48 Salim, Z. (2021, January 6) How Hawker Chan Earned The World's Cheapest Michelin-Starred Meal With His S$2 Chicken Rice. *Vulcan Post.* https://vulcanpost.com/728350/hawker-chan-worlds-cheapest-michelin-starred-meal/

49 O'Connor, C. (2012, March 7) *Undercover Billionaire: Sara Blakely Joins The Rich List Thanks To Spanx.* Forbes

50 Badenhausen, K. (2020) The Inside Story of How Michael Jordan Became The World's Richest Athlete. *Forbes.* https://www.forbes.com/sites/kurtbadenhausen/2020/04/17/the-inside-story-of-how-michael-jordan-became-the-worlds-richest-athlete/?sh=2ec1a8475276

51 Gordon, J. (2018, December 11) A Biography of Michael Jordan as a High School Basketball Player. *SportsRec.* https://www.sportsrec.com/7568006/a-biography-of-michael-jordan-as-a-high-school-basketball-player

52 Stewart, W. (2005) *The Little Giant Book of Basketball Facts.* New York, Sterling Publishing Co, Inc.

53 Sultan, K. (2015, February 20) Last Minute of Game 6 1998 NBA Finals Jazz vs Bulls. *YouTube.* https://www.youtube.com/watch?v=vabPVUpjdrk

54 Sultan, K. (2015)

55 Selena Roberts, S., 1998. THE N.B.A. FINALS; Pippen's pain pushes Jordan to greatest feat, The New York Times, June 15.

56 *The Last Dance.* Director by Jason Hehir, performance by Phil Jackson, Michael Jordan, David Aldridge, Scottie Pippen. Netflix, 2020. https://www.netflix.com/za/title/80203144

57 Lifshin, U., Greenberg, J., Weise, D. and Soenke, M., 2016. It's the end of the world and I feel fine: Soul belief and perceptions of end-of-the-world scenarios. Personality and Social Psychology Bulletin, 42(1), pp.104-117.

58 Zestcott, C.A., Lifshin, U., Helm, P. and Greenberg, J., 2016. He dies, he scores: Evidence that reminders of death motivate improved performance in basketball. Journal of Sport and Exercise Psychology, 38(5), pp.470-480.

59 Jobs, S., 2005. Steve Jobs' 2005 Stanford Commencement Address. Standford. June 12,

60 Cable, D., Lee, J.J., Gino, F. and Staats, B.R., 2015. How Best-Self Activation Influences Emotions. Physiology and Employment Relationships.

61 Cable, D., Lee, J.J., Gino, F. and Staats, B.R., 2015. How Best-Self Activation Influences Emotions. Physiology and Employment Relationships.

62 American Heritage Dictionary of the English Language, Fifth Edition. (2016). Houghton Mifflin Harcourt Publishing. https://www.thefreedictionary.com/inviters

63 Vindolanda Charitable Trust. https://www.vindolanda.com/roman-vindolanda-fort-museum

64 Sci News (2016) *Bloomberg Tablets: Hundreds of Roman 'Notepads' Unearthed in London.* http://www.sci-news.com/archaeology/bloomberg-tablets-roman-notepads-london-03925.html

65 Archaeology (2013) *A tablet bearing a birthday party invite includes the earliest Latin script penned by a woman.* https://www.archaeology.org/issues/106-1309/artifact/1171-writing-tablet-roman-fort-northumberland

66 https://romaninscriptionsofbritain.org/inscriptions/TabVindol291

67 Amiri, F. (2018, December 10) *'Fearless Girl' statue finds permanent home at New York Stock Exchange.* NBC News

68 Mandela, N. (1994) *Long Walk to Freedom.* Little, Brown Book Group: London

69 Nelson Mandela Foundation (2014) 50th anniversary of the sentencing of the Rivonia trialists. https://www.nelsonmandela.org/news/entry/12-june-1964-50th-anniversary-of-the-sentencing-of-the-rivonia-trialists

70 Robben-Island Museum (2013) *Integrated Conservation Management Plan 2013-2018.* https://www.robben-island.org.za/files/publications/Integrated%20conservation%20management%20plan/icmp_chapt3.pdf

71 United States Institute of Peace. (1995) *Truth Commission: South Africa.* https://www.usip.org/publications/1995/12/truth-commission-south-africa#:~:text=The%20Truth%20and%20Reconciliation%20Commission,1995%2C%20July%2026%2C%201995.

72 Goldman, A.L. (2002) *Percy Yutar, 90, Prosecutor Of Mandela in South Africa.* The New York Times

73 Mandela, N. & Langa, M. (2017) *Dare Not Linger: The Presidential Years.* Farrar, Straus and Giroux, New York

74 PBS. Causes of the Civil War. (History Detectives: Special Investigations) https://www.pbs.org/opb/historydetectives/feature/causes-of-the-civil-war/#:~:text=What%20led%20to%20the%20outbreak,was%20central%20to%20the%20conflict.

75 Parsons, E.F. (2015) *Ku-Klux: The Birth of the Klan during Reconstruction.* The University of North Carolina Press

76 Gordon. L. (2018) The Second Coming of the KKK: The Ku Klux Klan of the 1920s and the American Political Tradition. Liveright Publishing Corporation

77 FBI. *KKK Series.* https://www.fbi.gov/history/famous-cases/kkk-series

78 Davis, D. (2020, March 18) Klan We Talk. *TED Talks.* https://www.ted.com/talks/daryl_davis_klan_we_talk

79 Duwe, M. (2020) Daryl Davis: The black musician who converts Ku Klux Klan members. *The Guardian.* https://www.theguardian.com/music/2020/mar/18/daryl-davis-black-musician-who-converts-ku-klux-klan-members

80 Davis, D. (2020)

81 Davis, D. (2020)

82 Ferkany, M.A., 2019. *The Moral Limits of Open-Mindedness.* Educational Theory, 69(4), 403-419.

83 Mandela, N. (1994) *Long Walk to Freedom.* Little, Brown Book Group: London

84 The New York Times. (2013) *Nelson Mandela, South Africa's Liberator as Prisoner and President, Dies at 95.* https://www.nytimes.com/2013/12/06/world/africa/nelson-mandela_obit.html

85 Mandela, N. (2010) *Conversations With Myself.* New York: Farrar, Straus and Giroux

86 Davis, D. (2017, September 29). I wanted to understand why racists hated me. So I befriended Klansmen. *The Washington Post* https://www.washingtonpost.com/outlook/i-wanted-to-understand-why-racists-hated-me-so-i-befriended-klansmen/2017/09/29/c2f46cb8-a3af-11e7-b14f-f41773cd5a14_story.html

87 Davis, D. (2005) *Klan-destine Relationships.* New Horizon Publishing

88 Letters from Las Cruces. (2019) *Befriending the Klan: The Daryl Davis Story.* https://lettersfromlascruces.wordpress.com/2019/10/10/befriending-the-klan-the-daryl-davis-story/#:~:text=Invite%20your%20enemies%20to%20sit,ground%20 becomes%20fertile%20for%20fighting.%E2%80%9D

89 Aruna, R. & MKSS Collective. (2018) *The RTI Story: Power to the People.* Bombay: Roli Books

90 Bhutto, B. (1989) *Daughter of Destiny: An Autobiography.* New York: Simon & Schuster

91 Bridges, F. (2019, April 29) *5 Ways To Be Brave According to Brené Brown's Netflix Special 'The Call To Courage'.* Forbes

92 Howard, M.C. & Cogswell, J.E. (2017) *The left side of courage: Three exploratory studies on the antecedents of social courage.* The Journal of Positive Psychology. doi.org/10.1080/17439760.2018.1426780

93 Online Etymology Dictionary. *courage (n.)* https://www.etymonline.com/word/courage

94 Lopez, S.J., Pedrotti, J.T. & Snyder, C.R. (2014) *Positive Psychology: The Scientific and Practical Explorations of Human Strengths – 3rd Edition.* London: SAGE Publications.

95 Duckworth, A. (2016) *Grit: The Power of Passion and Perseverance.* New York: Scribner Book Company

96 Howard, M. & Cogswell, J. (2018) The Left Side of Courage: Three Exploratory Studies on the Antecedents of Social Courage. *The Journal of Positive Psychology*, 14(10):1-17. https://doi.org/10.1080/17439760.2018.1426780

97 Detert, J.R. & Bruno, E.A. (2017). Workplace courage: Review, synthesis, and future agenda for a complex construct. *The Academy of Management Annals, 11*(2), 593–639. https://doi.org/10.5465/annals.2015.0155

98 Howard. M.C. & Kent, K.A. (2014). Does the courage measure really measure courage? A theoretical and empirical evaluation. *The Journal of Positive Psychology*, Volume 9, Issue 5. https://doi.org/10.1080/17439760.2014.910828

99 Kipling, R. (2016) *Kipling: 'If-' and Other Poems.* London: Michael O'Mara Books

100 Mandela, N. (1995) *Long Walk to Freedom: The Autobiography of Nelson Mandela.* Boston: Back Bay Books

101 Goleman, D. (1995) *Emotional Intelligence: Why It Can Matter More Than IQ.* New York: Bantam

102 Schumann, C. M., Bauman, M. D., & Amaral, D. G. (2011). Abnormal structure or function of the amygdala is a common component of neurodevelopmental disorders. *Neuropsychologia*, 49(4), 745-759. https://doi.org/10.1016/j.neuropsychologia.2010.09.028

103 Lindquist, K. A., Wager, T. D., Kober, H., Bliss-Moreau, E., & Barrett, L. F. (2012). The brain basis of emotion: a meta-analytic review. *The Behavioral and brain sciences*, 35(3), 121.

104 Saarimäki, H., Ejtehadian, L. F., Glerean, E., Jääskeläinen, I. P., Vuilleumier, P., Sams, M., & Nummenmaa, L. (2018). Distributed affective space represents multiple emotion categories across the human brain. Social cognitive and affective neuroscience, 13(5), 471-482.

105 Weymar M and Schwabe L (2016) Amygdala and Emotion: The Bright Side of It. *Front. Neurosci.* 10:224. doi: 10.3389/fnins.2016.00224

106 Siegel, E. H., Sands, M. K., Van den Noortgate, W., Condon, P., Chang, Y., Dy, J., ... & Barrett, L. F. (2018). Emotion fingerprints or emotion populations? A meta-analytic investigation of autonomic features of emotion categories. Psychological bulletin, 144(4), 343.

107 Bocchio M., McHugh S.B., Bannerman D.M., Sharp T. & Capogna M. (2016) *Serotonin, Amygdala and Fear: Assembling the Puzzle.* Front. Neural Circuits 10,24. doi: 10.3389/fncir.2016.00024

108 Salay, L.D., Ishiko, N. & Huberman, A.D. (2018) A midline thalamic circuit determines reactions to visual threat. *Nature* 557, 183–189. https://doi.org/10.1038/s41586-018-0078-2

109 Stanford Medicine. (2018, May 2) *Scientists find fear, courage switches in brain.* https://med.stanford.edu/news/all-news/2018/05/scientists-find-fear-courage-switches-in-brain.html

110 Finding Mastery. (2020, August 12) *Dr Andrew Huberman on How the Brain Makes Sense of Stress, Fear, and Courage.* https://findingmastery.net/andrew-huberman/

111 Gilmartin, M. R., Balderston, N. L., & Helmstetter, F. J. (2014). Prefrontal cortical regulation of fear learning. *Trends in neurosciences*, 37(8), 455-464.

112 Kahneman, D. (2013) *Thinking, Fast and Slow.* New York: Farrar, Straus and Giroux

113 Schipani, S. (2018, September 25) *The Brain's "Bravery Cells" Encourage Risky Behavior.* Smithsonian Magazine

114 McGonigal, K. (2015, May 13) *How to Transform Stress into Courage and Connection.* Greater Good Magazine

115 https://www.researchgate.net/publication/317341217_An_Identity-Based_Motivation_Framework_for_Self-Regulation

116 De Bruin, L.R. (2019) *Improvising musicians' self-regulation and distributed creativities: A phenomenological investigation.* Thinking Skills and Creativity, Volume 32, pages 30-41. https://doi.org/10.1016/j.tsc.2019.03.004

117 Warrell, M. (2020, June 18) *You've Got This! Eight Ways to Build Courage For Touch Times.* Forbes. https://www.forbes.com/sites/margiewarrell/2020/06/18/youve-got-this-how-to-find-your-courage-in-challenging-times/?sh=51f442ca7114

118 Camus, A. (2020) *Personal Writings.* New York: Knopf Doubleday Publishing Group

119 Cuddy, A. (2012, October 1) *Your body language may shape who you are.* TED (YouTube) https://www.youtube.com/watch?v=Ks-_Mh1QhMc

120 Zelano, C., Jiang, H., Zhou, G., Arora, N., Schuele, S., Rosenow, J. & Gottfried, J.A. (2016) Nasal Respiration Entrains Human Limbic Oscillations and Modulates Cognitive Function. *Journal of Neuroscience*, 2016; 36 (49): 12448 DOI: 10.1523/JNEUROSCI.2586-16.2016

121 Kets De Vries, M.F.R. (2020, May 12) *How to Find and Practice Courage.* Harvard Business Review

122 Marsh, A. (2020, June 23) How we can keep fear from spiraling out of our control. *The Washington Post.* https://www.washingtonpost.com/opinions/2020/06/23/era-covid-19-our-fear-doesnt-have-define-us/?arc404=true

123 Albrecht, K. (2012, March 22) The (Only) 5 Fears We All Share. *Psychology Today.* https://www.psychologytoday.com/intl/blog/brainsnacks/201203/the-only-5-fears-we-all-share

124 Collins, J. & Hansen, M.T. (2011) *Great by Choice: Uncertainty, Chaos, and Luck – Why Some Thrive Despite Them all.* New York: Harper Business

125 Mandarin Morning (2020) *Chengyu Story: Man of Qi fears the sky falling.* http://www.mandarinmorning.org/News/2020/1015/10932.html

126 Lukin, K. (2020, February 6) *How to Stop Your Endless Worrying.* Psychology Today. https://www.psychologytoday.com/us/blog/the-man-cave/202002/how-stop-your-endless-worrying

127 Neuroscience News. (2016, April 7) *Is Risk-Taking Behavior Contagious?* https://neurosciencenews.com/behavioral-neuroscience-risk-taking-3993/

128 Rogers, C.R. (1995) *On Becoming a Person: A Therapist's View of Psychotherapy*. Boston: Mariner Books

129 Levitt, A. (2013, July 26) *Science proves love and fear are two sides of the same thing*. Chicago Reader

130 Finding Mastery. (2020)

131 Moran, J. (2018) *Aristotle on Eudaimonia ('Happiness')*. Think, Volume 17, Issue 48, Spring 2018, pp. 91-99 DOI: https://doi.org/10.1017/S1477175617000355

132 Nin, A. & Stuhlmann, G. (2009) *The Diary of Anais Nin, Vol. 3, 1939-1944*. Boston: Houghton Mifflin

133 Rogers, C.R. (1995) *On Becoming a Person: A Therapist's View of Psychotherapy*. Boston, Mariner Books

134 Clark, T.R. (2020, October 13) *To Foster Innovation, Cultivate a Culture of Intellectual Bravery*. Harvard Business Review. https://hbr.org/2020/10/to-foster-innovation-cultivate-a-culture-of-intellectual-braveryy

135 Lussenhop, J. (2020, August 25) *Mark and Patricia McCloskey: What really went on in St Louis that day?* BBC News

136 Cook, D. (2010) *I Did My Best – Greatest Hits*. Comedy Central Records

137 Nagesh, A. (2020, July 31) *What exactly is a 'Karen' and where did the meme come from?* BBC News

138 BBC News. (2020, 31 July) *Domino's New Zealand drops 'free pizza for Karen' offer after backlash*.

139 Santos, H.C., Varnum, M.E. & Grossmann, I. (2017) Global increases in individualism. *Psychological science*, *28*(9), pp.1228-1239

140 Carlson, R.W., Maréchal, M.A., Oud, B. *et al.* Motivated misremembering of selfish decisions. *Nature Communications* 11, 2100 (2020). https://doi.org/10.1038/s41467-020-15602-4

141 Hathaway, B. (2020, April 29) *Memory misfires help selfish maintain their self-image*. YaleNews

142 Jordan, J., Leliveld, M.C. & Tenbrunsel, A.E. (2015). The moral self-image scale: Measuring and understanding the malleability of the moral self. *Frontiers in Psychology*, 6, Article 1878.

143 Legg, T.J. (2018, May 30) What is a self-service bias and what are some examples of it? *Healthline*

144 Gabay, R., Hameiri, B., Rubel-Lifschitz, T. & Nadler, A. (2020) The tendency for interpersonal victimhood: The personality construct and its consequences. Personality and Individual Differences, Volume 165, 110134

145 Kaufman, S.B. (2020, June 29) Unraveling the Mindset of Victimhood. *Scientific American*

146 Ellison, J. (2020, November 7) *Lockdown Two unleashes the selfish gene.* Financial Times

147 Zappulla, J. (2019, August 25) Bolsonaro's selfishness is destroying the Amazon, but can international cooperation save it? The Independent Florida Alligator

148 Ahmad, T. (2020, June 29) *Self-Absorbed, Uncaring, Incompetent: COVID Has Exposed Populist Leaders for What They Are.* The Wire

149 Lammers, J., Stapel, D.A. & Galinsky, A.D., 2010. Power increases hypocrisy: Moralizing in reasoning, immorality in behavior. *Psychological science, 21*(5), pp.737-744. DOI: https://journals.sagepub.com/doi/full/10.1177/0956797610368810

150 The Economic Times. (2019, April 15) *Jack Ma, Bezos, Travis Kalanick: Top Bosses Who Promoted Hostile Work Culture.*

151 McClean, S., Courtright, S.H., Smith, T.A. & Yim Junhyok. (2021, January 19) Stop Making Excuses for Toxic Bosses. *Harvard Business Review*

152 McIntosh, C (2013). *The Cambridge Dictionary of English Grammar*. Cambridge: Cambridge University Press

153 Dambrun, M. and Ricard, M., 2011. Self-centeredness and selflessness: A theory of self-based psychological functioning and its consequences for happiness. *Review of General Psychology, 15*(2), pp.138-157.

154 Barth, F.D. (2016, February 25). *What's the Best Way to Deal With Rude and Selfish People?* Psychology Today

155 Ridley, M. (2016) In retrospect: The Selfish Gene. *Nature* 529, 462–463. https://doi.org/10.1038/529462a

156 Yanai, I. & Lercher, M.J. (2016) Forty years of The Selfish Gene are not enough. *Genome Biol* 17, 39. https://doi.org/10.1186/s13059-016-0910-7

157 Ågren JA, Clark AG (2018) Selfish genetic elements. PLoS Genet 14(11): e1007700. doi:10.1371/journal.pgen.1007700

158 Gershenson S. (1928) A New Sex-Ratio Abnormality in Drosophila obscura. *Genetics.* Nov;13(6):488-507. PMID: 17246563; PMCID: PMC1200995.

159 Östergren, G. (1945) Parasitic nature of extra fragment chromosomes. Botaniska Notiser 2: 157-163.

160 Burt, A, & Trivers, R. (2006) *Genes in Conflict: The Biology of Selfish Genetic Elements*. Harvard University Press

161 Ehrlich, P.R.; Dobkin, D.S. & Wheye, D. (1988) *Brood Parasitism*. Stanford Education

162 Gabbatiss, J. (2016, July 19) *There is no such thing as a truly selfless act*. BBC Earth

163 Nuwer, R. (2014, May 1) *This Bird Tricks Other Animals Into Handing Over Their Meals*. Smithsonian Magazine

164 Rand, A., Branden, N. & Greenspan, A. (1986) *Capitalism: The Unknown Ideal*. New York: Signet

165 Rand, A. (1964) *The Virtue of Selfishness: A New Concept of Egoism*. New York: Signet

166 Baker. P. (2019, March 27) *To Barbara Bush, Donald Trump Represented 'Greed, Selfishness'.* The New York Times

167 Raine, A. & Uh, S. (2019) The Selfishness Questionnaire: Egocentric, Adaptive, and Pathological Forms of Selfishness. *Journal of Personality Assessment*, 101:5, 503-514, DOI: 10.1080/00223891.2018.1455692

168 Pohjanpalo, K. (2021, March 19) *Finland Defend Title as World's Happiest Nation in 4th Straight Win*. Bloomberg

169 Trotter, S.R. (2015) *Breaking the law of Jante*. eSharp 23: 1-24

170 Harrison, F. (2020, April 1) *Who decides the common good?* Mail & Guardian

171 The Manchester Guardian (1905, January 23) *Revolution? Street Fighting in St Petersburg.*

172 Heller, A.C. (2009) *Ayn Rand and the World She Made*. New York: Nan A. Talese

173 Khazan, O. (2015, June 13) *Ayn Rand: In Love, Be Selfish*. The Atlantic

174 Svanberg, C. (2014, May 22) The 'virtue of selfishness'? Ayn Rand's Ethics of Egoism in your own life [video]. Ayn Rand Institute

175 Rand, A. (1964) *The Virtue of Selfishness: A New Concept of Egoism*. New York: Signet

176 Kakutani, M. (1981, March 29) *Life as Ellington' son was mostly 'mood indigo'*. The New York Times.

177 Williams P. (2004) *Quotable Michael Jordan: Words of Wit, Wisdom and Inspiration by and about Michael Jordan, Basketball's Greatest Superstar*. Lanham, Maryland: Taylor Trade Publishing

178 RIKEN. (2019, December 13) *Deepening our understanding of selfish behaviour*. Neuroscience News

179 Mugumbate, J. & Nyanguru, A. (2013) *Exploring African Philosophy: The Value of Ubuntu in Social Work*. African Journal of Social Work, Volume 3, Number 1

180 Feenstra, N. (2020, May 5) *Does Covid-19 Change My Acts of Strategic Selfishness?*

181 Feenstra, N. (2017, October 2) *The Art of Strategic Selfishness*. LinkedIn

182 Senge, P.M. (1990) *The Fifth Discipline: The Art and Practice of the Learning Organization*. New York: Doubleday

183 Cindy Smith's name has been changed to protect the innocent.

184 Oudeyer, P-Y. & Kaplan, F. (2007). What is intrinsic motivation? A typology of computational approaches. *Front. Neurorobot*. 1:6. doi: 10.3389/neuro.12.006.2007

185 Meet the Boss. (2014, May 9) *The Man Who Rescued Lego – Full Version*. YouTube.

186 Eriksson, K., Vartanova, I., Strimling, P. & Simpson, B. (2018) Generosity Pays: Selfish People Have Fewer Children and Earn Less Money. Journal of Personality and Social Psychology. http://dx.doi.org/10.1037/pspp0000213

187 Travers, M. (2019, September 4) *Why Selfishness Only Gets You So Far*. Forbes.

188 Treviqo, A.J. & Tilly, C. (2015) *George C Homans: History, Theory and Method*. New York: Paradigm Publishers

189 Tulane University. (2018, April 2020) *What Is Social Exchange Theory?*

190 Bullock, D. & Sanchez, R. (2021) *How to Communicate Effectively With Anyone, Anywhere: Your Passport to Connecting Globally*. Franklin Lakes: Career Press

191 History.com. (2020, February 21) *Code of Hammurabi*

192 King. L.W. (translator) (2008) *The Code of Hammurabi*. The Avalon Project, Yale Law School

193 Fareri, D.S. (2019) *Neurobehavioral Mechanisms Supporting Trust and Reciprocity*. Front. Hum. Neurosci. 13:271. doi: 10.3389/fnhum.2019.00271

194 Candia, C., Landaeta-Torres, V., Hidalgo, C.A. & Rodriguez-Sickert, C. (2019). Strategic reciprocity improves academic performance in public elementary school children. *arXiv preprint arXiv:1909.11713*

195 Covey, S.R. (1989) *The Seven Habits of Highly Effective People: Restoring the Character Ethic*. New York: Simon and Schuster.

196 Schacter, D.L., Benoit, R.G. & Szpunar, K.K. (2017) *Episodic Future Thinking: Mechanisms and Functions*. Curr Opin Behav Sci. 2017, Oct; 17: 41-50

197 Pinakin, D.J., Kumar, V., Kumar, A., Gat, Y., Suri, S. & Sharma, K. (2018) Mahua: A boon for Pharmacy and Food Industry. Curr Res Nutr Food Sci 2018; 6(2). http://dx.doi.org/10.12944/CRNFSJ.6.2.12

198 Naidu, T.A. (2021) *A hamlet that thrives on the ancient barter system*. The Hindu.

199 Turner, N. (2022) *Clothing Goes to War: Creativity inspired by scarcity in World War II*. www.nanturner.com

200 Jones, J. (2020, August 27) *Could bartering become the new buying in a changed world?* BBC Worklife

201 Strauss, I.A. (2016, February 26) *The Myth of the Barter Economy*. The Atlantic

202 Graeber, D. (2011) *Debt: The First 5000 Years*. Brooklyn: Melville House

203 Donne, J. & Fallon, K (ed). (1970) *No Man is an Island: Selected from the Writings of John Donne*. New York: Random House

204 Alam, M. (2018) *Les Brown: Terrible Student, Radio DJ, and Motivational Speaker*. The Minority Mindset. https://theminoritymindset.com/blog/les-brown-terrible-student-radio-dj-motivational-speaker/

205 Ali, S.R.C. (2020, February 25) *Empowering Yourself to Success With Les Brown*. Solomon RC Ali Corporation. https://www.solomonrcali.com/empowering-yourself-to-success-with-les-brown/

206 Goalcast (2018) Why it Pays to be Hungry: Les Brown's Motivational Speech. *YouTube*. https://www.youtube.com/watch?v=xFrOFKnaLDk

207 Goalcast (2018)

208 Bennett, T. (2009, September 9) *Les Brown Story of Persistence and Preparation*. https://tybennett.com/les-brown-story-of-persistence-and-preperation/

209 Neck, C. P., & Manz, C. C. (1992). Thought self-leadership: The influence of self-talk and mental imagery on performance. *Journal of organizational behavior*, *13*(7), 681-699.

210 Ali, S.R.C. (2020, February 25) *Empowering Yourself to Success With Les Brown*. Solomon RC Ali Corporation. https://www.solomonrcali.com/empowering-yourself-to-success-with-les-brown/

211 The History Makers. (2007, October 17) *The Honourable Less Brown*. https://www.thehistorymakers.org/biography/honorable-les-brown

212 Aurelius, M. (2019) *Meditations: The Casaubon Translation*. New York: Logos Books

213 Stroud, S. R. (2012). William James and the impetus of Stoic rhetoric. *Philosophy & rhetoric*, *45*(3), 246-268.

214 James, W. (1984) Principles of Psychology (Briefer Course). Cambridge: Harvard University Press

215 Yao, X. (2000) *An Introduction to Confucianism (Introduction to Religion)*. Cambridge: Cambridge University Press

216 African Proverbs in African Literature: A Critical Resourcebase (2012). https://proverbsafricanliterature.wordpress.com/interpretation/interpretation-3/

217 Biko, S. (1987) *I Write what I Like: A Selection of His Writings*. Chicago: University of Chicago Press

218 McLean, S. (2005). *The basics of interpersonal communication*. Pearson/A and B.

219 Kross, E., Bruehlman-Senecal, E., Park, J., Burson, A., Dougherty, A., Shablack, H., et al. (2014). Self-talk as a regulatory mechanism: how you do it matters. *J. Pers. Soc. Psychol*. 106, 304–324. doi: 10.1037/a0035173

220 Winsler, A.; Diaz, R. M.; Montero, I. (1997). "The role of private speech in the transition from collaborative to independent task performance in young children". *Early Childhood Research Quarterly*. **12**: 59–79.

221 Sibonney, C. (2019, November 19) *Is it normal for your kids to talk to themselves?* Today's Parent. https://www.todaysparent.com/kids/preschool/is-talking-to-yourself-normal/

222 George Mason University (2008, March 2019). *Preschool Kids Do Better When They Talk To Themselves, Research Shows*. ScienceDaily. https://www.sciencedaily.com/releases/2008/03/080328124554.htm

223 Fogarty, M. & Whitman, N. (2018, November 30) *Does Your Language Influence How You Think?* Scientific American. https://www.scientificamerican.com/article/does-your-language-influence-how-you-think/

224 Boroditsky, L. (2001) Does language shape thought?: Mandarin and English speakers' conceptions of time. *Cognitive psychology*, *43*(1), pp.1-22.

225 TED. (2018, May 2) How language shapes the way we think – Lera Boroditsky. *YouTube*. https://www.youtube.com/watch?v=RKK7wGAYP6k

226 Boroditsky, L. & Gaby, A. (2010, October 19) *Remembrances of Times East: Absolute Spatial Representations of Time in an Australian Aboriginal Community*. SAGE Journals. https://doi.org/10.1177/0956797610386621

227 David, T. (2014) *Magic Words: The Science and Secrets Behind Seven Words That Motivate, Engage, and Influence*. Hoboken: Prentice Hall Press

228 Hermans, H.J., & Gieser, T. (Eds.). (2011). *Handbook of dialogical self theory*. Cambridge University Press

229 Hermans, H.J. (2015). Dialogical self in a complex world: the need for bridging theories. *Europe's journal of psychology*, *11*(1), -4.

230 Oleś, P. K., Brinthaupt, T. M., Dier, R., & Polak, D. (2020). Types of Inner Dialogues and Functions of Self-Talk: Comparisons and Implications. *Frontiers in psychology*, *11*, 227.

231 Lester, D. (2010) A multiple self theory of personality. Hauppauge, NY: Nova Science

232 Carter, R. (2008) *Multiplicity: The New Science of Personality, Identity, and the Self*. New York: Little, Brown Spark

233 Kelly, G., 1955. Personal construct psychology. *Nueva York: Norton*.

234 Boeree, C.G. (2006) *Personality Theories: George Kelly 1905-1967*. https://webspace.ship.edu/cgboer/kelly.html

235 Chetty, K. (2020) *Personal Construct Theory Overview*. Very Well Mind. https://www.verywellmind.com/what-is-personal-construct-theory-2795957

236 Duckworth, A. (2017). Grit: Why passion and resilience are the secrets to success, London, Vermilion,

237 Berkovich-Ohana, A., Wilf, M., Kahana, R., Arieli, A., & Malach, R. (2015). Repetitive speech elicits widespread deactivation in the human cortex: the "M antra" effect? *Brain and behavior*, *5*(7), e00346.

238 Chamine, S., 2012. *Positive intelligence: Why only 20% of teams and individuals achieve their true potential and how you can achieve yours*. Greenleaf Book Group.

239 TEDx Talks. (2013, June 21) *Know your inner saboteurs: Shirzad Chamine at TEDxStanford*. YouTube. https://www.youtube.com/watch?v=-zdJ1ubvoXs

240 Gould, W.R. (2018, October 19) *Go ahead, talk to yourself. It's normal – and good for you*. Better by Today. https://www.nbcnews.com/better/health/talking-yourself-normal-here-s-how-master-it-ncna918091

241 Lupyan, G. and Swingley, D., 2012. Self-directed speech affects visual search performance. *Quarterly Journal of Experimental Psychology*, 65(6), pp.1068-1085.

242 Mayfield, J., Mayfield, M. and Neck, C.P., 2021. Speaking to the self: How motivating language links with self-leadership. *International Journal of Business Communication*, 58(1), pp.31-54.

243 Hatzigeorgiadis, A., Bartura, K., Argiropoulos, C., Comoutos, N., Galanis, E. and D. Flouris, A., 2018. Beat the heat: effects of a motivational self-talk intervention on endurance performance. *Journal of Applied Sport Psychology*, 30(4), pp.388-401.

244 Walter, N., Nikoleizig, L. and Alfermann, D., 2019. Effects of self-talk training on competitive anxiety, self-efficacy, volitional skills, and performance: An intervention study with junior sub-elite athletes. *Sports*, 7(6), p.148.

245 Latinjak, A.T., Masó, M., Calmeiro, L. and Hatzigeorgiadis, A., 2020. Athletes' use of goal-directed self-talk: Situational determinants and functions. *International Journal of Sport and Exercise Psychology*, 18(6), pp.733-748.

246 Kross, E., Vickers, B.D., Orvell, A., Gainsburg, I., Moran, T.P., Boyer, M., Jonides, J., Moser, J. and Ayduk, O., 2017. Third-person self-talk reduces Ebola worry and risk perception by enhancing rational thinking. *Applied Psychology: Health and Well-Being*, 9(3), pp.387-409.

247 Orvell, A., Vickers, B.D., Drake, B., Verduyn, P., Ayduk, O., Moser, J., Jonides, J. and Kross, E., 2020. Does Distanced Self-Talk Facilitate Emotion Regulation Across a Range of Emotionally Intense Experiences?. *Clinical Psychological Science*, p.2167702620951539.

248 Moser, J.S., Dougherty, A., Mattson, W.I., Katz, B., Moran, T.P., Guevarra, D., Shablack, H., Ayduk, O., Jonides, J., Berman, M.G. & Kross, E., 2017. Third-person self-talk facilitates emotion regulation without engaging cognitive control: Converging evidence from ERP and fMRI. *Scientific reports*, 7(1), pp.1-9.

249 Klemp, N. (2019, August 7) *The Neuroscience of Breaking Out of Negative Thinking (and How to Do it in Under 30 Seconds)*. Inc. https://incafrica.com/library/nate-klemp-try-this-neuroscience-based-technique-to-shift-your-mindset-from-negative-to-positive-in-30-seconds

250 Solberg, N.L., Evans, D.R. & Segerstrom, S.C. (2009). Optimism and College Retention: Mediation by Motivation, Performance, and Adjustment 1. *Journal of Applied Social Psychology*, 39(8), pp.1887-1912.

251 Bauer, J.J., McAdams, D.P. & Pals, J.L., 2008. Narrative identity and eudaimonic well-being. *Journal of happiness studies*, 9(1), pp.81-104. https://link.springer.com/article/10.1007/s10902-006-9021-6

252 Sweeny, K. (2017, February) *The downsides of positivity.* The Psychologist. https://thepsychologist.bps.org.uk/volume-30/february-2017/downsides-positivity

253 Schein, M. (2018, July 5) *Positive Psychology Is Garbage (And Why You Should Follow Its Founder's Lead).* Forbes. https://www.forbes.com/sites/michaelschein/2018/07/05/positive-psychology-is-garbage-and-why-you-should-follow-its-founders-lead/?sh=7cd6373071a9

254 Scully, S.M. (2020, July 22) *'Toxic Positivity' Is Real – and It's a Big Problem During the Pandemic.* Healthline. https://www.healthline.com/health/mental-health/toxic-positivity-during-the-pandemic

255 Ehrenreich, B. (2010) *Bright-sided: How Positive Thinking Is Undermining America.* Paperback, Picador; First edition

256 Turner, M. J., Kirkham, L., & Wood, A. G. (2018). Teeing up for success: The effects of rational and irrational self-talk on the putting performance of amateur golfers. *Psychology of Sport and Exercise*, 38, 148-153.

257 Van Raalte, J.L., Vincent, A., & Brewer, B.W. (2016). Self-talk: Review and sport-specific model. *Psychology of Sport and Exercise,* 22, 139–148. doi:10.1016/j.psychsport.2015.08.004

258 Tod, D., Hardy, J., & Oliver, E. (2011). Effects of self-talk: A systematic review. *Journal of Sport and Exercise Psychology*, 33(5), 666-687.

259 DeWolfe, C. E., Scott, D., & Seaman, K. A. (2020). Embrace the challenge: Acknowledging a challenge following negative Self-Talk improves performance. *Journal of Applied Sport Psychology*, 1-14.

260 TEDxCambridge. (2018, May) *Cultivating Wisdom: The Power of Mood.* YouTube. https://www.ted.com/talks/lisa_feldman_barrett_cultivating_wisdom_the_power_of_mood

261 Reijula, S. & Hertwig, R. (2020). Self-nudging and the citizen choice architect. *Behavioural Public Policy*, 1-31.

262 Swart, T. (2019). *The Source: The Secrets of the Universe, the Science of the Brain.* HarperCollins.

263 Stephan, E., Shidlovski, D. & Sedikides, C. (2018). Self-prospection and energization: The joint influence of time distance and consideration of future consequences. *Self and Identity*, *17*(1), 22-36.

264 Fogg, B. J. (2019). *Tiny habits: The small changes that change everything*. Eamon Dolan Books.

265 TEDGlobal. (2012) *Your body language may shape who you are*. YouTube. https://www.ted.com/talks/amy_cuddy_your_body_language_may_shape_who_you_are/up-next

266 Kelly, J. (2015, August 27) *How 'MacGyver' become a verb*. BBC News.

267 Walsh, D. (2019, May 21) *What makes someone a great leader in the digital economy?* MIT Management. https://mitsloan.mit.edu/ideas-made-to-matter/what-makes-someone-a-great-leader-digital-economy

268 Zlotoff, L.D. & Seifert, C. (2016) *The MacGyver Secret: Connect to Your Inner MacGyver and Solve Anything*. Pinehurst: MacGyver Solutions

269 Balok, C. (2019, August 28) *MacGyver's Secret You Can Use to Solve ANY Problem!* The Colt Balok Show, YouTube. https://www.youtube.com/watch?v=nk9B7wJpbhw

270 Basbanes, N.A. (2006, September 23) *Cicero's rise, from someone who was there*. Los Angeles Times. https://www.latimes.com/archives/la-xpm-2006-sep-23-et-book23-story.html

271 Houston, K. (2013) *Shady Characters: The Secret Life of Punctuation, Symbols and Other Typographical Marks*. Manhattan: WW Norton & Company

272 Bathroom Readers' Institute. (2018) *Uncle John's New & Improved Briefs: Fast Facts, Terse Trivia & Astute Articles*. San Diego: Portable Press

273 Classic FM. (2021) *Discovery The Great Composers – Monteverdi*. https://www.classicfm.com/composers/monteverdi/guides/discovering-great-composers-monteverdi/

274 Gardiner, J.E. (2015, August 3) *Monteverdi's Orfeo: 'a brilliant and compelling fable to the inalienable power of music'*. The Guardian.

275 Spitzer, J., & Zaslaw, N. (2004). *The birth of the orchestra: History of an institution, 1650-1815*. Oup Oxford.

276 McPherson, A. (2016, July 10) *Germany snatches orchestral world record from Aus*. LIMELIGHT. https://limelightmagazine.com.au/news/germany-snatches-orchestral-world-record-from-aus/

277 Russian News Agency. (2019, September 2) *Record number of musicians gather in St Petersburg to play national anthem.* https://tass.com/society/1075962

278 AFP (2016, July 10) *World's biggest orchestra of 7,500 musicians performs in German stadium.* The Straits Times. https://www.straitstimes.com/world/europe/worlds-biggest-orchestra-of-7500-musicians-performs-in-german-stadium

279 Hindustan Times (2016, July 12) *Frankfurt sets record for the world's largest orchestra'.* YouTube. https://www.youtube.com/watch?v=PrFjybczCSs

280 Joly, J. (2021, November 23) *Venezuela wins Guinness record for world's largest orchestra with 12,000 musicians.* Euronews. https://www.euronews.com/culture/2021/11/23/venezuela-wins-guinness-record-for-world-s-largest-orchestra-with-12-000-musicians

281 Berman, E. (2014, November 3) *Watch the Danish National Chamber Orchestra Perform After Eating World's Hottest Chili Peppers.* TIME. https://time.com/3555296/danish-national-orchestra-chili-peppers/

282 Chili Klaus. (2014, October 31) *Chili Klaus & Classical Orchestra.* YouTube. https://www.youtube.com/watch?v=MuvUaFp_qMQ

283 Pinkfong Baby Shark – Kids' Songs & Stories. (2016, June 18) *Baby Shark Dance.* YouTube. https://www.youtube.com/watch?v=XqZsoesa55w

284 Knowledge@Wharton. (2013, March 13) *'Contagious': Johan Berger on Why Things Catch On.* https://knowledge.wharton.upenn.edu/article/contagious-jonah-berger-on-why-things-catch-on/

285 Stillman, J. (2021, February 23) *He Studied the Behavior of 150 Million People and Found There Are Only 8 Reasons Things Go Viral.* Inc. https://www.inc.com/jessica-stillman/viral-content-james-currier.html

286 Berman, N. (2019, August 29) *Heavy metal and classical music have more in common than you think.* CBC. https://www.cbc.ca/music/heavy-metal-and-classical-music-have-more-in-common-than-you-think-1.5262655

287 Hanson, C. (2020, August 19) *These Fusion-Food Mashups Are Like Tasting the Future.* All Recipes. https://www.allrecipes.com/gallery/these-fusion-food-mashups-are-like-tasting-the-future/?

288 Hadamard, J. (1954) *An essay on the psychology of invention in the mathematical field.* Courier Corporation.

289 Einstein, A., Seelig, C., Bargmann, S., Unna, I. & Wolff, B. (1954). *Ideas and opinions.* New York: Wings Books

290 Kahney, L. (2008) *Inside Steve's Brain: Business Lessons from Steve Jobs, the Man Who Saved Apple*. London: Atlantic Books

291 Davis, J. (2017, June 4) *How Lego clicked: the super brand that reinvented itself*. The Observer. https://www.theguardian.com/lifeandstyle/2017/jun/04/how-lego-clicked-the-super-brand-that-reinvented-itself

292 Meet the Boss. (2014, May 9) *The Man Who Rescued Lego*. YouTube. https://www.youtube.com/watch?v=O-CiwT2ZTKc

293 Liu, R., Li, X., & Lam, K.S. (2017). Combinatorial chemistry in drug discovery. *Current opinion in chemical biology, 38*, 117-126.

294 Keeley, L., Walters, H., Pikkel, R. and Quinn, B., 2013. *Ten types of innovation: The discipline of building breakthroughs*. John Wiley & Sons.

295 Grant. A. (2013) *Give and Take: A Revolutionary Approach to Success*. London: Penguin Publishing Group

296 Marcus, A. (2018) *Own the Day, Own Your Life: Optimized Practices for Waking, Working, Learning, Eating, Training, Playing, Sleeping, and Sex*. Chicago: Harper Wave

297 Aubrey Marcus. (2019, September 30) *How Do You Own The Day?* YouTube. https://www.youtube.com/watch?v=iEiOfCmiqlA

298 Thurmon, D. (2016) *Off Balance On Purpose: Embrace Uncertainty and Create a Life You Love*. Georgia: Motivation Works, Inc.

299 Dan Thurmon. (2021) *How I Became A Juggling Motivational Speaker*. https://danthurmon.com/how-i-became-a-juggling-motivational-speaker/

300 Ben & Jerry's (2021) *The 10 Weirdest Ben & Jerry's Flavours Ever*. https://www.benjerry.co.uk/whats-new/2015/10-weirdest-flavours

301 Federal Aviation Administration. (2021, August 12) *Satellite Navigation – GPS – How It Works*. Retrieved from https://www.faa.gov/about/office_org/headquarters_offices/ato/service_units/techops/navservices/gnss/gps/howitworks/

302 Blakemore, E. (2019, March 22) What was the Cold War? *National Geographic*. Retrieved from https://www.nationalgeographic.com/culture/article/cold-war

303 BBVA OpenMind. (2020, October 6) *The Birth of GPS, an Unexpected Child of the Space Race*. https://www.bbvaopenmind.com/en/technology/visionaries/the-birth-of-gps-an-unexpected-child-of-the-space-race/

304 Hein, G.W. (2020, August 3) Status, perspectives and trends of satellite navigation. *Satellite Navigation* 1, 22. https://doi.org/10.1186/s43020-020-00023-x. https://satellite-navigation.springeropen.com/articles/10.1186/s43020-020-00023-x#citeas

305 Johnson, V.J. (1984) *Geodesy for the layman*. Washington DC: Defense Mapping Agency. https://www.ngs.noaa.gov/PUBS_LIB/Geodesy4Layman/TR80003A.HTM#ZZ0

306 Tewelow, W. (2020, September 16) The evolution of GPS satellites and their use today. *GPS World*. https://www.gpsworld.com/the-evolution-of-gps-satellites-and-their-use-today/

307 White, K. & Lehman, D.R. (2005, October 1) Looking on the Bright Side: Downward Counterfactual Thinking In Response to Negative Life Events. *Personality and Social Psychology Bulletin*. https://doi.org/10.1177/0146167205276064. https://journals.sagepub.com/doi/10.1177/0146167205276064

308 Joseph, S. (2019, January 2) What Is Eduaimonic Happiness. *Psychology Today*. https://www.psychologytoday.com/za/blog/what-doesnt-kill-us/201901/what-is-eudaimonic-happiness

309 Health, C. & Health, D. (2017) *The Power of Moments: Why Certain Experiences Have Extraordinary Impact*. New York City: Simon & Schuster

310 Pickup, O. (2016, November 25) Seven fascinating facts about the South Pacific. *The Telegraph*. https://www.telegraph.co.uk/films/moana/south-pacific-islands-fascinating-facts/

311 SurferToday. (2021) *What does Teahupoo mean?* https://www.surfertoday.com/surfing/what-does-teahupoo-mean

312 Gibbons, A. (2016, October 3) 'Game-chaning' study suggests first Polynesians voyaged all the way from East Asia. *Science*. https://www.science.org/content/article/game-changing-study-suggests-first-polynesians-voyaged-all-way-east-asia

313 Marshall, M. (2020, July 8) Polynesians and Native Americans met 800 years ago after epic voyage. *NewScientist*. https://www.newscientist.com/article/2248337-polynesians-and-native-americans-met-800-years-ago-after-epic-voyage/

314 Eckstein, L. & Schwarz, A. (2018, December 20) The Making of Tupaia's Map: A Story of the Extent of Mastery of Polynesian Navigation, Competing Systems of Wayfinding on James Cook's Endeavour, and the Invention of an Ingenious Cartographic System. *The Journal of Pacific History*. https://doi.org/10.1080/00223344.2018.1512369.

315 Vermillion, S. (2021, July 27) Polynesia's master voyagers who navigated by nature. *BBC*. https://www.bbc.com/travel/article/20210726-polynesias-master-voyagers-who-navigate-by-nature

316 Rapp Learn, J. (2021, June 16) The Viking Longship: An Engineering Marvel of the Ancient World. *Discover*. https://www.discovermagazine.com/planet-earth/the-viking-longship-an-engineering-marvel-of-the-ancient-world

317 Lynch, A. (2017, July 3) The first European settlement in the New World. *BBC*. https://www.bbc.com/travel/article/20170629-the-first-european-settlement-in-the-new-world

318 Sobel, D. (1995, January) Mihaly Csikszentmihalyi. *Omni* (Vol 17, Issue 4) https://go.gale.com/ps/i.do?id=GALE%7CA16045733&sid=googleScholar&v=2.1&it=r&linkaccess=abs&issn=01498711&p=AONE&sw=w&userGroupName=anon%7Ebfb32250

319 Geirland, J. (1996) Go With The Flow. *Wired*. https://www.wired.com/1996/09/czik/

320 Csikszentmihalyi M. (1997) *Finding Flow: The Psychology of Engagement with Everyday Life*. New York: Basic Books.

321 TED. (2008, October 25) Mihaly Csikszentmihalyi: Flow, the secret to happiness. https://www.youtube.com/watch?v=fXIeFJCqsPs

322 Bonaiuto, M., Mao, Y. & Roberts S, et al. (2016, November 7) Optimal Experience and Personal Growth: Flow and the Consolidation of Place Identity. *Front Psychol*. 2016;7:1654. doi:10.3389/fpsyg.2016.01654. https://www.frontiersin.org/articles/10.3389/fpsyg.2016.01654/full

323 Koehn, S. & Morris, T. (2012, August) The relationship between performance and flow state in tennis competition. *J Sports Med Phys Fitness*, 52(4): 437-47. https://pubmed.ncbi.nlm.nih.gov/22828465/

324 Šimleša, M., Guegan, J., Blanchard, E., Tarpin-Bernard F. & Buisine S. The Flow Engine Framework: A Cognitive Model of Optimal Human Experience. *Eur J Psychol*. 2018;14(1):232-253. doi:10.5964/ejop.v14i1.1370. https://ejop.psychopen.eu/index.php/ejop/article/view/1370

325 Kotler, S. & Wheal, J. (2017) *Stealing Fire: How Silicon Valley, The Navy SEALs, and Maverick Scientists Are Revolutionizing the Way We Live and Work*. New York: Dey Street Books

326 Katahira, K., Yamazaki, Y., Yamaoka, C., Ozaki, H., Nakagawa S. & Nagata, N. (2018, March 9) EEG Correlates of the Flow State: A Combination of Increased Frontal Theta and Moderate Frontocentral Alpha Rhythm in the Mental Arithmetic Task. *Front Psychol.* 2018;9:300. doi:10.3389/fpsyg.2018.00300. https://www.frontiersin.org/articles/10.3389/fpsyg.2018.00300/full

327 Gold, J. & Ciorciari, J. A Review on the Role of the Neuroscience of Flow States in the Modern World. *Behav Sci (Basel).* 2020;10(9):137. doi:10.3390/bs10090137. https://www.mdpi.com/2076-328X/10/9/137

328 Csíkszentmihályi, M., Khosla, S. & Nakamura, J. (2017). Flow at Work. *The Wiley Blackwell Handbook of the Psychology of Positivity and Strengths-Based Approaches at Work*, 99-109.

329 Zhang, Y. & Chen, M. (2018, June 29) Character Strengths, Strengths Use, Future Self-Continuity and Subjective Well-Being Among Chinese University Students. *Front. Psychol.* https://doi.org/10.3389/fpsyg.2018.01040.

330 Chamorro-Premuzic, T. (2016, January 4) Strengths-Based Coaching Can Actually Weaken You. *Harvard Business Review.* https://hbr.org/2016/01/strengths-based-coaching-can-actually-weaken-you

331 Flade, P., Asplund, J. & Elliot, G. (2015, October 8) Employees Who Use Their Strengths Outperform Those Who Don't. *Gallup.* https://www.gallup.com/workplace/236561/employees-strengths-outperform-don.aspx

332 Van Woerkom, M. & Kroon, B. (2020). The effect of strengths-based performance appraisal on perceived supervisor support and the motivation to improve performance. *Frontiers in Psychology, 11*, 1883. https://www.frontiersin.org/articles/10.3389/fpsyg.2020.01883/full

333 Corbu, A., Peláez Zuberbühler, M.J. & Salanova, M. (2021). Positive Psychology Micro-Coaching Intervention: Effects on Psychological Capital and Goal-Related Self-Efficacy. *Frontiers in Psychology, 12*, 315. https://www.frontiersin.org/articles/10.3389/fpsyg.2021.566293/full

334 Seligman, M.E.P. & Csikszentmihalyi, M. (2000). Positive psychology: an introduction. *Am. Psychol.* 55, 5–14. doi: 10.1037/0003-066X.55.1.5

335 Feloni, R. (2016, April 29) Facebook's lead HR consultant explains how the company radically changed the way it trains managers. *INSIDER.* https://www.businessinsider.com/marcus-buckingham-explains-how-facebook-trains-managers-2016-4?IR=T

336 Connley, C. (2021, April 29) The go-to interview question Facebook's head of global recruiting always asks – and how to answer it. *CNBC*. https://www.cnbc.com/2021/04/29/facebooks-head-of-global-recruitings-go-to-interview-question.html

337 Peterson, C. & Seligman, M.E.P. (2004). *Character Strengths and Virtues: A Handbook and Classification*. New York, NY: Oxford University Press.

338 Peterson, C. & Seligman, M. (2004) *Character Strengths and Virtues: A Handbook and Classification*. American Psychological Association/Oxford University Press. First Edition.

339 Littman-Ovadia, H., Dubreuil, P., Meyers, M.C. & Freidlin, P. (2021, April 8) Editorial: VIA Character Strengths: Theory, Research and Practice. *Front. Psychol.* https://doi.org/10.3389/fpsyg.2021.653941.

340 Freidlin, P., Littman-Ovadia, H. & Niemiec, R.M. (2017). Positive psychopathology: Social anxiety via character strengths underuse and overuse. *Personality and Individual Differences, 108*, 50-54. https://www.viacharacter.org/pdf/Overuse-underuse-optimal_use__SAD_-_Freidlin_Littman-Ovadia__Niemiec_(2017).pdf

341 Bachik, K., Carey, G. & Craighead, W.E. (2021). VIA character strengths among US college students and their associations with happiness, well-being, resiliency, academic success and psychopathology. *The Journal of Positive Psychology, 16*(4), 512-525. https://www.tandfonline.com/doi/abs/10.1080/17439760.2020.1752785?journalCode=rpos20

342 Peterson, C.; Park, N.; Hall, N. & Seligman, M.E.P. (2009). Zest and work. *Journal of Organizational Behavior*. 30 (2): 161–172. https://doi.org/10.1002/job.584

343 Peterson, C., Park, N., Hall, N., & Seligman, M. E. (2009). Zest and work. *Journal of Organizational Behavior: The International Journal of Industrial, Occupational and Organizational Psychology and Behavior, 30*(2), 161-172. https://onlinelibrary.wiley.com/doi/abs/10.1002/job.584

344 Chan, D.W. (2009). The hierarchy of strengths: their relationship with subjective well-being among Chinese teachers in Hong Kong. *Teaching and Teacher Education*. 25 (6): 867–875. https://doi.org/10.1016/j.tate.2009.01.010

345 Sezgin, F. & Erdogan, O. (2015). Academic optimism, hope and zest for work as predictors of teacher self-efficacy and perceived success. *Educational Sciences: Theory and Practice, 15*(1), 7-19. https://doi.org/10.12738/estp.2015.1.2338

346 Peterson, C., Park, N., Hall, N. & Seligman, M. E. (2009). Zest and work. *Journal of Organizational Behavior: The International Journal of Industrial, Occupational and Organizational Psychology and Behavior*, *30*(2), 161-172. https://onlinelibrary.wiley.com/doi/abs/10.1002/job.584

347 Gander, F., Proyer, R.T., Rush, W. & Wyss, T. (2012, January 20). The good character at work: an initial study on the contribution of character strengths in identifying healthy and unhealthy work-related behavior and experience patterns. *Int Arch Occup Environ Health*. **85** (8): 895–904. doi:10.1007/s00420-012-0736-x. PMID 22261976.

348 Peterson, C., Park, N., Hall, N. & Seligman, M. E. (2009). Zest and work. *Journal of Organizational Behavior: The International Journal of Industrial, Occupational and Organizational Psychology and Behavior*, *30*(2), 161-172. https://onlinelibrary.wiley.com/doi/abs/10.1002/job.584

349 Park, N. & Peterson, C. (2009). Character strengths: Research and practice. *Journal of college and character*, *10*(4), 1-10. https://doi.org/10.2202/1940-1639.1042

350 Peterson, C., Ruch, W. Beermann, U., Park, N. & Seligman, M.E.P. (2007) Strengths of character, orientations to happiness, and life satisfaction. *The Journal of Positive Psychology* 2, no. 3: 149-156. https://doi.org/10.1080/17439760701228938

351 Park, N. & Peterson, C. (2006). Character strengths and happiness among young children: Content analysis of parental descriptions. *Journal of Happiness Studies*, *7*(3), 323-341. https://doi.org/10.1007/s10902-005-3648-6

352 Park, N. & Peterson, C. (2006). Moral competence and character strengths among adolescents: The development and validation of the Values in Action Inventory of Strengths for Youth. *Journal of adolescence* 29, no. 6: 891-909. DOI:10.1016/j.adolescence.2006.04.011

353 Martínez-Martí, M.L. & Ruch, W. (2017). Character strengths predict resilience over and above positive affect, self-efficacy, optimism, social support, self-esteem, and life satisfaction. *The Journal of Positive Psychology*, *12*(2), 110-119. https://doi.org/10.1080/17439760.2016.1163403

354 Shahram, S.Z., Smith, M.L., Ben-David, S., Feddersen, M., Kemp, T.E. & Plamondon, K. (2021). Promoting "Zest for Life": A Systematic Literature Review of Resiliency Factors to Prevent Youth Suicide. *Journal of research on adolescence*, *31*(1), 4-24. DOI:10.1111/jora.12588

355 Graziosi, M., Yaden, D. B., Clifton, J.D., Mikanik, N. & Niemiec, R. M. (2020). A strengths-based approach to chronic pain. *The Journal of Positive Psychology*, 1-9. DOI:10.1080/17439760.2020.1858337

356 Tversky, A. & Kahneman, D. (1974). Judgment under uncertainty: Heuristics and biases. *Science, 185*(4157), 1124-1131. https://apps.dtic.mil/sti/pdfs/AD0767426.pdf

357 Eagleman, D. (2012) *Incognito: The Secret Lives of the Brain*. New York City: Vintage

358 Brush, J.E. (2015, January 15) Decision-Making Shortcuts: The Good and the Bad. *NEJM Knowledge+*. https://knowledgeplus.nejm.org/blog/decision-making-shortcuts-good-bad/

359 Ambady, N. & Rosenthal, R. (1992). Thin slices of expressive behavior as predictors of interpersonal consequences: A meta-analysis. *Psychological Bulletin*. 111 (2): 256-274. https://www.semanticscholar.org/paper/Thin-slices-of-expressive-behavior-as-predictors-of-Ambady-Rosenthal/df0c9ca7be20ee0b7c5436332c20dcf46b2109d7

360 Gladwell, M. (2007) *Blink: The Power of Thinking Without Thinking*. New York City: Back Bay Books

361 Brighton, H. & Gigerenzer, G. (2012). Homo heuristicus: Less-is-more effects in adaptive cognition. *The Malaysian journal of medical sciences: MJMS, 19*(4), 6.

362 Morgan, A. & Piccinini, G. (2018). Towards a cognitive neuroscience of intentionality. *Minds and Machines, 28*(1), 119-139. https://link.springer.com/article/10.1007/s11023-017-9437-2

363 MyBroadband. (2021, June 5) *How we built a R4-billion company*. https://mybroadband.co.za/news/motoring/399901-how-we-built-a-r4-billion-company.html

364 WeBuyCars. (2021) *Our Story*. https://www.webuycars.co.za/our-story

365 UT News. (2014, May 16) *Adm. McRaven Urges Graduates to Find Courage to Change the World*. https://news.utexas.edu/2014/05/16/mcraven-urges-graduates-to-find-courage-to-change-the-world/

366 Tough, P. (2013) *How Children Succeed: Grit, Curiosity, and the Hidden Power of Character*. Boston: Mariner Books

367 Tough, P. (2011, September 14). What if the Secret to Success is Failure? *The New York Times*. https://www.nytimes.com/2011/09/18/magazine/what-if-the-secret-to-success-is-failure.html

368 Fletcher, D. & Sarkar, M. (2016). Mental fortitude training: An evidence-based approach to developing psychological resilience for sustained success. *Journal of Sport Psychology in Action, 7*(3), 135-157. DOI:10.1080/21520704.2016.1255496

369 Duckworth, A. (2016) *Grit: The Power of Passion and Perseverance*. New York: Scribner Book Company

370 Lucas, K. & Buzzanell, P.M. (2004). Blue-collar work, career, and success: Occupational narratives of sisu. *Journal of Applied Communication Research*, *32*(4), 273-292. DOI:10.1080/0090988042000240167

371 Freud, S. (1958). The dynamics of transference. In *The standard edition of the complete psychological works of Sigmund Freud, Volume XII (1911-1913): The case of Schreber, papers on technique and other works* (pp. 97-108).

372 Rath, T. & Clifton, D.O. (2004, October 14) The Big Impact of Small Interactions. *Gallup*. https://news.gallup.com/businessjournal/12916/big-impact-small-interactions.aspx

373 Trafton, A. (2014, January 16) *In the blink of an eye*. MIT News. In the blink of an eye | MIT News | Massachusetts Institute of Technology

374 Pulvermüller, F., Shtyrov, Y. & Hauk, O. (2009). Understanding in an instant: Neurophysiological evidence for mechanistic language circuits in the brain. *Brain and language*. 110. 81-94. 10.1016/j.bandl.2008.12.001.

375 Levitin, D.J. (2014). *The organized mind: Thinking straight in the age of information overload*. Penguin.

376 Thinkers50. (2021) *Thinkers50 Hall of Fame: Clayton Christensen*. https://thinkers50.com/biographies/clayton-christensen/

377 Christensen, C.M., Allworth, J. & Dillon, K. (2012) *How Will You Measure Your Life?* New York City: Harper Business

378 Age-of-the-sage.org. (2021) *Marcel Proust quotation having/seeing with new eyes*. http://www.age-of-the-sage.org/quotations/proust_having_seeing_with_new_eyes.html

www.ingramcontent.com/pod-product-compliance
Lightning Source LLC
Chambersburg PA
CBHW072045110526
44590CB00018B/3045